DR FRANCIS PRYOR, author of the acclaimed *Seahenge* and *Britain BC*, has spent more than thirty years studying the prehistory of the Fens. He has excavated sites as diverse as Bronze Age farms, field systems and entire Iron Age villages, as well as barrows, 'henges' and a large ceremonial centre dating to 3800 BC. In 1982, while working in a drainage dyke at Flag Fen, on the outskirts of Peterborough, he discovered the waterlogged timbers of a Bronze Age religious site. In 1987, with his wife Maisie Taylor, he set up the Fenland Archaeological Trust, which opened Flag Fen to the public.

He is President of the Council for British Archaeology, and frequently appears on Channel 4's popular archaeology programme *Time Team*. In 2003 he wrote and presented a two-part television series on *Britain BC*, and in 2004 made a three-part series on *Britain AD*.

For automatic updates on Francis Pryor visit harperperennial.co.uk and register for AuthorTracker.

From the reviews of *Britain AD*:

'Controversial, deceptively clever and a damn good read'
BBC History Magazine

'Pryor's opinionated (yet fairly argued) text rollicks along, informed by a great deal of recent research and new discoveries ... Eminently readable'
British Archaeology

'Francis Pryor has been an eloquent advocate for a new, fascinating vision of the prehistoric past. After *Seahenge* and *Britain BC*, this book completes an exhilarating trilogy in which the received ideas of far too long are swept away'
Scotsman

By the same author

Seahenge
Britain BC

BRITAIN A.D.

*A Quest for Arthur, England
and the Anglo-Saxons*

FRANCIS PRYOR

HARPER PERENNIAL
London, New York, Toronto and Sydney

Harper Perennial
An imprint of HarperCollins*Publishers*
1 London Bridge Street, London SE1 9GF

www.harperperennial.co.uk

This edition published by Harper Perennial 2005

First published by HarperCollins*Publishers* 2004

Copyright © Francis Pryor 2004

PS section copyright © Louise Tucker 2005, except 'Why
Archaeology Matters' by Francis Pryor © Francis Pryor 2005

PS™ is a trademark of HarperCollins*Publishers* Ltd

Francis Pryor asserts the moral right to
be identified as the author of this book

Maps and diagrams by Leslie Robinson and Rex Nicholls

A catalogue record for this book
is available from the British Library

ISBN 978 0 00 718187 2

Set in PostScript Linotype Minion with Photina display by
Rowland Phototypesetting Limited,
Bury St Edmunds, Suffolk

MIX
Paper from
responsible sources
FSC   FSC® C007454

Printed and bound by CPI Group (UK) Ltd, Croydon, CR0 4YY

For Maisie

CONTENTS

CONTENTS

PLATES

A view of Hadrian's Wall, running east from Birdoswald fort, Cumbria.

A view west towards the main street or *via principalis* of Birdoswald fort.

A reconstructed 'Anglo-Saxon' hall at Bede's World, near Jarrow, Northumberland.

A reconstructed 'sunken feature building' or *Grubenhaus* at Bede's World.

The churchyard of the parish church at Rudston in the Wolds of East Yorkshire contains the tallest Neolithic standing stone in Britain.

The remains of the fourteenth-century church tower of Barlings Abbey, in the Witham Valley, near Lincoln.

The medieval ruins of Tupholme Abbey in the Witham Valley.

View from the ruins of Tupholme Abbey, looking across the Witham Valley.

An Ogham stone in County Wicklow, Ireland.

TEXT ILLUSTRATIONS AND MAPS

ACKNOWLEDGEMENTS

I must start by acknowledging the small group of people who made the three fifty-minute programmes on which this book is loosely based: Charles Furneaux, commissioning editors at Channel Four, Roy Ackerman of Diverse Productions (executive producer), Tim Copestake (producer/director), Rowan Deacon (assistant producer), Melanie Wangler (production manager), Colin Clarke (lighting cameraman) and Peter Eason (sound recordist). Rowan Deacon was particularly helpful with the research behind Chapters 2 and 3. The writing of this book was greatly aided by my agent, Bill Hamilton at A.M. Heath; publisher Richard Johnson and editor Robert Lacey, both at HarperCollins. The excellent line drawings in the text are by Rex Nicholls. The picture editor was Caroline Hotblack. Special thanks go to Lotte Kramer for kind permission to reproduce her poem 'See-saw' in Chapter 9.

Many archaeologists and other scholars have helped me come to terms with a very thorny subject; they include: Paul Budd, Barry Cunliffe, Ken Dark, Guy de la Bédoyère, Mike Fulford, Martin Henig, Nicholas Higham, Catherine Hills, David Howlett, Sam Lucy, Richard Morris, Andrew Pearson, Dominic Powlesland, Richard Reece, Charles Thomas, Roger White and Tony Wilmott. Drafts of various chapters have kindly been looked over by Dr Nicholas Higham and Guy de la Bédoyère in an attempt to catch the worst 'howlers'. I am deeply indebted to everyone mentioned, but I also freely acknowledge that any mistakes or omissions in this book are my responsibility alone.

FRANCIS PRYOR
Flag Fen
Peterborough, Cambridgeshire
May 2004

Britain AD is in a sense the third volume of an informal trilogy on the archaeology and early history of Britain. It was not planned as a trilogy from the outset, because the idea only came to me gradually, as I was writing the first of the three books, *Seahenge*. I knew then that I had to write *Britain* BC, and in my heart of hearts I also wanted very much to tackle the challenge posed by the collapse of Roman rule and the onset of the so-called 'Dark Ages' of the fifth to seventh centuries AD. But I felt more than a little daunted by the task. It was the writing of *Britain* BC that gave me the broader perspective and confidence to undertake the present work.

As I worked on *Seahenge*, I became aware that I was writing a book about what archaeologists refer to as 'process': the methods, approaches and techniques whereby archaeology is actually done. In that sense, *Seahenge* is a book less specifically about Britain than the other two; but if you read *Seahenge* first you will derive more from the *Britain* books, because you will better understand the thought processes behind the work of the various archaeologists and historians involved. Incidentally, I should add here that Mark Brennand and Maisie Taylor have written the full detailed, academic report on that most remarkable of sites.[1] Their detailed analysis of the fifty-five timbers – the way they were worked and how they were positioned – has given us a unique insight into the way Early Bronze Age people viewed their world. I do not think it is an exaggeration to say that it has transformed our understanding of Early Bronze Age ritual and religion, and has confirmed many theories that had hitherto been based largely on speculation.

My approach is a personal one. I believe with some passion that archaeology is a personal discipline, and consider it misleading to suggest that there are such things as impersonal, dispassionate or objective archaeological books, just as there are no absolute facts in archaeology, other than the objects themselves. The objects are facts, but anything we attribute to them is interpretation. You may think that a term like 'cremation urn' has to be factual; but that presupposes that we all agree on what constitutes a cremation – and here, as elsewhere, there are many grounds for argument. If archaeologists and historians care about their subject, they will have axes to grind, and I prefer to sharpen mine in public.

In all my books I have tried to think and write in time-depth, because I am convinced that the fundamental attitudes underlying human society take a long time to change. Such a long-term view of British history and prehistory would have been impossible without the work of the Venerable Bede, who was one of the ablest minds of all time. It was Bede, in his great *Historia Ecclesiastica Gentis Anglorum* (Ecclesiastical History of the English People), which he completed in the year 731, who introduced the system of BC/AD to British history.[2]

In *Britain BC* I used archaeology to give an impression of what it might have been like to have been alive in the supposedly anonymous and faceless world of prehistoric times. Prehistory, incidentally, is the name given to the study of human history before the advent of writing and written records, which arrived in Britain with the Roman Conquest of AD 43. Too often it is portrayed as a time when individuals, who of course could not be identified, did not matter. So they have tended to be forgotten, their humanity replaced by explanations that assume that prehistoric people somehow lacked free will. In the past prehistorians were too ready to attribute social and cultural innovation to external processes such as migration, economic collapse and environmental change. By approaching their subject in this cold-blooded way, they dehumanised it and made ancient people appear like machines that merely responded to various stimuli in a predictable fashion. This was far too mechanistic for my taste: I prefer my archaeology, like my friends, to be human, fallible and hard to explain. But for some reason nearly all archaeologists detest unsolved mysteries; they would prefer *any* explanation to no explanation.

Archaeologists dealing with the period covered by *Britain AD* have also fallen, too often, into a mechanistic explanation of change and the denial of free will to the so-called 'Anglo-Saxons'. But there is an important difference between the so-called 'Dark Ages' and prehistory, because now we are no longer wholly reliant on archaeology. In the present book I have tried to reconcile the contrasting views of ancient life provided by historians and archaeologists; and I conclude that in many significant respects the two are irreconcilable. I do not believe that this matters a great deal, because the authors of the only 'historical' sources available were not writing history at all: they were writing polemic, with a well-defined audience and purpose. I shall have more to say on that in Chapters 1 and 2.

In this book I will suggest that in the fifth and sixth centuries AD there are, if anything, rather too many faces: unreliable ancient authors, semi-mythical leaders and one impossible hero called Arthur. These faces have been dominant for far too long, and the voices that have attended them – sometimes their own, more often those of their modern academic supporters – have tended to drown out the quieter, subtler, and to me far more persuasive, stirrings of archaeology. In this book I have made a conscious effort to redress this imbalance.

I have tried to write about more than just the lives of people in the past. I have attempted to make my work relevant to the world around us today. If archaeology is only about antiquity it will soon wither and die, as a pointless, self-serving pursuit. This trilogy addresses themes that matter in the twenty-first century: questions about ideology, the role of religion in daily life, problems of identity and sense of place. In the present book I have also grasped the nettle of what it means to be British – but I do not offer solutions, because there aren't any. I also avoid the easy way out of saying that there is no such thing as Britishness. Popular definitions of Britishness certainly vary, but that does not invalidate them. Some of them may be jingoistic, or worse, but I believe that a sense of community, however one chooses to define that term, is something worth holding on to in a crowded world that is growing increasingly self-centred.

Finally, I write about something that is surely quintessentially British, namely the keeping up of appearances. Over the years I have become increasingly convinced that the British use their past as a surface coating, a facing, to prevent them from thinking about who they really are as individuals. You can see a rather extreme expression of this tendency if you visit Glastonbury. Anyone who stood outside the Abbey Gates with a loudhailer and proclaimed that Arthur never existed, and that Camelot and Avalon were not intended to be taken as literal truth, would be jeered to the echo, before the rocks began to fly.

Much of the Arthurian New Age 'philosophy' is actually quite closely linked to early-twentieth-century views on racial purity, in which people like the Celts were seen to have an actual, ethnic identity. In today's New Age, the ancient Celt is seen to possess mystical virtues that your average Irish Dark Age warlord would have found less than attractive. Half-baked, wishy-washy mysticism would not have appealed to him.

In the first two chapters of this book we will see how Druidism, Arthur and what is called the 'Celtic Twilight' are largely modern inventions. This already grossly distorted view of early British history has been further elaborated by the New Agers. I wouldn't object to this – after all, everyone is free to believe what they choose – were it not for the fact that I detect whiffs of quasi-racism in much of this muddled thinking. I get very wary when I hear talk of how wonderful the Celts were. The unlamented Aryans lurk not far below the Arthurian surface, in legends such as Tristan and Yseult; if, that is, one treats these stories as anything other than fiction, pure and simple.

In *Seahenge* I played down the full horror of some of the events surrounding the lifting of the timbers from the beach at Holme-next-the-Sea in Norfolk, as I was writing principally about archaeology, and did not want to chase what I then regarded as a red herring.[3] It was also both too close and too unpleasant even to attempt to write about with any degree of objectivity. Readers may however recall that the unfortunate archaeologists on the beach had to face the wrath of neo-Pagans and Druids, which they did with dignity and not a little courage. I remember how one of the Druids proclaimed angrily that he was a 'British Aboriginal', and that we were desecrating 'his' religious site. I replied, in a foolish attempt to use humour to defuse the situation, that that was fine, because I was descended from Vikings and was therefore allowed to do a little light pillaging. This made him apoplectic with rage. He genuinely believed in his racial purity, and that that gave him certain rights. The linking of rights to race is just a blink away from Nazi beliefs.

Although it is not my main purpose, I do hope to debunk some of these spurious half-truths, and in the process help people come to their own conclusions about what it meant to be British in the past, what it means in the present, and what it will mean in the future – and of these three, the future is the one that matters most.

I have had a lot of fun writing this book. I have visited remote and extraordinary places, and met many old friends and some fascinating new people. The old friends were generally archaeologists, and the new people were mainly historians or specialists in fields of study that a prehistorian such as myself is unlikely to encounter. *Britain AD*, and the making of the three television films that have accompanied it, has been a wonderful journey of discovery. Having said that, I must sound a note of warning.

Journeys of discovery lead one into uncharted territory, but in the present instance that territory is not the true *terra incognita* one encounters during academic research. Instead this quest has taken me into realms of the past that have been thoroughly studied by many archaeologists, historians and, more recently, scientists. These scholars might reasonably enquire what business a prehistorian of the Neolithic, Bronze and Iron Ages has with post-Roman Britain. In my defence I can only say that sometimes a fresh view, one rooted in a lifetime's experience in a different, but closely related, field, can sometimes provide unexpected insights.

I do not think it hurts to view the three or so centuries of the misnamed 'Dark Ages' (i.e. from the official end of the Roman Empire in Britain to, say, the mid-seventh century: AD 410–650) as what they were: an insular development out of Later Iron Age culture, following some 350 years of Roman influence.[4] In archaeology it is always a good idea to examine origins and consequences: too often we fix our gaze on one period on its own. Chronological isolationism is just as bad as its geographical equivalent; indeed, when it comes to the study of post-Roman Britain it is essential to take a broad view of both time and space.

In this book I have tried to view the events of the post-Roman epoch in greater time-depth than previously. To my mind what happened in Dark Age Britain is not particularly surprising when placed against the backdrop of prehistory. What is strange, however, is the variety of ways in which the post-Roman period has been interpreted by subsequent generations, including our own. I suspect this has something to do with identity: the identity of various élites, including royalty. It also has to do with emerging and beleaguered national identities. Again, I touch on these themes further in the first two chapters.

For myths to arise they often require mystery, and the post-Roman period has always been seen in the popular imagination as particularly mysterious. I was brought up to believe that chaos and anarchy followed the collapse of Roman civilisation in Britain. Out of this primordial cultural soup arose a new form of life which in southern Britain was to be called England. The magic ingredient, the yeast of the brew, was hordes of Continental immigrants who by the early seventh century had transformed post-Roman anarchy into the rugged, no-nonsense world of the Anglo-Saxons. As national origin myths go, that of England is pretty good. It explains why the English are – or think they are – so different from the other nations of Britain. It's also an excellent story. But whether it's true or not is another question altogether.

Today most people with even a passing interest in the past are broadly familiar with what one might call the cultural aspects of medieval times. We enjoy their great buildings, their paintings, sculpture and increasingly their music. As a result, we believe we can identify with them. The post-Roman period lurks on the misty, romantic fringes of that world. It's a period that we wish we could identify with, but sadly we cannot. This is frustrating, because for better or worse the Dark Ages lie at the threshold of the period that gave rise to our own times. As a consequence of this, over the centuries we have recast the Age of Arthur in our own image. This is because historians, story-tellers and others are very good at reshaping the past in ways which reflect contemporary concerns. Today, for example, some of us look to Arthur to supply the mysticism which seems to have vanished from modern life, for whatever reason: perhaps the rationality of science, growing secularism, or even the dogmatic certainties of evangelical religion. These surely are some of the reasons why the Arthur industry is thriving. I have no wish to debunk the hundreds of books, films and videos that appear every year on Arthur and his court. Rather my intention is to think about the contexts of that time and to consider what might actually have happened, given what we know about previous and subsequent epochs from both archaeology and history.

I have already mentioned that the Romans introduced writing to Britain. Of course most people were not aware of it at the time, but this process had already given rise to the discipline of history, which one might define as the study of the past from written sources. These sources can be as diverse as wills, letters, accounts, inscriptions, military commands or ecclesiastical texts, but they are all grist to the historian's mill. The historian's tradition is to paint with a broad brush and to seek causes for historical events. Historians also have a tradition of superb writing: open Edward Gibbon's magisterial *The Decline and Fall of the Roman Empire* (written between 1776 and 1788) at random, and some resounding passage will tumble forth. This is what Gibbon says about King Arthur. I quote it at length both because it makes excellent sense and because it reads so beautifully:

> But every British name is effaced by the illustrious name of
> ARTHUR,* the hereditary prince of the Silures, in south Wales,
> and the elective king or general of the nation. According to the
> most rational account† he defeated, in twelve successive battles,
> the Angles of the North and the Saxons of the West; but the
> declining age of the hero was embittered by popular ingratitude
> and domestic misfortunes. The events of his life are less interesting
> than the singular revolutions of his fame. During a period of five
> hundred years the tradition of his exploits was preserved, and
> rudely embellished, by the obscure bards of Wales and Armorica
> [Brittany], who were odious to the Saxons, and unknown to the
> rest of mankind. The pride and curiosity of the Norman conquerors
> prompted them to inquire into the ancient history of Britain; they
> listened with fond credulity to the tale of Arthur, and eagerly
> applauded the merit of a prince who had triumphed over the Saxons,
> their common enemies. His romance, transcribed in the Latin of
> Jeffrey of Monmouth, and afterwards translated into the fashionable

* Gibbon adds a footnote on his sources here, which concludes with the remark that 'Mr Whittaker . . . has framed an interesting and even probable, narrative of the wars of Arthur: though it is impossible to allow the reality of the round table.'
† By 'most rational account' he is probably referring to the Welsh author known as Nennius.

idiom of the times, was enriched with the various, though in-
coherent, ornaments which were familiar to the experience, the
learning, or the fancy of the twelfth century . . . At length the light
of science and reason was rekindled; the talisman was broken; the
visionary fabric melted into air; and by a natural, though unjust,
reverse of the public opinion, the severity of the present age is
inclined to question the *existence* of Arthur.[5]

That was going too far, even for Gibbon, who clearly believed in
Arthur as a real historical figure.

At first archaeologists followed this grand tradition, but it soon
became apparent that the writing of sweeping narrative did not work
for archaeology. It's not that our data do not allow us to draw general
conclusions; it's just that we should not attempt to mimic what historians do so well. As archaeologists we can indeed paint with a broad
brush, but we have learnt that it is best to confine our efforts to the
painting of archaeological pictures. Today archaeology tends to be
more concerned with the long-term processes of social change. We
prefer to work with landscapes rather than lineages, and we tend to
be less involved with one-off events than with more gradual change.
When we do try to pin down specific historical incidents we often
become unstuck. The classic case, which I will discuss in Chapter 6,
is that of the so-called Anglo-Saxon 'conquest' of England, and its
aftermath.

Because archaeologists work with data that are foreign to most
historians, we are sometimes accused of stretching the evidence too
far. I was once kindly, but rather patronisingly, told by a classicist that
I, and archaeologists like me, should take lessons on the limitations
of inference.[6] He did not believe that prehistoric data (i.e. sherds of
pottery, fragments of flint, or pieces of bone) were capable of sustaining
speculation about the manner in which prehistoric communities might
have viewed the world around them. Most prehistorians consider we
are 'speculating' from the safety of solid statistical or palaeo-
environmental data. We do not believe that we are flying kites. Having
said that, we do not believe either that we have actually hit on the
truth, because unless a day dawns when we can somehow get inside
the minds of long-dead people, we will never know how or what they
actually thought. Even then we will have to confront the many prob-

lems that face anthropologists when they try to explain what motivates tribal societies in various parts of the world today. In fact the long-established, innate conservatism of the archaeological profession makes it extremely hazardous for any prehistorian to espouse 'flaky' theories, or ideas that tend, however slightly, towards the crackpot. Recently, however, there has been a welcome freeing-up of attitudes. In the past two decades the intellectual climate in archaeology has become more liberal, and slightly less intolerant of dissent from within. Ironically, only history – in perhaps a century or two – will be able to judge the extent to which archaeology is actually revealing truths or is building castles in the air.

There is one important difference between history and archaeology which has nothing to do with the quality of the data we study, but rather its quantity. Written historical information on the post-Roman era in Britain is surprisingly scarce, and new discoveries happen very rarely; when they do, it is often in the course of archaeological excavation. By contrast with the essentially static historical 'database', that of archaeology is constantly increasing. Hardly a day goes by without some new discovery. Often these discoveries might appear routine and unimportant, such as the exposure of the footings of yet another Saxon-period house, but these isolated pieces of information can be fitted together to form a coherent pattern. It's a process that can take years, as we will see (Chapter 8) in the case of Dominic Powlesland's work at West Heslerton in Yorkshire, but that does not make it any less reliable. The progress of archaeological research tends to be gradual and cumulative; it can only be measured from time to time. That is why it is sometimes necessary to step back in both time and space to take a broader view.

When I started writing this book, I intended to organise it much as we had done the three television films, for the simple reason that it seemed to work very well. I also liked the process that gave rise to the structure of the films. In many ways the making of the television series was like an archaeological project, being based on a small and closely integrated team. As the months passed its structure grew in complexity: stories nested within stories in a way that is only possible on film, where one can show one thing on screen, while telling another in commentary and flashback. I decided to arrange the book in a simpler fashion, that was only broadly based on the structure of the films. I start with two chapters on the ancient sources and modern origin myths of Britain, and the legends that surround King Arthur. In subsequent chapters I turn to the archaeological evidence, starting not in the Dark Ages of immediately post-Roman Britain, not even in the preceding Roman period, but in pre-Roman, or prehistoric, times, where the roots of the mythical King undoubtedly lie.[7]

Dates and Periods

Date	Period Name	Alternative Names	Period
	Post-medieval		
1500			
	Medieval (can start *c.* AD 800)	The Middle Ages	
1066			
800	Late Saxon	Early Medieval	
	Middle Saxon		
650			
	Early (or Pagan) Saxon ('Pagan' is an older usage)	Early Christian (in the south-west)	'The Dark Ages' or Migration Period
450			
410	Sub- or Post-Roman		
	The Roman Period		
43 AD			
BC	Late Iron Age		
150			
450	Middle Iron Age		
750	Early Iron Age		
1250	Late Bronze Age		
1500	Middle Bronze Age		
	Early Bronze Age		
2500			
	Neolithic or New Stone Age		
4200			
	Mesolithic or Middle Stone Age		
10,000			
	Palaeolithic or Old Stone Age		
500,000			

Archaeological Characteristics	Notes
	1485 *Le Morte d'Arthur* printed c. 1136 Geoffrey of Monmouth's *History of the Kings of Britain* 1066 Norman Conquest
Towns flourish	871–899 King Alfred reigns
Appearance of first towns in Britain	731 Bede's *History* finished 664 Synod of Whitby
	625 King Raedwald of Essex buried at Sutton Hoo 597 St Augustine's mission to the Anglo-Saxons lands in Thanet c. 475–550 Gildas writes
'Anglo-Saxon' pottery at end of 4th century	
Most of Britain a part of the Roman Empire	409 British reject Roman rule 367 great Barbarian Conspiracy 60–61 Boudica's revolt
Wheel-made pottery British Celtic Art flourishes	54–55 Caesar's two expeditions to Britain
Period of rapid population rise	
Appearance of earliest Celtic Art	
First construction of hillforts	
Era of metalwork hoards	
Era of round barrows Appearance of Beaker pottery	1600 Plank-built sea-going boats
2950 Stonehenge started First farming in Britain around 4200	
Hunter-gathering and fishing communities, using small flint implements and weapons	
	End of the last Ice Age
Hunter-gathering communities, using large flint implements and weapons	Ages of Ice
	Earliest people in what was later to become Britain

CHAPTER ONE

Origin Myths:
Britons, Celts and Anglo-Saxons

THE EARLY HISTORY of southern Britain has often been portrayed
as particularly tumultuous and difficult. Sir Roy Strong has summarised the conventional picture in characteristically elegant fashion:

> The fifth and sixth centuries still remain ones of impenetrable
> obscurity, fully justifying their designation as the Dark Ages. Britain
> was only one of many countries which suffered the consequences
> of the collapse of the Roman Empire. In England's case the effect
> was far more dramatic, for there was no continuity as two-thirds
> of the eastern parts of the island passed into the hands of German
> pagan and illiterate warrior tribesmen. Urban society collapsed,
> and the Latin language was abandoned in favour of British or
> primitive Welsh. Under the aegis of the British Church some form
> of Latin learning survived, but in the east a series of Anglo-Saxon
> petty kingdoms emerged whose cultural status can only be categor-
> ised as barbarian.[1]

If we examine the archaeological record it is hard to find convincing
evidence for the picture of post-Roman disjunction, anarchy and chaos
that is supposed to have led to the Anglo-Saxon invasions of the fifth
and sixth centuries AD. It is even harder to find actual evidence for
these invasions themselves. Instead, archaeology paints a picture of
rural stability in those parts of southern and eastern Britain that were
to become Anglo-Saxon England in the early seventh century.

This stability should be set against a background of increasing contacts with the Continental mainland that had been underway since at least the Iron Age, and that continued throughout the Roman period. After the departure of the Roman field army in AD 409, order in the one-time province of Britannia was maintained by existing local élites and by elements of the erstwhile Roman army who effectively 'privatised' their services. The Christian Church most probably played a significant role in local administration, even in the east of England, where Anglo-Saxon paganism was once believed to have reigned supreme. This picture differs dramatically from the conventional image of the period known, inappropriately, as the Dark Ages.

I believe that a number of long-held and popular, but ultimately false beliefs are obscuring what is actually a fascinating and highly creative period of British history. It was a time of huge change, but not of chaos. It was a period which witnessed the creation of a distinctive post-Roman European civilisation, and which also gave rise to some brilliantly executed and beautiful objects. Above all, it was never a Dark Age.

In the version of the past taught at most British schools in the second half of the twentieth century, and still widely accepted by the population at large, British history begins with the Ancient Britons. One would suppose these to have been the indigenous or 'native' people of the British Isles, who had been living there since they became islands after the Ice Age, around nine thousand years ago. It was believed, however, that Britain had been subject to a number of invasions from the Continent in pre-Roman times: first, a wave of people who brought with them the arts of farming and pottery manufacture in the Neolithic or New Stone Age; then another, smaller, influx of new and genetically distinctive people known as the Beaker folk, who were believed to have introduced the skills of bronze-working. The third and perhaps most significant invasion, or invasions, was supposed to have taken place in the Iron Age, after about 500 BC. These newcomers were known as the Celts. In addition to these three main 'invasions' there were a number of others of less significance – making a total of eight or nine.

It is not the purpose of this book to examine the earlier two of these three hypothetical prehistoric waves of immigration.[2] Suffice it to say that while modern archaeology does still accept that some incomers helped establish farming in Britain, the so-called 'Neolithic Revolution' was far more an invasion of ideas than of people. The later invasions of Beaker folk are simply discounted, although personally I believe that something was going on in the Early Bronze Age, which may well have involved high-status individuals travelling to and from Britain. This is supported by a number of scientific tests and other archaeological indications which suggest that the population of prehistoric Britain and Europe was far more mobile than would have been supposed fifty years ago. But while mobility – where people travel hither and thither – is one thing, prehistorians today are reluctant to attribute most major changes to a single cause, such as mass migration.

In the accepted picture of early British history, Iron Age (by now 'Celtic') Britain was visited by Julius Caesar in 55 and 54 BC, and was finally conquered by the Romans in AD 43. There was a major revolt against Roman rule, led by the East Anglian queen of the Iceni, Boadicea (today Boudica) in AD 60–61. Christianity was made legal in the Roman Empire by the Emperor Constantine the Great in AD 324, with the Edict of Milan. The Roman period in Britain ended nominally in or just before the year AD 410. There was then a period of about four decades, sometimes known as the 'sub-Roman' period, when a sort of insular Roman rule continued; but Anglo-Saxon migration had started, and the Romanised British population in eastern England were powerless to resist it.

The following period, of two or so centuries, was known variously as the Pagan Saxon period or the Dark Ages (today most scholars prefer the term 'Early Saxon'). It was characterised by waves of invasion by various people, including Angles, Saxons and Jutes. This was the age of the legendary King Arthur. Arthur was supposed to have been a Romanised Briton, based in the West Country, who led British/Celtic resistance to the Anglo-Saxons, who were expanding their domination of England westwards. He won a famous victory at the Battle of Mount Baddon or Badon, some time at the beginning of the sixth century, but was eventually defeated and slain at the Battle of Camlan in AD 539.

Missionaries under St Augustine reintroduced Christianity to Britain in AD 597, and the Pagan Saxon period was followed by the Christian Saxon period, which came to an end with the Norman Conquest of 1066. Differences between St Augustine's Roman Church and the British or Celtic Churches were resolved, largely in favour of the Roman Church, at the Synod of Whitby in 664. The Christian Saxon period witnessed the birth of England; its first widely acknowledged king was Alfred, who ruled from his capital Winchester in Wessex from 871 to 899. Alfred's reign was largely given over to wresting eastern England back from Viking domination. Viking raids had become a serious problem from the late eighth century: the famous abbey on Lindisfarne island was sacked in 793, and the 'great raiding army' of Viking warriors invaded East Anglia in 866.

It will be clear from this highly compressed synopsis of conventional British prehistory and early history that the Arthur stories are not the only examples of what one might term British origin myths. None of them attempts to explain British origins directly. In other words, they are not British equivalents of the biblical story of Creation. But they do nonetheless address themes that are closely bound up with a sense of emerging national identities. The problem is whether they are actually about the time in which they are supposed to have taken place, or the times in which they are told, retold or elaborated. My own view is that it's the latter, if only because the real origins of British culture – whether or not it was ever perceived by prehistoric people as such – lie hidden in the mists of antiquity.

I do not believe that it is necessary to define a culture to be part of one; it would be absurd to suggest that the people who created Stonehenge five thousand years ago were without a developed culture – indeed, a highly developed culture. It probably had many points in common with similar cultures in Scotland, Ireland and Wales, but we do not know whether these communities saw themselves as either British or as part of a series of insular cultural traditions. I believe that the many parallels that can be observed in the layout of ceremonial and other ritual sites and monuments across Britain and Ireland reflect a shared cosmology or system of beliefs. That, however, is not to say that they shared a common culture. Take language. The people of the various tribal kingdoms of Britain would have understood the dialects of the kingdoms around them, but the leaders of, say, the Iceni in Norfolk would probably not have understood their equivalents in Wales, Northumberland or Devon.

It is unlikely that the Ancient Britons saw themselves as Britons.

By the Later Iron Age, in the century or so prior to the Roman Conquest, the upper echelons of southern British tribal societies would have been aware of the Channel and of Gaul (France) beyond it. Some would probably have had relatives there. At what point did a sense of 'Britishness' develop? If we are to answer that, which is essential to a proper understanding of Arthur's role, we must first tackle the vexed question of the Celts, who are often seen as being synonymous with the Ancient Britons. Arthur was a Romanised Briton, and it follows that he must also have been a Romanised Celt. Who were they, then, these romantic-sounding Celts?

They have had an excellent press. In 1970 the historian Nora Chadwick wrote, in a best-selling paperback on the subject:

> Celtic culture is the fine flower of the Iron Age, the last phase of European material and intellectual development before the Mediterranean world spread northwards over the Continent and linked it to the world of today ... Common political institutions gave them a unity bordering on nationality, a concept which the Mediterranean peoples could understand. They realised that the Celts were a powerful people with a certain ethnic unity, occupying wide and clearly defined territories, in process of expansion, and that they were possessed of internal political organisation and formidable military strength.[3]

At this point I should say a few words about culture and ethnicity, as they are understood in archaeology. 'Culture' is the harder of the two to pin down. At times I will use the word in its accepted contemporary sense: as a description of a given group of people with shared outlooks and values. At other times it will be clear from the context that I am using it in its narrower, archaeological sense. An archaeological 'culture' is one represented by a recurring assemblage of artefacts which are believed by archaeologists (although not necessarily by the people who made and used them) to represent a particular set of activities, or a particular group of people. For example, the widespread occurrence in Early Bronze Age Europe of highly decorated drinking vessels, together with bronze and copper daggers, was believed to represent people of the distinctive 'Beaker Culture'. Today the word 'culture' is finding less favour; most archaeologists try to avoid it, as it carries so many other meanings. This has led to unhappy-sounding terms such as the 'Beaker phenomenon' or the 'Beaker presence', neither of which has any meaning at all.

The term 'ethnicity' is less vague, and does not have a specialised archaeological definition. Nonetheless, the one I prefer is taken from the *Oxford Dictionary of Archaeology*: 'The ascription, or claim, to belong to a particular cultural group on the basis of genetics, language or other cultural manifestations.'[4]

The Celts were seen as an ethnically distinct group of people whose origins lay around the upper Danube and Alpine regions. There are passing references to them by the great classical Greek historian Herodotus, writing in the fifth century BC. Their presence was also noted near the Greek colony at Massilia (Marseilles) by a slightly earlier writer, Hecataeus.[5] From approximately the fifth century BC it was believed that they spread north, east, south and west from their central European heartland.[6] By the end of the third century BC the process of expansion was drawing to a close. Then the Roman Empire came and went, and in post-Roman times Celtic culture continued to flourish mainly in western Britain and in neighbouring parts of north-western France.[7] Given this view of history we can only assume that elsewhere in Europe Celtic culture simply vanished in the centuries following the collapse of the Western Roman Empire (the Eastern or Byzantine Roman Empire continued until the fall of Constantinople in 1453).[8]

The identification of the Celts as a distinct entity was largely based on a wonderful art style that came into existence in Early Iron Age Europe.[9] Celtic art, as it is generally known, did indeed begin in Continental Europe – as, centuries later, did Impressionism – but the spread of neither style of art involved the migration of people. Art is, after all, about ideas which can be communicated both by example and by word of mouth. The term 'Celtic art' has, however, stuck, and I do not think it can easily be dislodged. Personally, I would prefer a less culturally loaded term, like 'Iron Age art'. But whatever one calls it, it is superb: it features vigorous, swirling plant and animal figures that possess an extraordinary grace and energy. The standards of design and craftsmanship are outstanding. Some of the finest examples of Celtic art were produced in Britain in the decades prior to the Roman Conquest of AD 43.[10]

The art was both very distinctive and widespread throughout Europe, but there is little evidence for the spread of an actual people. This fact first came to prominence in 1962, when Professor Roy Hodson published a paper in the learned journal the *Proceedings of the Prehistoric Society*. Two years later he wrote another in the same journal. In essence his argument was simple: the numerous invasions of Iron Age Britain that had been suggested by leading scholars such as Professor Christopher Hawkes of Oxford simply hadn't happened. Hodson proposed that the changes in, for example, pottery styles that are evident in the British Iron Age merely reflect changes in style, taste and sometimes in technology (for example the introduction of the potter's wheel in the first century BC). He argued persuasively that an invasion of new people from abroad would have brought with it widespread changes: in house shape, in burial customs, in farming practices and so forth – but that had not happened. British Iron Age houses remained resolutely round, whereas their counterparts on the Continent, where the invaders were supposed to have originated, were rectangular. It wasn't enough to base the existence of hypothetical migrations on such slight evidence. Today Roy Hodson's reinterpretation of the British Iron Age as a largely insular phenomenon is universally accepted by prehistorians. It has become the new orthodoxy.

If there were no Iron Age invasions, then how did the Celts reach Britain? The answer can only be that they didn't come from outside. In other words, they were always there. In that case, what was happening on the Continental mainland? What about the art? What about classical references to Celts in, for example, the area around Marseilles? How one answers these questions depends on one's point of view. If you believe in an ancient people that shared a common ethnicity, and perhaps similar Indo-European languages and culture, it doesn't really matter what you call them. 'Celts' will do nicely. 'Prehistoric Europeans' would be even better – or worse. The point is that retrospectively applied labels that are believed to have cultural or ethnic validity are pointless.

In common with most of my colleagues, I take a position which acknowledges, for example, that there may indeed have been a tribal group living near Marseilles who called themselves Celts, but that the evidence for a vast pan-European Celtic culture simply isn't there. Certainly people were moving around, as they have always done and will continue to do, but there is no evidence for large-scale, concerted folk movements in the fifth to third centuries BC. If you examine a given tract of landscape, as I have done in the Peterborough area over the past thirty years, there is no sign whatsoever that the population changed some time in the mid-first millennium BC with the arrival of the Celts. It simply did not happen. Everything, from the location and arrangement of fields, settlements and religious sites to ceremonial rites, bespeaks continuity. In Chapter 3 I will look at another, very different, Iron Age landscape in Hampshire, and again there is no evidence for a change of population.

Today most prehistorians take the view that changes in the archaeological record are a reflection of technological advance, population growth and evolving social organisation. Societies were becoming more hierarchical and their leaders were becoming more powerful. These élites maintained contacts with each other by various means, such as the exchange, often over long distances, of high-status objects, many of which were examples of the best Celtic art. In short, one can substitute the words 'Iron Age culture' for 'Celtic culture'. The big difference is that Iron Age culture was actually Iron Age cultures – plural. That applied in Britain as much as anywhere else. Archaeologically speaking, it would be misleading to talk about pre-Roman Celtic Britain as if it was a unified society. In fact the reverse was true, as we will see in Chapter 3.

A side-effect of the debunking of the ancient Celts has been to deprive us of a species of archaeological book that was often very well-written and coherent. As the authors of Celtic histories believed they were describing a lost people, they were quite happy to draw together disparate strands of evidence to paint a vivid picture in a way we would hesitate to do today.[11] The origins and consequences of the Celtic myth have recently been reviewed by the archaeologist Simon James. He takes a decidedly minimalist view of the Celts, with which I am in complete agreement:

The term 'Celtic' has accumulated so much baggage, so many confusing meanings and associations, that it is too compromised even to be useful as a more general label for the culture of these periods. The peoples in question organised themselves in a diversity of ways . . . and, it seems, spoke a variety of languages and dialects, which were not all mutually intelligible. The undoubted similarities and relations between them are best explained in terms of parallel development of many societies in intimate contact, rather than of radiation from a recent single common origin.[12]

James considers that the notion of British identity is remarkably recent, and did not develop until the later Middle Ages.[13] It is an idea that might be thought to have its roots in the Act of Union between England and Scotland in 1707, as that was the time when it became politically important to start thinking in terms of a broader British nation. But in fact there was little public enthusiasm for the idea until the 1770s, following the loss of the American colonies. Unsuccessful foreign wars can have unifying effects at home. The emergence of a broader British identity was given further impetus by the late-eighteenth-century development of the second British Empire, based on India, which was beneficial to the interests of both Scotland and England. So any differences between the two countries were placed on hold.

Archaeologists are part of modern society, and reflect the norms of that society; that is how the Celtic myth came into existence. It was then given intellectual substance by prehistorians, who have since been the first to debunk it. The modern notion of 'Celticity' or 'Celticness' has its origins in British insular independence movements. Many people in Ireland and Wales did not feel part of a Britain that was dominated by England. The situation in Scotland was more complex, because regional differences and traditional frictions between Lowlands and Highlands, Protestants to the east and Roman Catholics to the west, tended to smother the emergence of popular anti-British/English feeling until the second half of the twentieth century.

The victory of William of Orange at the Battle of the Boyne in 1690 set the seal of Protestant domination in Ireland. In the north this domination came from Scotland, in the south from England. During the eighteenth and subsequent centuries opposition to Protestant domination in Ireland was largely expressed through the Roman Catholic faith and the revival of a Gaelic or Celtic identity. Today the notion of Celticity still gives rise to strong feelings in Ireland, where the wrongs of the recent past are very keenly felt. Even in academic circles the archaeological debunking of the ancient Celts meets with strong resistance.

The situation in Wales was perhaps even more complex than in Ireland. In Wales, Protestantism was the dominant religion, and the chapel formed the focus of many industrialised communities. The expression of an anti-British Welsh identity began, ironically enough, among London Welsh in the last decade of the eighteenth century. The stimulus was provided by economic migration from rural areas (mainly to the New World); this in turn was accompanied by a huge movement of English people to work in the industrialised south of Wales.

In the 1790s there was a revival of their literature and history by the Welsh population resident in London, and it took a strangely archaeological course. The following appeared in the *Gentleman's Magazine* in October 1792:

> This being the day on which the autumnal equinox occurred, some Welsh bards, resident in London, assembled in congress on Primrose Hill, according to ancient usage ... A circle of stones formed, in the middle of which was the *Maen Gorsedd*, or Altar, on which a naked sword being placed, all the Bards assisted to sheath it.[14]

The celebration of Welsh identity which accompanied the literary revival was focused on a colourful figure known as Iolo Morganwg, born Edward Williams in 1747. Williams was a Glamorganshire stonemason who had been working in London since the 1770s and was a member of a group of Welshmen who took an active interest in the literature, history and antiquities of their native land. He adopted the bardic name Iolo Morganwg ('Iolo of Glamorgan') and set about reviving (and sometimes forging) documents, and creating new customs that bolstered his passionately held views on Welsh politics and identity – which owed much to the ideas of radical political theorists like Thomas Paine, author of *The Rights of Man*. Morganwg linked his 'Gorsedd' (circle of stones or pebbles), and the ceremonies associated with it, to ancient times – even as far back as the Druids.

Morganwg achieved something quite remarkable: he managed to have his largely invented Gorsedd ceremonies attached to the genuinely antique Eisteddfod. The Eisteddfod was (and is) an annual meeting that celebrates Welsh music, literature and poetry. The first recorded Eisteddfods took place in the fifteenth and sixteenth centuries at a time when the Welsh poets (Welsh *Beirdd*) were still a distinct and ancient class with their own 'orally transmitted rules and norms'.[15] By the eighteenth and nineteenth centuries, however, the tradition of the Eisteddfods was flagging, and the addition of the politically loaded Gorsedd rituals had a galvanising effect on their popularity.

The first Gorsedd Circle bardic ceremonies to be held in Wales took place at the end of the three-day Eisteddfod in Carmarthen in 1816. The grafting of the 'dignified nonsense' of the Gorsedd rituals onto the Eisteddfod has given subsequent students of Welsh history serious headaches.[16] What cannot be denied, however, is that while the reinvention of Welsh identity represented by Morganwg and his followers was very popular, it was an essentially middle-class phenomenon. The bulk of the Welsh population were English-speakers, and they expressed their identity and shared values through the chapel, choirs and active involvement in Labour politics.

What are we to make of the modern invention and reinvention of a Celtic identity? The first point is that it owes little or nothing to the ancient Celts, who, as we have seen, did not exist as a single cultural or ethnic entity. So is it still valid? I believe it is, but only time will tell how long it will last. I would agree with Simon James that the modern concept of Celticness matters because it is an expression of self-identity. It is also a shared sense of difference from the English/British who were (and are) seen as a threat. And it cannot be denied that the people concerned share, or more usually shared, languages whose ancient roots were related. Maybe their view of a common early history is flawed, but then so is that of the English. Simon James would go further: 'That this tradition [of the ancient Celts] is now under attack does not invalidate *modern* Celtic identity, because to some degree *all* modern ethnic and national identities create essentially propagandist histories.' Writing about the people of the British Isles, he notes:

Ethnicity and nationhood depend on *self*-identity, on being aware of larger groupings and their interactions, and feeling *involved* in

one of them. I would argue that, until the rise of the four historic
nations in the medieval period, and even long after, a clear sense
of large-scale ethnic or national identity – of belonging to an
imagined community like the Scots, Welsh, Irish or English – was
usually weakly developed among the mass of the people, who rarely
had to deal with such issues.[17]

If the concepts of Britain and Britishness are seen by many Welsh,
Scottish and Irish people as no more than ways of referring to England
and Englishness, what of the English? Even if they wanted to, they
could not identify themselves with the Celts, as they themselves are
the Other, the forces of opposition, which played a key role in the
birth of the modern Celtic identity. They have had to look somewhere
else. The Vikings and Normans are already spoken for by the Danes
and the French, which leaves only the Germanic presence of the Anglo-
Saxons – a choice which was made very much easier, in Georgian and
Victorian times, by the presence on the English throne of a German
royal family.

The idea that the origins of the English nation could be found in
a massive influx of Anglo-Saxon people first became popular around
AD 700–1100.[18] Its widespread acceptance was due to a number of
contemporary accounts, including those of Gildas (sixth century), the
Venerable Bede (c.731) and the *Anglo-Saxon Chronicles* (from c.890).[19]
Then, some time around 1136, the highly influential author and creator
of the principal Arthurian stories, Geoffrey of Monmouth, wrote in
his *Historia Regum Britanniae* (History of the Kings of Britain) an
origin myth which traced the foundation of Britain back to the Trojans
– of all people.[20] This wonderful flight of fantasy described how Brutus,
great-grandson of Aeneas of Troy, landed at Totnes, subdued the race
of giants who lived there, and gave his name to the country he had
pacified (Britain = Brutus). During his visit he founded London,
calling it New Troy. Even the creation of the Arthur stories seems drab
by comparison with the Brutus myth, but both were widely accepted
throughout the medieval period, during which Geoffrey's history was
held in high regard as an accurate historical source.

After about 1600 the Brutus myth fell from favour, to be replaced
by a new set of semi-mythic principal characters, including Hengist,

Horsa and Alfred the Great.[21] Alfred is of course a known historical figure, whose achievements are well documented. Perhaps it is sad that today he is better known for burning cakes than for his administration or government. The brothers Hengist and Horsa are indeed semi-mythic. They make their first appearance in that magnificent work of early propagandist history, Bede's *Historia Ecclesiastica Gentis Anglorum* (*c.*731), where they are portrayed as the founders of the royal house of Kent. Bede tells us they were leaders of Germanic forces invited to Britain by Vortigern, a Romanised southern British king, in the year 449. According to Bede, their arrival signalled the *adventus Saxonum*, or coming of the Saxons, who originally appeared as mercenaries, or *foederati*.

During the 450s we learn that the mercenaries turned against their client, Vortigern, to establish their own rule. It seems a straightforward enough story, and it was later taken up and elaborated by other sources, including the *Anglo-Saxon Chronicles*; but Bede, like all subsequent historians, had his own motives for writing in the way he did. He did not see himself as writing 'pure' or unbiased history in the sense that we would understand it today. In writing his great work he was also delivering a message; and the invasion of the Anglo-Saxons was part of that message.

In the early eighteenth century the Anglo-Saxonist view of history was strongly influential. It was widely believed, for example, that institutions such as Parliament and trial by jury were ultimately Germanic. But this view changed as the political scene itself altered in the late eighteenth and early nineteenth centuries. We have seen in the case of the Celts how issues to do with nationalism and self-identity came to the fore at this time, but it was by no means a straightforward picture. France was perceived as the great enemy, not just as another powerful nation, but one with the potential to subvert the entire structure of British government, as witnessed by French attitudes to the American colonies, the Revolution of 1789 and of course the subsequent Napoleonic Wars. There were pleas for British unity. The great Whig politician and conservative thinker Edmund Burke, in his highly influential *Reflections on the Revolution in France*, published in 1790, did not play down national differences within Britain, but placed great emphasis on the antiquity of the British system of government. A few years earlier, in 1756, the antiquarian and pioneering archaeologist of the Old Stone Age, John Frere, also worried about contemporary political developments; he 'called for the English, Lowland Scots and the Hanoverian Kings, all of whom were descendants of the Saxons, to live in harmony with the Ancient Britons (the Welsh)'.[22] Ancient history was being brought into contemporary affairs in a way that we would find extraordinary today.

We have already seen that archaeological and historical research is affected by the climate of thought prevailing at the time, and I cannot avoid a brief discussion of the two World Wars, both of which saw Britain pitted against Germany: in theory, at least, Anglo-Saxon versus Teuton. The First World War did not have a major impact on Anglo-Saxon research in Britain. Before it, opinion was divided as to whether the Anglo-Saxons were large-scale military invaders or true immigrants, and in the 1920s and thirties an essentially similar debate continued. However, after the horrors perpetrated by the Nazis in the Second World War, the English began to feel uncomfortable with their supposed Germanic roots.

The end of the war also saw the effective end of the British Empire, for a number of reasons. This led to a change in historical attitude: a world view centred on Anglo-Britishness was no longer possible. Nicholas Higham has described the effects of the post-war/post-Empire situation well:

One result was the final overthrow of the old certainties provided by a belief in the inherent superiority of English social and political institutions and Germanic ancestry, by which the British establishment had been sustained for generations. This provided opportunities for the revival or construction of alternative visions of the past. Historically, insular Germanism was rooted in the enterprise of legitimising the early and unique rise of the English Parliament to supremacy in the seventeenth and eighteenth centuries, but its fragility was now revealed.[23]

We will discuss the problems inherent in 'insular Germanism' later; here I merely want to note that today the world of Anglo-Saxon archaeology is divided over the question of large-scale invasions in post-Roman times. More conservative opinion still favours mass folk movements from the Continent to account for the widespread changes in dress style, funeral rites and buildings. Other scholars point out that such changes can be brought about by other means. This alternative view, which I support, would have been inconceivable thirty years ago. Viewed as a piece of archaeological history, it seems to me that the Anglo-Saxon invasions are the last of a long list of putative incursions that archaeologists of the nineteenth and twentieth centuries used as catch-all explanations when they encountered events they could not explain. It is far more healthy, intellectually speaking, to admit sometimes that we don't fully understand a particular phenomenon, rather than to rush to an off-the-peg 'solution'. Doubts can sometimes prove wonderfully stimulating.

As has been noted, however, wherever archaeologists have taken a close look at the development of a particular piece of British landscape, it is difficult to find evidence for the scale of discontinuity one would expect had there indeed been a mass migration from the Continent. We will see this in several case studies, including the Nene Valley (Chapter 4), West Heslerton in Yorkshire, and in the Witham Valley near Lincoln (both Chapter 8). I believe it will be a close study of the landscape that will clinch the archaeological case against large-scale Anglo-Saxon invasions, just as it did for their supposed 'Celtic' predecessors.

CHAPTER TWO

The Origins and Legacy of Arthur

LIKE MANY CHILDREN, I found the tales of King Arthur enthralling. Everything about him seemed to fire the imagination. I did not fully understand the rather murky business surrounding his conception in Tintagel Castle; nor did I realise that the various elements of the tales came from different sources and periods. That didn't matter, because the whole epic was driven by the energy that comes from a good story.

Arthur was the son of Uther Pendragon (King of Britain) and Igraine, the beautiful wife of Duke Gorlois of Cornwall. This union was made possible by the wizard Merlin, who altered Uther's appearance to resemble that of the Duke, who was away fighting. Conveniently he was killed in battle shortly after Arthur's conception. Uther married Igraine and Arthur became their legitimate son, growing up to be a handsome, generous, brave and virtuous prince.

According to legend, Britain could not find a king, so Merlin devised a test: the man who could withdraw a sword embedded in a stone was the rightful heir. Arthur duly accomplished the task. His reign was a busy one. As King of the Britons he fought the invading Anglo-Saxons, and won a famous victory at Mons Badonicus (Mount Badon). His final battle was at Camlann, where he opposed his usurping nephew Mordred. Arthur may have been killed on earth, but he was taken to the magic island of Avalon by the indispensable Merlin, where his wounds were cured. Other versions have only Arthur and one of his knights, Sir Bedevere, surviving the battle. Arthur proceeds to Avalon, while Bedevere is charged with returning his sword Excalibur to the Lady of the Lake. Arthur resides on Avalon to this day, and will return if Britain is ever in need of him.

Arthur's capital was at Camelot, which in the Middle Ages was supposed to have been at Caerleon on the Welsh borders, and his court was organised around the Knights of the Round Table. All the knights were equal in precedence but they all vowed to uphold a code of ethics laid down by Arthur, who was one of their number. The best-known of the Knights of the Round Table were Bedevere, Galahad, Gawain, Lancelot, Mordred, Percival and Tristan. From Camelot the knights set out on their adventures, of which the most famous was the quest for the Holy Grail, the mystical chalice used by Christ at the Last Supper. The myth was centred around Percival, Galahad and Glastonbury, where the Grail was supposed to have been taken by Joseph of Arimathea, who looked after Christ's body after the Crucifixion. Joseph's staff, driven into the ground at Glastonbury, took root as the Holy Thorn.

Apart from Arthur and Merlin, the most celebrated character is Sir Lancelot, Arthur's most trusted adviser. Lancelot had many adventures, of which the most hazardous was his love for Guinevere, Arthur's Queen, which was foretold by Merlin. She returned his love, and they had a protracted adulterous relationship. Despite Arthur's anger when he learned the truth he was strangely forgiving of his old friend. Lancelot missed the Battle of Camlann and subsequently learned that Guinevere had become a nun at Amesbury. He himself became a monk at Glastonbury, where he was told in a dream that he should ride at once to Amesbury. He arrived too late to be present at Guinevere's death, and died of grief soon after.

If the myths surrounding the arrival in Britain of the ancient Celts, and perhaps the Anglo-Saxons too, have been discredited or are beginning to crumble, what of King Arthur? One might suppose that as he is portrayed as a heroic, mythical figure he would have been particularly vulnerable to critical assault. Strangely, however, the reverse seems to be the case: Arthur and his legends stubbornly refuse to die, despite everything that is hurled at them.

One reason for this is that the Arthurian legends are suffused with strange echoes of antiquity which seem to possess more than a faint ring of truth. The stories contain elements which would have been completely at home in the Bronze and Iron Ages: the importance of the sword Excalibur, its 'disposal' in a lake in which lived the Lady of the Lake, and the fact that Avalon is an island: Arthur's 'peerless sword, called Caliburn', in the twelfth-century account of Geoffrey of Monmouth, 'was forged in the Isle of Avalon'.[1] Swords, lakes and islands were of known religious significance in prehistoric times, not just in Britain but across most of northern and central Europe. These are ancient myths, and there is good evidence to suggest that they survived in Britain throughout the Roman period too; that they even flourished during the Dark Ages, and survived well into medieval times.

Another element in the story with an ancient feel to it is the tale of the sword in the stone. The story does not appear in the principal earlier medieval writers, Geoffrey of Monmouth, Wace, Layamon or Chrétien de Troyes, and seems to have been introduced by writers of the Old French 'Vulgate Cycle', which I will discuss shortly. It must surely be explained as a mythic reference to the casting of a bronze sword. I have witnessed this process, and it is most spectacular: the orange-glowing sword is actually pulled from a two-piece stone mould by the metal-smith. It's rather like the process of birth itself, and is altogether different from the shaping of an iron sword, which is fashioned by repeatedly hammering out and reheating an iron bar. Other early components in the Arthurian story include the tales surrounding the Holy Grail, although, as we will see, these are rather less ancient, and may contain Late Roman and Early Christian elements.

It could be argued that it was the popularity of the Arthurian legends that kept these myths alive, but there is an increasing body of evidence to suggest that a great deal of pre-Roman religion and ideology survived, in one form or another, into post-Roman times. These tales would have been recognised as being ancient, and would have been selected for inclusion within the Arthurian tradition for that very reason. The Roman period, in other words, does not represent a clean break with earlier traditions; we will see in Chapter 9 that certain important and supposedly 'Anglo-Saxon' introductions were actually earlier traditions continuing in altered forms – as one might expect after nearly four centuries of Roman rule.

Perhaps the main point to emphasise is that these ancient observances were living traditions that were shaped and recreated by subsequent generations for their own purposes. In many instances they were not intended to be taken literally, as history. They always existed within the realms of legend, myth and ideology. People in the past would have understood this. Sadly, we appear to have lost that sense of wonder or transcendence that can accept different realities for their own sake, without feeling obliged to burden them with the dead hand of explanation.

The principal modern proponent of King Arthur has been Professor Leslie Alcock, who believes that South Cadbury Castle in Somerset was the site of Arthur's court, Camelot. This acceptance of Arthur's historicity (i.e. historical truth) colours much of his writing, both archaeological and historical. Although he acknowledges that there are many unsolved problems, he belongs to what David Dumville has termed the 'no smoke without fire' school of recent Arthurian historians.[2] Adherents of this school may have doubts about Arthur's historicity, but they believe that so much was written about him, albeit long after his lifetime, that there *has* to be a core of truth to it. Alcock has also argued, moreover, that early sources such as the British Easter Annals mentioned St Patrick, St Bridget and St Columba by name, and nobody today doubts their historicity – so why doubt Arthur, who is mentioned in the same sources?[3] Unfortunately, historians do not work like that: each person's claim to veracity must be examined on its own merits, preferably using a number of independent sources. It is not good enough to claim that if A is known to have existed, then B must have lived too.

I knew Alcock when he was still actively engaged in archaeology, and I know many of the people who worked with him at his excavations on South Cadbury in the late sixties and early seventies. His excavations were of the highest standard, and the subsequent publications were also first-rate. Why did he become so involved with what was ultimately to prove a wild-goose chase? I don't think anyone knows precisely why, although Nicholas Higham has plausibly suggested that Alcock's was essentially a post-war reactive response: he was looking for a non-Germanic origin for British culture.[4] A cynic, however, might suggest that the Camelot/Arthur stuff helped keep Alcock's much-loved South Cadbury project financially alive. Maybe, but neither he nor the very distinguished people on his Research Committee were particularly worldly or ambitious in that way. It was a *bona fide* academic research project, and certainly not a mere money-making ploy. So, to return to my original question, why did he become so preoccupied with Arthur?

I can only suppose that something of the Arthurian magic touched him and fired his imagination. Maybe too he was intellectually predisposed to accept Arthur as a result of the horrors of the Second World War. There is no doubt that, even if at times flawed, Alcock's writing on the history of Arthur can be remarkably persuasive. For a long time he clearly believed in the importance of what he was doing, even if he did eventually radically rethink his original ideas about Cadbury and its supposed identification with Arthur's Camelot.[5] Whatever the truth about Arthur and Camelot at South Cadbury, the excavations were superb, and have given rise (as we will see in Chapter 8) to an important and continuing project of fieldwork.

What is it about the Arthurian legends that so many people find appealing? Is it just that he has been used as a historical metaphor to explain something as nebulous as the origins of Britain? Or is it more than that? Does Arthur express something deep within ourselves, something we do not fully understand, but which we feel matters? Or are the myths surrounding the Once and Future King just very good stories? My own feeling is that while it may be possible to deconstruct the historiography (i.e. the history of the history) of the Arthur myths, that process will not necessarily explain their enduring appeal, and it certainly will not explain why they are so extraordinarily popular with so many people of different nationalities today. Let me give a single example of the phenomenon.

Anyone who has been touched by the power of the Arthur myths never forgets the experience. It happened to me back in 1974, in Toronto, when I was an Assistant Curator at the Royal Ontario Museum. It was a time when there was a great upsurge of Arthurian interest, brought about by Leslie Alcock's claim that a Somerset hillfort at South Cadbury was probably the site of Camelot.[6] Geoffrey Ashe's popular analysis of the myths and stories surrounding the Grail legends had appeared in paperback,[7] and of course there were other publications, some good, some less so.[8] It was widely assumed that, as an

English archaeologist, I would know about the Dark Ages. In fact I was a prehistorian working on the outskirts of prosaic Peterborough, not at glamorous Glastonbury – but like a fool I kept quiet about that. In any case, the museum's PR people thought it would be a good idea if I gave a public lecture on the subject of 'Arthur's Britain'. Little did I know what I was letting myself in for.

My suspicions should have been roused when the BBC contacted me in late summer while I was digging in Peterborough; my lecture in Toronto was scheduled for some time around Christmas. The BBC had received a tip-off from someone in Canada, but as I was still reading the first chapters of Leslie Alcock's *Arthur's Britain*, I couldn't answer the questions they asked me. So they left me in peace.

Back in Toronto, I soon realised that my Arthur talk was going to be very big indeed. The publicity was huge, and was developing swiftly. In the mid-1970s the over-commercialised AM radio stations of North America were being replaced by more laid-back FM stations, playing music by bands like the Mothers of Invention, Pink Floyd and so forth. King Arthur was meat and drink to this audience, and I had several extended chat sessions with DJs on air.

On the day of the lecture I arrived at the museum, but the crowd around the main entrance was so big that I had to go down to the basement and enter through the goods entrance. I clutched my slides in what was rapidly becoming a very sweaty palm. Upstairs, the main lecture theatre was already packed, and there was still half an hour to go. I handed my slides to the audio-visual technician, who was visibly shaken by the huge crowd. He was Welsh, and the quiet words 'Good luck, boyo' came from an uncharacteristically dry mouth. Out on the stage a crew was rapidly rigging up a sound system that would relay my voice to a crowd standing in the huge rotunda just inside the museum's main entrance. I later learned that additional loudspeakers were positioned outside the building – and remember, this was Canada in the winter.

I think the lecture was successful, but I was so dazed that I can't in all honesty remember how it went. Arthur had worked his magic, and had left me an older and a wiser young man. After that experience, I simply will not accept that the appeal of Arthur is just about British origin myths or the romance of chivalry. I do not believe that there is a rational explanation, but I am convinced that there is a power to these stories that cannot be explained away.

We have seen how two of the British origin myths, the Celts and the Anglo-Saxons, owe their current popularity to a series of re-inventions in the eighteenth, nineteenth and twentieth centuries. The same can be said of Arthur, but his story has a far longer history of creation, recreation and adaptation. By contrast, whether or not one believes there was ever an ethnic group called the ancient Celts, it cannot be denied that Britain was home to a diverse group of Iron Age cultures with their own highly original style of art. Similarly, even if, as I believe, they did not invade *en masse*, a few 'Anglo-Saxons' (or people like them) probably did come to Britain in the post-Roman period – either that, or perhaps as well as that, influential British people repeatedly travelled to northern Germany, where they were influenced by what they saw.

But when it comes to Arthur, one fact cannot be sidestepped: there is no mention of a character of that name in any ancient account of Britain written between AD 400 and 820 – and Arthur is supposed to have lived in the fifth century.[9] There are sixth- and seventh-century accounts of battles and other events in the fifth century which have been linked to Arthur by modern authors, with more or less credibility, but none with certainty. There are also later accounts which hark back to earlier times and hypothetical lost authors; but nobody, either at the time or within a few generations of his death, wrote about him by name until some four centuries later – fifteen or twenty generations after the event. To put that in context, it is as if Simon Schama was the first historian ever to mention Oliver Cromwell by name.

Today Arthur is essentially a literary phenomenon, and there is an enormous subsidiary literature devoted to the legends surrounding him.[10] Here I will concentrate on the early writing that actually gave birth to the legends that still continue to be recreated and elaborated.[11]

We cannot embark on even a short review such as this without first questioning whether our hero did or did not exist.[12] Given the lack of direct evidence prior to the ninth century, it seems to me that the question cannot be answered. Derek Pearsall puts it well: 'Proving that Arthur did not exist is just as impossible as proving that he did. On this matter, like others, it is good to think of the desire for certainty as the pursuit of an illusion.'[13] What we can say, however, is that the fifth century was a time when strong individual leaders were needed and had come to the fore – as we will see when we discuss the Late Roman frontier fort at Birdoswald on Hadrian's Wall (Chapter 9). It seems to me that if Arthur did not exist, which seems more likely than not, he ought to have done. It is equally probable that there were several Arthurs. The trouble is, we have no evidence either way. If we cannot establish the truth of Arthur the man, what can we say about Arthur the myth? The stories and legends of the Arthurian cycle may tell us only a little about post-Roman Britain, but they can tell us something about the times in which they were written. More importantly, they can throw a great deal of light on the way in which British history has been expropriated by powerful people and political factions for hundreds of years. It is a process which continues to thrive.

The earliest account of events that were later linked to Arthur was written in a sixth-century history by a man named Gildas. Gildas is a shadowy figure, but we do know that he was a British monk of the Celtic Church, that he was thoroughly fluent in Latin, and that he died around 570 or 571. He spent his life in south Wales and Brittany, where he is revered as a saint. The oldest existing manuscript of his work dates to the eleventh century. Its title, *De excidio et conquestu Britanniae* (Concerning the Ruin and Fall of Britain), gives away the reasons why Gildas wrote his history: he was in fact preaching something of a political diatribe.[14] Gildas wrote in a particularly high-flown, flowery style of Latin that does not translate very comfortably. The distinguished archaeologist and historian Professor Leslie Alcock was driven to write: 'If ever there was a prolix, tedious and exasperating work it is Gildas' *De excidio*.'[15] Even so, his message is abundantly clear: Anglo-Saxon expansion is divine retribution for the moral laxity of the Celtic/British nobility.

The absence of any mention of Arthur in this important early source is surprising – the more so since Gildas is the first to mention the Battle of Mons Badonicus (Mount Badon), which was supposedly the most significant event of Arthur's life. If he wanted a stick with which to castigate his audience, Arthur would have been ideal for the purpose. But his name is never mentioned. Instead we are told that the victor of Mount Badon was one Ambrosius Aurelianus – although Alcock, a strong advocate of Arthur being the victor at Badon, doubts whether that was what Gildas meant. Alcock does not deny, however, that Gildas does say that Ambrosius Aurelianus was a successful leader of the Britons in battle.

According to some readings of his text, Gildas mentions that Badon was fought in the year of his own birth, which was probably around, or shortly after, AD 500. In a difficult passage, Gildas appears to imply that he is writing forty-four years later. Some dispute this, and believe (as did Bede, who had access to earlier and more authoritative versions of Gildas) that what is referred to as having occurred forty-four years earlier is some event other than the author's birth. But, taken together, the evidence suggests that Mount Badon was fought in the decades on either side of the year 500.

The name Arthur probably derives from the Latin *gens* or family name Artorius, although in manuscripts it often appears as Arturus. It may also be derived from *artos*, the Celtic word for a bear. The first account of a person named Arthur is by the anonymous author (once believed to have been Nennius) of the *Historia Brittonum* (History of the Britons), a collection of source documents written and assembled around 829–30. Although the *Historia* draws on many earlier Welsh sources, it is its 'highly contemporary political motives'[16] that are most important if we are to understand it – and indeed nearly all medieval and earlier Arthurian literature. In this instance the motives relate to politics in ninth-century Wales.

The author of the *Historia Brittonum* was writing for the particular benefit of King Merfyn of Gwynedd, in north-west Wales, and his supporters, who were resisting English conquest and Anglicisation. They needed a heroic Celtic leader that people could look back to, and the *Historia* provided one. The *Historia* was also created as a counter to the 'Englishness' of the Venerable Bede's history, which was then very popular. As Nicholas Higham points out, the élite surrounding King Merfyn resisted external pressures successfully: 'The separate existence of Wales is a lasting tribute to their achievement.'[17]

It is always difficult to make use of documents that only exist in the form of later copies or translations, as subsequent copyists may have added their own personal touches to flesh out the events being described. Arthur was very popular in the early medieval period, and it is probable that his name was interposed in earlier histories in this way. One example of this is the account of two important Arthurian battles in the *Annales Cambriae* (Welsh Annals), written around 1100, but drawing on earlier sources. Historians and others have tended to concentrate their attention on Arthur, but these documents, which were probably produced in south-west Wales, are actually far more concerned with the threat from Gwynedd, to the north, which completely overshadowed the issue of 'racial' struggle with England.[18]

The Welsh Annals, a record of significant events, were included in the *Historia Brittonum* of Nennius.[19] The two crucial references are to the two most famous battles of the Arthur cycle: that at Mons Badonicus, or Mount Badon, in which Arthur and his British army defeated the Anglo-Saxons; and Arthur's final battle at Camlann. In translation they read as follows:

> *[Year 516]* Battle of Badon in which Arthur carried the cross of Our Lord Jesus Christ on his shoulders for three days and three nights and the Britons were victors.
> *[Year 537]* The strife of Camlann in which Arthur and Modred perished. And there was plague in Britain and Ireland.[20]

Modred (or Mordred) was Arthur's nephew, who is supposed to have usurped his throne. There is little doubt about the historicity of Badon, as the battle is mentioned by name in Gildas, who was not writing to promote the British cause. That is not to say of course that Arthur was the British leader – and plainly, if he did carry a cross on his shoulders for three days, he could not have done much actual fighting. The problem is to know when these accounts were written. Were the references to Arthur added later, when the Annals were compiled? Or were the individual annual entries indeed written year-on-year, in which case they would have a greater claim to historical accuracy? Leslie Alcock opts for year-on-year composition, but most historians now believe that the Badon entry was actually written around 954, some 450 years after the event itself.

Given the strong political motives that we know lay behind the writing and compilation of the *Historia Brittonum*, we must treat these entries with enormous caution. The substitution of Arthur for Gildas'

Ambrosius Aurelianus as the victor of Mount Badon might partially be explained by the political impossibility – given the *Historia*'s intended audience – of citing a general with a Roman name as a heroic British leader.

As I have said, these events have been discussed interminably. The Welsh Annals state that Camlann took place twenty-one years after Badon, but there is no absolute agreement as to the date of Badon, except, as we have seen, that it probably happened in the decades on either side of 500, and probably not after 516. The Welsh Annals add further confusion to an already confused picture by mentioning '*Bellum baronies secundo*' (the second Battle of Badon), which Alcock believed was fought in the year 667. The actual sites of the two battles are also unknown.

The most distinguished writer and scholar of the eighth century was the Venerable Bede. This remarkable man was born near Monk-wearmouth, County Durham, some time around 673, and died about 735. He is widely associated with the then new monastery at Jarrow, near Newcastle in Northumberland, where he was ordained priest in 703, but he probably lived most of his life at the monastery that was twinned with Jarrow, at Monkwearmouth. His major work, which tradition has it was written at Jarrow, is the *Historia Ecclesiastica Gentis Anglorum*, which he finished in 731.[21] Bede's Ecclesiastical History is a highly important source of early English history. It is both well written and well researched, but like the man, Bede's intentions in writing it were complex.

Bede's primary motive was the salvation of his people, and he saw the Church as the means of achieving it. Although not an ethnic Anglo-Saxon himself, he wrote from their perspective, and his history is essentially about the anarchy and power vacuum that followed the end of Roman rule. He describes a period when southern Britain was subject to marauding bands from the Continent. The conversion of the Anglo-Saxons to Christianity by St Augustine in 597 was for Bede the great turning point. As he saw it, the Church imposed order in a world where structure was lacking. He was hostile to the British, whom he saw as chaotic, and he used the writings of their own historian, Gildas, against them – in the process he edited and greatly improved the overelaborate language of the *De excidio*. Bede fails to mention

Arthur, and follows Gildas, his source, in attributing the victory at Mount Badon to Ambrosius Aurelianus.

The *Anglo-Saxon Chronicle*, the last of the major pre-Norman histories of Britain, was established by King Alfred some time in the 890s. In form it was an annal, written in Old English, and was maintained and updated at major ecclesiastical centres. It begins with the Roman invasion and was still being updated in the mid-twelfth century. Surviving manuscripts are associated with Canterbury, Worcester, York and Abingdon. The Chronicle can be patchy as a source on early events, but it is much better in its later coverage, of the reigns of Alfred (871–99), Aethelred (865–71), Edward the Confessor (1042–66) and the Norman kings. It is also an important document for the study of the development of Old English; but while it is not particularly relevant to the Arthur myths, it does provide a useful account of the early Anglo-Saxon histories of south-eastern England, especially Sussex and Kent.

The first major source of full-blown Arthur stories is the *Historia Regum Britanniae* (History of the Kings of Britain), written by Geoffrey of Monmouth in the 1130s.[22] It would be fair to call Geoffrey (*c.*1100–55) the father of the mythical King Arthur, who was largely his invention. He did, however, use the principal earlier authors Gildas, Bede and Nennius, together with current oral sources, which as we will see could have had very much older roots. His History was also based on an unnamed earlier British or Welsh work which he had seen and which is often assumed to have been the 'source' for his own considerable inventions. This famous 'lost source' has itself become a Holy Grail of modern Arthurian enthusiasts and theorists.[23] Geoffrey's book was to prove enormously popular and influential, particularly as an inspiration for the later Arthurian literature in the medieval courtly tradition.

In the previous chapter we saw how Geoffrey produced the Brutus legend to account for the origins of Britain; Arthur was by no means his only invention. Later in his life he wrote a less successful Latin epic poem about the life of the prophet Merlin, the *Vita Merlini*. Geoffrey was undoubtedly a very capable author, but like everyone else concerned with Arthur, he had his own motives for writing. He lived in very troubled times. England was in the throes of a civil war between the followers of King Stephen and those of Matilda, daughter of Henry I; the war started when Stephen seized the throne in December 1135, and ended when he died in 1154 and Henry II ascended the throne. During this period, generally known as the Anarchy, the country grew weary of warfare and strife. There was a widespread desire for peace, which may help to explain why Geoffrey's largely fictional history met with such success both in Britain and on the Continent, where it provided the source for a rich tradition of medieval Arthurian romances.

Geoffrey wrote his history in order to provide an honourable pedigree for the kingship of England that was then being fought over so keenly. He was writing for the benefit of the Anglo-Norman aristocratic élite, and he set out to show how their predecessor, King Arthur, had performed mighty deeds. Arthur had, according to Geoffrey, defeated the Roman Emperor and conquered all of Europe except Spain. That went down well with an audience of Norman knights whose families, friends and relations controlled not just England and Normandy, but large parts of Europe too.

But Geoffrey's work went further. Significantly, he made use of earlier sources to give the appearance of authenticity for those who possessed some historical knowledge. As Nicholas Higham puts it:

> It provided the new Anglo-Norman kings with a predecessor of heroic size, a great pan-British king in a long line of monarchs capable of countering pressures for decentralisation, as had occurred in France, and reinforcing claims of political superiority over the Celtic lands. Existing claims that the Normans were descended from the Trojans gelled easily with the descent of the Britons from the same stock . . . At the same time Arthur offered an Anglo-Norman counterbalance to . . . Charlemagne as an historical icon.[24]

Geoffrey's account of Arthur and his exploits is both remarkably full and detailed, and hard to put down. These, however, are more than mere tales of adventure; there is something transcendent about them. It seems to me beyond doubt that Geoffrey intended to create this sense of 'otherness', of the stories being somehow close to the supernatural.

Most reviews of Arthurian history talk in terms of pre- and post-

Galfridic sources.* Pre-Galfridic sources are seen as having more historical value than Geoffrey's own work and those that followed him. All, however, are chronologically separated from the events in question by several centuries. All their authors, too, have their own motives for writing. Nicholas Higham was the first to point out that pre-Galfridic sources such as the *Historia Brittonum* or the *Annales Cambriae* should not 'be treated very differently from, for example, Geoffrey's *Historia*, or other later texts. All are highly imaginative works, none of whose authors saw their prime task as the reconstruction of what actually happened in the distant past. Rather, in all cases, then as now, the past was pressed into the service of the present and was subject to the immediate, and highly variable, purposes of political theology.'[25]

The story of Arthur's conception at Tintagel Castle, which involves magical changes of identity, harks back to Biblical tradition and the miraculous conception of the Virgin Mary. As Pearsall and others have noted, there is more than a little of the British Christ to King Arthur. Even given the extraordinary power of Geoffrey's writing, it is still remarkable just how rapidly the Arthurian tradition took off not in Britain alone, but in Europe too. This is largely down to two gifted translators of the original, and to a French writer whose literary skills were the equal of Geoffrey's.

Geoffrey's *Historia Regum Britanniae* was translated into French by Robert Wace, a churchman who was originally from Jersey, but who lived at Caen in Normandy. He called his translation the *Geste des Bretons* (History of the Britons), but it was renamed the *Roman de Brut* (a topical reference to Romance and Britain/Brutus) by the scribes who copied it out for a wider readership. The new title stuck. Wace's was a very free translation, with many additions – Pearsall describes it as an 'expanded adaptation' – but it was a very successful one. It was presented to Eleanor of Aquitaine, the imperious and flamboyant new queen of England's Henry II, in 1155. This puts the work at the heart of European courtly culture, for the court of Henry II (1154–89)† and the glamorous divorcee Eleanor was the most exciting

---

* In Latin Geoffrey of Monmouth translates as 'Galfridus Monemutensis', hence 'Galfridian'.
† All royal dates refer to the period on the throne.

in Europe. Henry's power extended over most of France as well as England, and the court and literary language of his kingdom was French.[26] Wace added much new and important material to the Arthur story, including the Round Table, and he renamed Arthur's magical sword – Geoffrey of Monmouth's Caliburn – Excalibur.

It was another author-cum-translator, a rural priest near Worcester named Layamon ('lawman'), who took the Arthurian tradition, or *Brut* as it was now known, and transferred it to Middle English verse around 1200. Layamon's *Brut* stands as an extraordinary work of literature in its own right. It takes a different course from the courtly vision of Wace. Layamon was inspired by strong feelings of patriotism. He clearly loved traditional Anglo-Saxon battle poetry, heroism and what Pearsall calls 'kingliness, steeped in religious awe'.[27] Pearsall sums up the differences between Wace and Layamon thus: 'Throughout Wace is calm, practical, rational, with an eye for the realities of war and strategy; Layamon is aggressive, violent, heroic, ceremonial and ritualistic.'[28]

Post-Galfridian writers on Arthur take the romance forward wholly in the realms of fiction. Arthur was hugely popular in Anglo-Norman circles in France, where his exploits were further elaborated in verse by Chrétien de Troyes, a prolific author of Arthurian romance. Between 1160 and 1190 his works included *Lancelot ou Le Chevalier de la charette*, *Yvain ou le Chevalier au lion*, and the unfinished *Percival ou Le conte del graal*. Chrétien may have used Breton verbal sources in the composition of his works, which were important because they lifted Arthur and his court out of a narrowly British context.

It was Chrétien who introduced the quest for the Holy Grail, but at this stage in the development of the story the Grail was still just the mystical chalice that had been used by Christ in the Last Supper. It had yet to acquire its connection with the Holy Blood, a fascinating process to which I will return later. Effectively, Chrétien made Arthur a figure of heroic romance who transcended nationality. Derek Pearsall notes: 'Geoffrey of Monmouth gave shape and substance to the story of Arthur, but it was Chrétien who invented Arthurian romance and gave to it a high-toned sensibility, psychological acuteness, wit, irony and delicacy that were never surpassed.'[29]

It is not my intention to provide a history of the Arthurian literature which thrived on both sides of the Channel in the medieval period,* nor can I attempt to cover the wealth of creative writing he has given rise to in more recent times, ranging from Tennyson's cycle *The Idylls of the King* to T.H. White's novel sequence *The Once and Future King*. However, one author, Sir Thomas Malory (*d*.1470), must be mentioned if we are to understand how the Arthurian legends were subsequently used in Britain.

Malory's great work, written in English, was *Le Morte d'Arthur*.[30] The original title, given to it by the author himself, was *The Book of King Arthur and his Knights of the Round Table*. This title has the not inconsiderable merit of describing the contents to a T, but it is hardly marketable, which Malory's astute publisher and editor William Caxton realised immediately. Caxton (*c*.1420–*c*.1492) was, of course, England's first successful printer and publisher, working from his press in Westminster. It was he who gave Malory's great work its mysterious-sounding and slightly ominous title, which he lifted from the last tale in the book, 'The Death of Arthur', and it was his inspiration to translate it into French. Malory wrote *Le Morte d'Arthur* as a loosely connected cycle of tales. Caxton edited them together into a single text, which he published in 1485.[31]

As we have seen throughout this chapter, the various authors of Arthurian tales had their own, sometimes complex, agendas and motives. This is true of Malory too. *Le Morte d'Arthur* was written some fifteen years before it was published. 1485 happened to be the year of the Battle of Bosworth, in which Richard III was killed and a new royal dynasty began under Henry Tudor (Henry VII). Bosworth signalled the final phase of the Wars of the Roses, which ended when Lancastrian forces under Henry VII defeated a Yorkist army at Stoke, near Newark in Nottinghamshire, in 1487. It was of course in the Tudor interest to portray the Wars of the Roses as being long, drawn-out and bloody, and Malory wrote *Le Morte d'Arthur* around 1470 as a tribute to an earlier and now vanishing age of heroism, honour and Christian chivalry. Like Bede and Gildas before him, he saw the past as providing an example to the present that could not be ignored. It was perhaps

---

* There were differences in French and English readers' appreciation of the stories, however. For example, the tale of Gawain and the Green Knight was more popular in England than the exploits of Sir Lancelot, who was particularly favoured in France.

an accident of history that the Tudors should have shared his vision, if in an altogether more self-interested fashion.

Just who Thomas Malory was is far from certain. There are four contenders, of which perhaps the most likely is a Sir Thomas Malory of Newbold Revell in Warwickshire. He was knighted in 1445, and elected to Parliament the same year, but he seems to have been an unsavoury character. In 1440 he was accused of robbery and imprisoning (although we know nothing about any consequent court case). Then in 1450 he was accused, along with several others, of lying in wait to attack Sir Humphrey Stafford, Second Duke of Buckingham and one of the richest men in England. Again, the allegations were never proved. After this Malory appears to have pursued a life of crime, which included cases of extortion with menaces and straight robbery. Then rapes start to appear on the list of offences he was accused of committing, along with yet more robbery and violence.

Several attempts were made to catch him, and he spent some time in custody – sometimes managing to escape from it. Eventually the law caught up with him and in 1452 he was held in London's Marshalsea Prison, where he is supposed to have written his masterpiece. He died on 14 March 1470, and was buried at Greyfriars Chapel near Newgate Prison, from which he had been released following a pardon from Edward IV in 1461. Towards the end of his life he appears to have acquired some degree of wealth, but we have no idea whether this was from his previous life of crime or from a patron such as Richard Neville, Earl of Warwick (known as 'Warwick the Kingmaker').

Was this unpleasant individual the author of the *Morte d'Arthur*? Certainly the events of his life were colourful, and the book itself is nothing if not colourful. But could a thug and a rapist be the creator of a work which espouses high ideals of honour and chivalry? Frankly, I cannot answer that question. But I earnestly hope that some other plausible candidate will one day be found. Meanwhile we must make do with the flawed Sir Thomas of Newbold Revell.[32]

Malory used two main sources as inspiration for his work. Both were written in the past, and harked back to an age of heroic chivalry. In the mid-fifteenth century, when Malory was writing, most people must have been aware that the world around them was changing. Today, with the advantage of hindsight, we can appreciate that the medieval epoch (the Middle Ages) was in the process of dying.* A new period, and with it a new way of thinking about the world – ultimately a new cosmology – was coming into existence. It was a process that had been fuelled by the release of the knowledge contained within the libraries of Constantinople, which fell to the Ottoman Empire in 1453. Archaeologists refer to this as the post-medieval period, but to most people it will be familiar as the time of the Tudors and the early Renaissance.

The first of Malory's sources was English. It consisted of two Morte d'Arthur poems written in the previous century. Each was distinguished by a particular pattern of rhyming. The so-called Alliterative *Morte Darthure* was based on Geoffrey of Monmouth, whereas the Stanzaic *Morte Darthur* was based on a Continental original, the *Mort Artu* of the so-called Vulgate Cycle of French romances† – which forms the second and more important of Malory's sources. The Vulgate Cycle was a huge collection of Arthurian romances that was put together 'by a number of authors and compilers, working *c.*1215–30 under the spiritual direction or influence or inspiration of Cistercian monastic teaching ... It survives in many forms and many manuscripts, and occupies seven large quarto volumes in the only edition that aims at completeness.'[33] Derek Pearsall considers that the main aim of Chrétien de Troyes and the compilers of the Vulgate Cycle was to include the story of the Holy Grail as an integral part of the Arthurian epic romance. Malory followed, with many embellishments, where they had led.

Perhaps Malory's most memorable addition to the legend was the linking of the Holy Grail to the Holy Blood. This has recently been examined by the historian Richard Barber in a fascinating study.[34] He concludes that the linking of the Grail to the blood which dripped from Christ's side during the Crucifixion was more than an act of literary creation by Malory. He can find no mention of the Holy Blood and the Holy Grail in Chrétien de Troyes or the copious works of the

---

* The notional date for the end of the medieval period is generally taken as 1485, the year of the Battle of Bosworth.

† The term 'Vulgate' refers to the fact that the romances were written in French, not Latin. French was the vulgar tongue, or language of the people. Both 'vulgate' and 'vulgar' derive from the Latin verb *vulgare*, to make public or common.

Vulgate Cycle, and comes to the surprising conclusion that Malory 'was influenced by the cult of the Holy Blood at Hailes [Abbey], not thirty miles from his Warwickshire home, which was a famous pilgrimage site in his day. If this is correct, the Grail reflects Malory's own piety, typical of a fifteenth-century knight.' It would suggest too that there was another side to the otherwise unpleasant knight from Newbold Revell. We will see later that there is another lesson to be learned from Richard Barber's remarkable observation.

Malory was working with a vast and rich set of sources. Faced with such an *embarras de richesses* he could easily have produced an unwieldy and ultimately unreadable mess of a book. Had he decided to prune away all the excess, we would have been left with a skeleton plot, devoid of atmosphere or romance. As it was he took the middle path, and the result is a literary masterpiece of enduring greatness, even if sometimes the complex interweaving of narrative and 'the almost narcotic or balletic repetition of the rituals of jousting or fighting is part of the dominant experience of reading'.[35] It can at times be very heavy going.

We have seen that Malory's printer and publisher, William Caxton, was an astute editor, but he was also an able businessman and book-seller, and he was aware that there was a public demand for an up-to-date account of Britain's most illustrious hero. He was also motivated by patriotism, and felt it was absurd that the most complete account of the Arthur saga should be contained in foreign sources. So he decided to do something about it, and wrote a fine Introduction which makes a persuasive sales pitch.

Le Morte d'Arthur is one of the earliest printed books, and several copies of Caxton's publication survive. The trouble with printed books is that the manuscripts on which they were based often perish, and we can lose sight of what the author intended to write, before the editors or censors made their changes. But in 1934 a manuscript of *Le Morte d'Arthur* was found in the library of Winchester College. It was apparent that in his desire to present Malory's work as a complete and continuous English account of the Arthur sagas, Caxton had removed most of Malory's internal text divisions and introduced his own, which obscured the original eight sections.[36] So we end this brief review of early Arthuriana with the master spinner of tales himself being spun, and it is ironic that, like the subject of his great work, the identity of Thomas Malory himself remains uncertain.

I want to turn now to the ways in which the legends of Arthur have been used in British public life. Royal dynasties change, and sometimes incomers seek legitimacy by harking back to a real or an imagined past. Unpopular monarchs try to ally themselves to legendary heroes, and popular ones seek to increase their public appeal in the same way. When the legends of Arthur were used politically they really did matter. Arthur, and what he stood for, was deadly serious.

We have seen how the composition of the pre-Gilfradic sources was influenced by political motives, especially in the case of the *Historia Brittonum* of Nennius, which was written and assembled to favour the cause of the Welsh monarchy and aristocracy, with Arthur as a potent symbol of Welsh identity and independence. By the same token, Geoffrey of Monmouth saw to it that Arthur was identified with the Anglo-Norman court in England.[37] He set about achieving this with what today we would see as barefaced sycophancy, but which was usual practice in medieval times: he dedicated editions of his *Historia Regum Britanniae* to key people: to Henry I's (1100–35) illegitimate son Robert, and even to the warring King Stephen. Geoffrey's version of the past, including the strange account of Brutus and the marginally less strange story of Arthur, remained the dominant version of British history until well into the Tudor dynasty.

King Stephen's successor, Henry II (1154–89), was the first and possibly the greatest of the Plantaganet kings of England. He took an active part in fostering the growth of the Arthurian myth by patronising Wace, author of the *Roman de Brut*, but he is best remembered as the probable instigator or supporter of a remarkable piece of archaeological theatre that took place at Glastonbury Abbey in 1191, two years after his own death. As we have seen, Arthur was an important symbol of Welsh resistance to the growing power of the English crown, and Henry II realised that something had to be done to lay this particular ghost. It happened that in 1184 the principal buildings of Glastonbury Abbey had been gutted by a catastrophic fire, and the monks were faced with the prospect of raising a huge sum of money to pay for the repairs. The story goes that shortly before his death Henry had been told by a Welsh bard that Arthur's body lay within the grounds of Glastonbury Abbey. So, with the support of Henry's successor Richard I (1189–99), top-secret excavations were carried out, and the monks announced their discovery of 'Arthur's bones' in 1191. In a successful attempt to make this farrago credible, a Latin inscription was found with the bones, which translates as:

> HERE IN THE ISLE OF AVALON LIES BURIED
> THE RENOWNED KING ARTHUR,
> WITH GUINEVERE, HIS SECOND WIFE

This fraudulent discovery seems to have had the desired effect. Pilgrims and visitors flocked to Glastonbury Abbey, and the idea – the magic – of Arthur was effectively removed out of Wales into the clutches of the Anglo-Norman ruling élite in England. It was a master-stroke. The appropriation of Arthur provided Richard I, whose domain was spreading beyond the borders of England into Ireland and the Continental mainland, with a hero to rival the cult of Charlemagne that was then so powerful across the Channel. As an indication of the Arthurian legends' power to impress outside Britain, Richard I gave his Crusader ally Tancred of Sicily a sword which he claimed was Excalibur.

Despite the fact that several English rulers have named their offspring Arthur, none of them has yet managed to sit on the throne. It's as if the name were jinxed. Henry II was the earliest case in point. His grandson Arthur was acknowledged by Henry's childless successor Richard I as his heir, and would eventually have succeeded to the throne had he not been murdered by King John in 1203.

Edward I (1272–1307) made considerable use of Arthur's reign as a source of political precedent and propaganda to be reformulated for his own purposes.[38] He likened himself to Arthur, and with his Queen Eleanor of Castile he presided over a grand reopening of the Glastonbury tomb in 1278; subsequently he organised the construction of a shrine to Arthur in the abbey church, which was destroyed during the Dissolution of the Monasteries in 1536. One can well understand the importance Edward I attached to an English Arthur, given his vigorous campaigns against the Welsh in 1277 and 1282–83. It was Edward too who encouraged the belief that Joseph of Arimathea had visited the sacred site at Glastonbury, taking with him the Chalice used in the

Last Supper. While he was there he drove his staff into the ground, and it miraculously took root as the Glastonbury Thorn. Finally, it seems likely that Edward I was also instrumental in the construction of the great Round Table at Winchester, which I will discuss shortly.

Edward I's grandson Edward III (1327–77) was one of England's most successful monarchs, and like his grandfather he was an admirer of all things Arthurian, making regular visits to Arthur's shrine at Glastonbury. He founded Britain's most famous order of chivalry, the Order of the Garter, on his return from his famous victory over the French at Crécy in 1348. Four years previously he had hoped to 'revive' the Order of the Round Table at a huge tournament at Windsor, but had to cancel this plan because of the expense. The Order of the Garter made a very acceptable substitute, as Nicholas Higham has pointed out: 'The new institution was an "Arthurian" type of secular order, albeit under a new name, established at Windsor, which was popularly believed to have been founded by Arthur.'[39]

Edward IV, whose claim to the English throne was hotly disputed during the Wars of the Roses, actually succeeded to the crown twice (1461–70 and 1471–83). If anyone required legitimation it was he. He bolstered his regal pretensions by showing that he was related to the Welsh kings (which he was), and through them, via Geoffrey of Monmouth's *Historia*, to Arthur, the rightful King of Britain. It was during Edward's reign that Malory finished his *Morte d'Arthur*.

Henry Tudor defeated Richard III (1483–85) at the Battle of Bosworth, and ruled as Henry VII (1485–1509). To legitimise his shaky claim to the throne, he asserted that his new Tudor dynasty united the previously warring houses of York and Lancaster, and also claimed legitimacy through his connection to Arthur and the real heroic king figure of seventh-century Wales, Cadwaladr (Anglicised as Cadwallader). Henry would have been aware of prophecies that predicted that both heroic figures would one day return to right ancient wrongs. In the second year of his reign he sought to strengthen his perceived ties to Arthur by sending his pregnant wife, Elizabeth of York, to Winchester, which was popularly believed to have been the site of Arthur's court. At Winchester she gave birth to Arthur, Prince of Wales. Sadly Arthur succumbed to consumption and died, aged fifteen, in 1502; he was elder brother to the future Henry VIII.

After this initial recourse to Arthur (which did not involve a serious attempt to prove that the Tudor dynasty really *was* descended from the mythical king), Henry VII does not appear to have made significant use of the legend later in his reign. Similarly his son Henry VIII generally stayed clear of Arthur, except when it came to the crisis of his divorce from Catherine of Aragon.[40] In order to establish his own, and his country's, independence from the Roman Catholic Church he resorted to Geoffrey's *Historia* as an account of English history that was free from direct foreign influence (apart from Brutus). He also had his own image, labelled as King Arthur, painted on Edward I's renowned Round Table at Winchester. A recent study of this portrait and the tabletop on which it was painted has thrown unexpected new light on Henry's view of himself, his court – and Arthur.

The Great Hall of Winchester Castle was built by King Henry III between 1222 and 1235; it is arguably the finest medieval aisled hall surviving in England. The vast painted tabletop resembles nothing so much as an immense dartboard of 5.5 metres diameter, with the portrait of King Arthur at the top (at the twelve o'clock position) and the places of his Knights of the Round Table indicated by wedge-shaped named segments. Today it hangs high on the hall's eastern gable-end wall, but originally it would have stood on the ground.

The Round Table was taken down from its position on the wall for the first time in over a hundred years on Friday, 27 August 1976. The reasons for removing it were to inspect its condition, carry out any necessary restoration and to check that the brackets which secured it to the wall were in sound condition. It also gave archaeologists, art historians and other specialists a chance to date the tabletop and its painting, and more importantly to form a consensus on why and how it had been constructed. The results of their work were edited together by the team leader, Professor Martin Biddle, into a substantial but fascinating volume of academic research.[41]

Tree-ring dates suggest that the Round Table was constructed in the second half of the thirteenth century, between 1250 and 1280, as the centrepiece for a great feast and tournament that took place at Winchester Castle in 1290.[42] It was probably made in the town from English oak by the highly skilled carpenters who were one of England's great assets in the medieval period. Visit the spire of Salisbury

Cathedral, the roof of Westminster Hall or the great lantern at Ely if you want to see examples of their work, which was unrivalled anywhere in Europe.[43] The purpose of the tournament was to celebrate, in Martin Biddle's words, 'the culmination of King Edward I's plans for the future of his dynasty and of the English crown'. The construction of the Round Table and the holding of the tournament also had the effect of transferring, in popular imagination, Arthur's fabled capital from Caerleon in Wales to Winchester in southern England. In other words, it was a major public relations coup.

It may seem improbable, but the impact of a round table on medieval sensibilities would have been considerable. Tables are important pieces of furniture. Around them take place meals and other social gatherings, and the shape of the table itself reflects the organisation and hierarchy of the gathering. Today many family dining tables are round or oval. This does not just reflect the fact that the shape is more compact and better suited to smaller modern houses; it also says something about the way modern family life is structured. In Victorian times, for example, long rectangular tables were the norm in middle-class households. This reflected the importance of the Master and Mistress of the house, who would have sat – or rather presided – at either end. Along the sides sat the children, poor relations and others. In medieval times dining arrangements in great houses were even more formal. The Lord and his immediate family would have eaten at a separate high table, probably raised on a dais at one end of the hall. Tenants, servants and others would have dined in the main body of the hall. The high table would have been separated from, but clearly visible to, all those present. To make the display even clearer, the Lord's family and retinue would probably all have sat along one side of the high table, facing out over the hall for everyone to see. The Winchester Round Table broke all these rules, and it must have had a shocking effect on the people who saw it: in the late Middle Ages a round table was not merely an offence against protocol, it challenged the rigidly hierarchical system in which the understanding of political reality was enshrined.[44]

Sixty years after the tournament Edward III had the legs removed and the tabletop hung high on the wall, for everyone to see and wonder at. I believe that the effect of this removal from the ground to a more remote spot, high on the wall, was deliberate. Yes, it was more visible, but it was also removed, like an altar in church, visible but separate, and – I can think of no other word – Holy. Although it was still unpainted, there is some evidence that it may have been covered by a rich hanging or cloth.

The painting of the Round Table took place in the sixteenth century, in the reign of Henry VIII. Apart from some later touching up, to everyone's surprise X-ray photos showed there to have been just one layer of paint. In other words, the design had not been built up over the century and a half or so between the time of Edward III and Henry. There were two known events attended by Henry at Winchester which could have led to the creation of the painting. The first was a visit he made in 1516; the second was a more grand state occasion, when the King came to Winchester with the Holy Roman Emperor Charles V in 1522. In a fascinating exercise in detailed art history, Pamela Tudor-Craig charted the history of Henry's beard.[45] This study was able to link the Round Table's portrait of Henry as King Arthur to the period of his second, of three, beards, characterised as 'square, relatively youthful and short-bearded', that Tudor-Craig dated to the period June 1520–July 1522.

Clearly Henry was out to impress the Holy Roman Emperor. But there was more to it than that. Pamela Tudor-Craig points out that by this stage of his reign he had rid himself of Cardinal Wolsey, who had failed to gain approval for the annulment of Henry's first marriage, and was

> directing attention to historical research whereby the case for independence from Rome can be bolstered by the citation of ancient and national roots. The image of a seated king on the Round Table in Winchester Great Hall is not only a prime example of the interest in British history evinced by Henry VIII and his advisors: it is a card in the game of international diplomacy that engaged the papacy, the Holy Roman Empire, and the French and English monarchies during most of Henry VIII's reign. The Roman Emperor had Charlemagne, Francis of France claimed Julius Caesar. Henry VIII called out the Round Table presided over by King Arthur, his own imperial ancestor.[46]

During the Renaissance people in intellectual circles were inclined to question ideas that had been widely accepted during the Middle Ages, and the concept of a long-dead king whose courtiers slipped in and out of the realms of religion and magic began to lose credibility as a historical fact. But Arthur continued to exercise a degree of influence in certain circles, as Nicholas Higham explains:

> Although it is quite easy to over-emphasise Arthur's importance, he was successively used for political and cultural purposes by Edward IV, Henry VII, Henry VIII, and Elizabeth, then James VI and I, variously as a source of dynastic legitimacy and imperial status, as a Protestant icon, as a touchstone of nationalism and the new identity of the realm with the monarch's own person, and as a source of courtly ideals and pageantry.[47]

By the seventeenth century a population that had embraced Protestantism and accepted first Oliver Cromwell and subsequently parliamentary government, by which the Divine Right of Kings was repudiated, would not willingly have embraced Arthur, despite the pretensions to equality suggested by the Round Table. Instead, attention shifted towards the more historically verifiable King Alfred as England's founding father. Alfred saw himself as a Saxon king, and from the eighteenth century onwards the Anglo-Saxons, rather than the semi-legendary Romanised British, became the preferred origin myth in England.

It is probably not stretching the truth to think of Alfred as the English or Anglo-Saxon Arthur. He is often represented in similar poses, looking noble, his head held proudly aloft. There is usually a large sword hanging from his belt or grasped in his right hand. He is portrayed as being rather more rugged than the somewhat fey image of Arthur. All in all, Alfred is seen as very English, and an altogether appropriate ancestor for someone like Queen Victoria.* Like Arthur, it would seem that Alfred acquired much of his reputation and many of his heroic legends after his lifetime.[48]

Ultimately it was the Renaissance that finished Arthur as a potent

---

* At Burgh Castle on the Norfolk coast there is a stained glass church window which celebrates the links that were believed to exist between Victoria and Alfred. When I first saw the window I thought Alfred was Arthur, until I read his name.

political symbol. Ironically, the freedom of thought engendered by that great change in intellectual attitudes liberated people's imaginations, and Arthurian legends were given a new and wholly fictitious life. The Arthur of history was replaced by the Arthur of fiction. Today that Arthur is still thriving, and has contributed to a new genre of literature by way of epics such as Tennyson's *Morte d'Arthur* and *Idylls of the King*, and the fantasies of J.R.R. Tolkien, which owe more than a nod in Arthur's direction. The world of Arthur has acquired a life of its own: the post-Industrial, pre-modern age has become an unlikely Avalon. It is, for me at least, a somewhat unsettling thought that one day Arthur might prove to be the most enduring character from British history.

CHAPTER THREE

Ancient Britons

IT IS MY BELIEF that one cannot understand what was happening in late-Roman and 'Dark Age' Britain unless one has a grasp of what life was like before the Roman Conquest. The Roman period was indeed important to the development of British history, but the actual number of incomers was relatively small, given a minimum estimated population in Britain then of about 1.5 million. Certainly large elements of the southern British populace were fully Romanised by the close of the period, but others outside the south-east were not. It makes no sense to discuss post-Roman events against a backdrop of Roman Britain alone. One must look farther back in time.

When the Roman legions came ashore in the first of Caesar's two visits to Britain in 55 BC, they encountered well-orchestrated and stiff resistance. The Roman army was the most formidable military machine in the ancient world, yet the British tribesmen were able to give almost as good as they got (as Edward Gibbon would not have put it). The great Caesar's second expedition to Britain a year later, in 54 BC, was on a much larger scale, and it met with greater military success. Then he departed. The Romans did not invade Britain again for three years short of a century, in AD 43. This time the Roman Emperor was Claudius, and the general who commanded the invading armies was one Aulus Plautius. South-eastern Britain was overrun relatively swiftly, between AD 43 and 47, which Barry Cunliffe puts down to 'a measure of incipient Romanisation'.[1] In other words, as we will see in Chapter 5, the invaders were not entirely unwelcome, especially to those tribal leaders who had already formed political alliances with the Roman Empire.

The facts, as baldly stated here, do not suggest that pre-Roman

Britain was a thinly populated peasant society with a weakly developed sense of political purpose. Far from it. What emerges from a study of pre-Roman Britain is that the islands featured a diverse mix of different societies. Often these cultural groupings were in conflict – or perhaps a state of rivalry – with each other, but there are archaeological reasons to believe that they were also united by strong bonds of belief and ideology. Put another way, it seems likely that the various inhabitants of later prehistoric Britain shared a common 'world view' or cosmology.[2] Many aspects of this world view would have been shared with Iron Age people on the Continental mainland, but in certain respects even Roman writers acknowledged that Britain was pre-eminent. For example the Druids, those politico-religious leaders perhaps best seen as the Iron Age equivalents of the Muslim Mullahs, helped rally resistance to the spread of Roman rule both in Britain and on the other side of the Channel.[3] Graham Webster describes the stiffening effect that Druidism had on British resistance to Roman rule:

> Perhaps it is not surprising that the most savage and devastating wars Rome ever fought were against the Jews and the Britons, since Judaism and Druidism had a strong political bias and the passions they aroused were directed against Rome with a fanaticism which could be broken only by a crushing defeat that destroyed the majority of the devotees.[4]

We will see, however, that while many of the most militant followers of Druidism were slaughtered by Roman troops, both during Boudica's revolt in AD 60–61 and on the island of Anglesey in AD 59, it takes more than martyrdom – albeit on a large scale – to destroy a society's long- and deeply-held religious convictions, especially if those beliefs are fundamental to one's world view. We will also see that the religious beliefs behind Druidism had roots that may well have extended as far back as the Bronze Age, or even earlier. There is increasing evidence for the survival of prehistoric British religious customs through, and indeed beyond, the Roman period. I will discuss this further in Chapter 5.

I remember being taught at university that the Druids had nothing whatsoever to do with Stonehenge, which had been built over a millennium before the Iron Age, the period when Druidism flourished. The emphasis on this chronological separation was a way of saying that the modern Druids and their New Age fellow-thinkers had got it all wrong. How laughable, we were told it was, that the latter-day Druids dressed up in sheets and pranced around the stones on the night of the midsummer solstice. How misguided they were! Today, however, most prehistorians would accept that the religious beliefs that formed the core of Druidism had very ancient roots indeed, at least as old as Stonehenge, and probably a great deal older.[5]

It came as no surprise when we found that the small Early Bronze Age timber circle known as Seahenge was entirely made from oak trees. The choice of oak must have been deliberate, because other locally occurring woods such as ash, willow, alder or poplar, would have been just as suitable, and rather less work to cut down. Oak was, and still is, the best British constructional timber, and it must have been held in high regard in prehistory. It was the structural steel of its day. Barry Cunliffe quotes a revealing passage from Pliny the Elder, writing about the Druid priesthood:

> They choose groves of oak for the sake of the tree alone and they never perform any sacred right unless they have a branch of it. They think that everything that grows on it has been sent from heaven by the god himself.[6]

Pliny goes on to describe how mistletoe is cut from oak trees, with a great deal of ceremony and the use of a golden sickle; a superb Late Bronze Age sickle, complete with its wooden handle, was found along-side a contemporary timber causeway through wet ground at Shine-water Park, near Eastbourne, and we now know of several sites in Britain where identical Bronze and Iron Age religious rituals continued without a break. When it comes to the matter of pre-Roman ritual and ideology, I'm now inclined to think that the much-derided people wearing sheets actually had a better idea of what was going on in prehistory than my lecturers at Cambridge, who were unable to take a sufficiently long or broad view of the way that prehistoric beliefs arose, developed and matured through the centuries of later prehistory.

Most prehistorians are now agreed that the modern Western dis-tinction between the sacred and the profane – between religion and domestic life – is a product of the way we organise our time. If you like, it reflects our world view, which is largely based around the need to work – and to work with the greatest possible efficiency. In medieval times the Church impinged on domestic life to a far greater extent than it does today, and a sizeable proportion of the population, who lived in the hundreds of monastic foundations across the land, devoted their entire lives to the service of God. The sixteenth-century Reformation was to change all that. Over succeeding generations religion became increasingly confined to church on Sunday. In most households today people no longer say grace before meals – the last vestige of religion within the domestic sphere.

In pre-Roman times religion and daily life were closely integrated. People would probably not have been aware of when their thoughts were within the realms of ideology or practicality, because the distinction was meaningless. The shades of the ancestors inhabited the countryside around them. Their presence within burial mounds along the edges of communal grazing ensured that animals were not allowed to stray too often onto pastures where they were not welcome. The prevailing cosmology in pre-Roman Britain seems to have been structured around the cycle of the seasons, and the movements of the sun and moon in the sky. These things gave form not just to the great religious (archaeologists prefer the term 'ritual') monuments such as Stonehenge, but to the arrangement of ordinary houses, which in Britain were almost invariably circular in plan. By the same token, the interior arrangement of communal tombs, such as Maes Howe in Orkney, replicated the way that houses were laid out. The one was seen as a reflection of the other – which tells us something about the way in which the sacred and the profane were seen as being part of the same entity.

If we see integration, we also see longevity, which suggests that prehistoric religious beliefs addressed themes that were deeply rooted within society. These themes doubtless included the role of the family as a means of structuring society, the place of human institutions within the natural world, and of course the continuing cycle of the seasons – and with it the replenishment of food, fuel and shelter. Today many of these concerns can be addressed through science and secularity. Religion does not need to be invoked. Having said that, prehistoric ideologies also addressed the traditional territory of religion, which may be seen as 'rites of passage', to use an anthropological term: birth, puberty, marriage and death.

When we look at prehistoric ritual activity it's hard not to see constant reiteration. There is a long-standing concern with water, for example: all sorts of things are placed in or thrown into rivers, bogs, lakes, ponds and wells – swords, shields, weaponry in general, pottery vessels, bones, bodies and so forth.[7] Sometimes these things are fabulously valuable, at other times they are more humdrum. Sometimes they have been deliberately smashed before being offered to the waters, at other times they are in perfect condition. Items used in the preparation of food, and particularly corn-grinding stones, known as quern stones, are often placed in the ground or in water as offerings.

It would be a mistake to regard the items placed in the ground or in water as mere things. Certainly they could be very beautiful, but like many objects they possessed a symbolic life of their own. Thus a sword could indeed be a weapon, but it could also be a symbol of an individual's rank or authority, so that its breaking before being offered to the waters would have symbolised that its owner had passed out of this life. Maybe the broken sword was thought to become whole again in the realm of the ancestors.

We can only speculate as to what these things originally symbolised, but there are now literally thousands – maybe tens of thousands – of prehistoric offerings known in Britain alone, and certain patterns are beginning to emerge. Water probably symbolised both separation and travel. Beneath it you died, yet it was also a substance in which you saw your own reflection – something we take for granted today, but which rarely happened in prehistory. A journey across water, whether by boat or on foot along a causeway, could symbolise the journey from this world to the next – or any other rite of passage. Prehistoric causeways which played an important ritual role often led to offshore islands, which again could be seen as symbolising other worlds or states of being. As for the corn-grinding stones, they possibly reflected the importance of the meal as a means of keeping the family together, but they could also have expressed a wealth of other ideas, including the role of women within society, motherhood or family life.

These rites first become evident archaeologically from around

4200 BC, at the onset of the New Stone Age or Neolithic period, but there is a growing body of evidence to suggest that their roots lie even further back in time – maybe even as far as post-Glacial times, around ten thousand years ago. The prevalence of certain themes over thousands of years does not indicate that a particular religion held sway for that length of time; it's doubtful whether one could have talked of 'a religion' in Neolithic times. What this longevity or persistence indicates is a phenomenon termed by French anthropologists the *longue durée*. Practices which persisted in certain cultures over huge stretches of time owed their longevity to the fact that they were embedded or rooted within aspects of society that were seen to be essential to that particular community. In prehistoric Britain, the most persistent theme was a concern with the cycle of time and the movement of the celestial bodies.

One could speculate endlessly on what it was that made the passage of the seasons, the sun and the moon so important in prehistoric Britain, but it may owe something to the prevalent way of life, which was based on animal husbandry, a choice which in turn was influenced by the British maritime climate, which grows grass superbly well. We always suppose that the ancient arable farmer worried about the germination of the next season's crops, and that this gave him an interest in seeing that the days lengthened after the midwinter solstice. The same goes for the livestock farmer: grass too effectively ceases to grow in winter, and the appearance of calves and lambs was, I am sure, as eagerly awaited as the first sprouts of a freshly germinated crop of wheat. Farmers have a natural concern for the passage of the seasons.

Nevertheless, I'm doubtful whether one can attribute something as fundamental as a society's world view merely to climate or livelihood. Such things come from deep within people themselves. Fully formed ideas need time to appear, but when they do, they are taken up very rapidly if they are right for the society and the times. This is what probably happened in the Later Neolithic period in Britain and Ireland, with the first appearance of circular tombs known as passage graves, whose entrances were often aligned on the sun at solstice. Before that time (say 3200 BC), many of what were later to prove persistent ritual themes had been in existence for several centuries or more, but it was the appearance of passage graves beneath round mounds, and slightly later the erection of the great henge monuments, that gave formal expression to these long-held beliefs.

The longevity of the religious ideas of pre-Roman Britain suggests they were deeply embedded within society. They were not mere superstitions. The placing of swords and shields in a river was not the pre-Roman equivalent of tossing coins in a fountain 'for luck'. We should think more in terms of christening, Holy Communion or the funeral service. If these rites were deeply rooted within British culture, they were also part and parcel of everyday life: they fitted that life and expressed the way people viewed themselves, their families and their world. They were, if you wish, a ceremonial or ritualised expression of the beliefs that motivated people to get up in the morning.

The idea of the *longue durée* also suggests that when we find pre-Roman rites surviving into Roman and post-Roman times, we are witnessing the survival of far more than mere ritual or superstition. We are actually seeing the survival of ancient patterns of social organisation, family structure and cosmology too – because you cannot separate the rituals from the societies and the belief systems that gave rise to them. Certainly some will have been modified through time and changing circumstances, but the core of the beliefs must remain constant, or the rites become irrelevant – in which case they wither and die.

With certain notable exceptions, such as Navan Fort in Northern Ireland, the religious sites of the last prehistoric period, the Iron Age, are less obviously eye-catching than the elaborate monuments of the Later Neolithic and Bronze Age periods such as Stonehenge and Avebury in England, Maes Howe in Orkney and Newgrange in Ireland.[8] By this period, too, the archaeological evidence for actual settlement is becoming more prominent, largely as a result of the steady growth of the British population. In this chapter I want to give an impression of what Britain might have looked like to a visitor arriving in, say, AD 42 – the year before the Roman Conquest. I start with a simple question: was Iron Age Britain very different from Roman Britain? I believe that it wasn't, for the simple reason that, setting aside short-lived introductions such as towns, the army and the imperial administration, Roman Britain *was* Iron Age Britain.

The survival of 'native' British culture and traditions into post-

Roman times only makes sense if we understand its age and scale. Take, for example, the longevity of British society before the arrival of Roman forces in AD 43. In common with other parts of Europe there had been well-organised societies living in settled communities for at least three thousand years before Christ. Before that there were two millennia or so when societies were less settled, but no less organised. Even in the millennia after the Ice Ages (around ten thousand years ago) the British population was thin, but the landscape was already being parcelled up by the people who inhabited it. Life for hunter-gatherer groups was by no means an anarchic free-for-all.

It is simply wrong to suppose that the Romans brought civilisation to a barbarian Europe: they brought their own *style* of civilisation, which was founded on ideas that flourished in classical Greece in the fifth century BC, and they imposed it, with greater or lesser success, on pre-existing settled populations who possessed their own social rules and regulations. The landscapes that Caesar's legions marched across were not dense primeval forests: most of them had been cleared of trees for several millennia. His men tramped their way through fields, roadways, farms and villages. I doubt whether the average modern person, if dropped into a rural village in pre- or post-Roman Britain, would be able to tell them apart. He would probably only spot that he was in Roman times if a visiting government or military official was in the neighbourhood, or if he happened to be shown a family's best dinner service (which seems somewhat unlikely).

If pre-Roman society consisted of a handful of skin-clad savages eking out a frugal existence on nuts and berries, its ideas and culture could not have survived into post-Roman times. There has to be a critical mass of people for their ideas to persist if their culture is overtaken by outsiders. In the case of pre-Roman Europe that critical mass certainly existed. Any lingering notions of skins, nuts or berries should be replaced by woven cloth, wine, beer, bread, cheese, mutton, lamb, beef and pork. Estimates of Britain's population in the last centuries BC are hard to arrive at, but few would place it much below 1.5 million, and some would put it as high as 2.5 million.[9] Whatever else it was, it was not a small handful. Who were these people, and what would it have been like to have lived in Britain during the century or so before the Claudian conquest of AD 43?

The second half of the last century BC and the first half of the first century AD is sometimes seen as a period of 'almost-' or 'proto-history', because although written records had yet to develop in Britain, Julius Caesar and other Roman authors were busily writing in Gaul (France) and elsewhere; sometimes they even referred to Britain. In Britain there are early indications of writing that did not simply arrive, fully finished, from elsewhere: there are, for example, numerous examples of Iron Age coinage, some of which bear clear inscriptions, such as 'CAM', which we know was an abbreviation (much needed) of Camulodunum, present-day Colchester in Essex. Writing, rather like farming, seems to have been an idea that people wanted to grasp even before they understood precisely how it worked. Maybe members of élite society in southern Britain liked the concept of literacy before they possessed it fully themselves.

The great Roman general and future Emperor Julius Caesar made two visits to England in 55 and 54 BC. These expeditions were essentially to gather intelligence, and should be seen as a part of his campaigns in Gaul, which began in earnest in 59 BC. Caesar's first expedition to Britain in 55 BC involved ninety-eight transport ships carrying two legions (each of ten thousand men), plus cavalry and many accompanying warships. The landing in Kent was resisted, and there were numerous skirmishes with the British. Eventually Caesar retreated back to Gaul. The following year he did things on a larger scale. This time there were eight hundred ships, transporting five legions and two thousand cavalry. This huge force met stiff resistance under Cassivellaunus, leader of the Catuvellauni, a tribe centred on Verlamion (St Albans) and parts of what is today called 'Mid-Anglia' (Hertfordshire and areas around). Caesar had a hard fight through Kent. He crossed the Thames into the Catuvellaunian heartland, and eventually British morale broke down and Cassivellaunus sued for peace. Caesar returned victorious, with many hostages, but he had met fierce opposition, and was probably relieved to leave Britain with his honour intact.

The history of relations between Britain and Roman Gaul after the second visit of Caesar is complicated. The leading authority on the period, Professor Barry Cunliffe, has distinguished two significant phases in Later Iron Age southern Britain.[10] During the earlier, or

Contact Period (120–60 BC), Britain was in regular contact with Europe and the expanding Roman Empire. Following the fall of Gaul and Caesar's two visits to Britain, Rome had made two physical impacts – hence the Impact Period. Cross-Channel relations in the Impact Period became a great deal less straightforward, and depended very much on the political skill, or otherwise, of the emerging tribal leaders, or kings, of southern Britain.

The numerous Iron Age issues of British coinage provide us with useful sources of information. It is still popularly believed that the Romans introduced the idea of coinage to Britain. Even in archaeological circles, where it has long been recognised that coinage began in Britain under the influence of Continental prototypes, it was thought that so-called Celtic coins were debased and misunderstood versions of their far more sophisticated classical (i.e. Greek and Roman) counterparts. It was held that Celtic coinage was both poorly executed and undisciplined; it is hard to avoid the conclusion that this opinion reflected current views of pre-Roman society when compared with a classical ideal. All that was changed, however, by a detailed study of British pre-Roman coinage by the numismatist R.D. Van Arsdell.[11]

The earliest coins imported to Britain arrived around 125 BC, and the first British-minted insular issues appeared just twenty-five years later. These were cast bronze coins, made in Kent. Another twenty-five years later the first struck British coins were produced. Casting is a crude method of producing coins, each one of which must be produced in an identical mould. Struck coins are produced using a design inscribed onto two dies, which are negative images of the coin face in a metal harder than the coin itself. The dies are hammered onto the front (obverse) and back (reverse) of each coin blank, which is of a specific weight and composition. The first actual coin die from pre-Roman Britain has recently been discovered near Alton in Hampshire.[12] It's a die for the obverse of the coin, and it shows a lively horse with a charioteer holding something looking like a lance, with a long shaft.

It used to be believed that British Celtic coins were not minted to controlled (i.e. specified) weights and compositions. In effect this meant that they could not have been used as money. Van Arsdell

Four examples of pre-Roman 'Celtic' coins with prancing horses. These are examples of Cunobelin so-called Wild Type (AD 10–20).

however convincingly showed that their weights and denominations were strictly controlled. It was also thought that the design of Celtic coinage, which often appears as a surreal but strangely harmonious disintegration of heads and legs, was uncontrolled, chaotic and barbaric. Again, Van Arsdell revealed that the art of the coins conceals messages that are relevant to their value. He has also shown, as we knew from other aspects of Celtic art, that Iron Age art in Britain was not simple. The artists were not attempting to draw an image that looked exactly like, say, a horse. Like Picasso and other modern artists, they were more concerned with illustrating what horses stood for: their grace, speed and ability seemingly to fly when jumping obstacles. In other words, their art had more to do with impression and expression than representation pure and simple.

Celtic pre-Roman coinage clearly illustrates the sophistication of Later Iron Age societies. The coins in question are numerous, possibly numbering tens of thousands. This suggests that maybe a hundred or a thousand times more than that were originally minted, indicating highly sophisticated, populous and well organised societies. This was the culture which the Romans sought to control. Thanks to their military might they were generally successful in this, but control should not be confused with the erasure of pre-existing societies. Roman control of large parts of the British Isles – most of Scotland, Cornwall, all of Ireland and parts of Wales – was tenuous or non-existent. In areas of southern Britain where their rule was most effective, they simply added a new layer to what was already there. They certainly affected the development of life in southern and central Britain, but by no means did they destroy British society.

If we regard the way that coinage was adopted as a response to a growing and widespread phenomenon that élite groups in Britain wanted to become involved with, there were other aspects of the Roman and classical world that also appealed to the same classes. In particular the personal appearance of British élites was changing. Quite literally, they were cleaning up their act. In the Late Iron Age we see the widespread appearance of items to do with personal hygiene: small bronze scoops for removing earwax, tweezers, razors and miniature pestles and mortars for grinding make-up. I found one of these tiny Roman pestle and mortar sets within the posts of the Bronze Age causeway at Flag Fen, presumably offered to the waters as a deliberate act – otherwise it is difficult to explain why the two things were found together. Personal appearance was now something that mattered, and was required to be taken seriously.

The British Museum Iron Age specialist J.D. Hill has made a study of these changes to people's appearance in the Late Iron Age.[13] Not only were they paying greater attention to personal hygiene, their clothes must have altered too. In the next chapter we will see examples of safety-pin- (or fibula) style brooches from an Iron Age and Roman site at Maxey, near Peterborough. These were by no means isolated finds. In the final centuries of the Iron Age we see the widespread adoption of these new Continentally-inspired ornaments, that must have been accompanied by a change towards finer clothing, if only for special occasions such as weddings. Hill has referred to this change as the 'fibula event horizon'. The important point to note here is that these changes marked more than just a new fashion. They marked a new attitude not just to personal appearance, but to personal perception: 'the end of one kind of body and the beginning of another kind of body', to quote the title of Hill's paper. We will see later that there was an equivalent of the 'fibula event horizon' in the fifth century AD, although this time the influences were to be from northern Germany rather than Roman Gaul.

We are now fully within the era of proto-history, verging indeed on history. During the Impact Period, contacts with the Continent grew stronger as Roman rule gave much-needed stability to Gaul. The Roman army was busy tackling Germany, and Britain, after Caesar's two bloody expeditions, was left alone. The result was prosperity and a measure of stability. Starting very early in the first years AD, a remarkable man called Cunobelin arose as High King of the Catuvellauni, ruling his kingdom from a new capital at Camulodunum (Colchester). His domain consisted of a confederation of tribes comprising most of East Anglia south of Norfolk (home of Boudica's Iceni), plus Kent and parts of southern England. His reign lasted over thirty years, which was no mean achievement – and very much longer than any of his contemporaries. He died some time around AD 40, and instability returned to the tribal kingdoms of southern Britain. Doubtless this political uncertainty was a significant factor behind the Roman decision to invade three years later.

At some point during the Impact or Contact Periods it seems probable that a sense of 'Britishness' developed among certain of the élites of southern Britain. This may not have amounted to a sense of shared belonging or solidarity, as in the modern Celt; nevertheless, informed people must have been aware that they lived on an island, and that the Continental mainland was different – it was an 'other', the scene of tumultuous political events. Maybe their sense of being British amounted to no more than a feeling of opposition to, or admiration of, the Romans. Perhaps it was no more than a feeling of opposition to that 'other' across the Channel. Certainly unity amongst the various tribal kingdoms that had emerged during the Contact Period is hard to find: each had its own policies with regard to the Romans, and radical policy shifts could happen overnight. It was a fickle world.

Attacks on Brittany in 57 BC as part of Caesar's campaign against Gaul effectively finished off the flourishing trade that then existed between Britain and the Continent, which was not to resume for some time. When it did, the focus shifted from the south-west of Britain eastwards towards the Thames estuary, to Hertfordshire, Essex and Kent, which were becoming politically and economically more important. While Britain tended to provide raw materials and slaves in exchange for wine and other high-status commodities, it was not always as simple as that. Simon James describes how the contacts between Britain and mainland Europe were complex; the British provided ideas and political inspiration for their cousins across the Channel.[14]

By Late Iron Age times and into the first years AD, Roman authors record that the Druidic religion flourished in Britain, and had an important influence on the Continent.[15] Certainly the Romans saw it as a threat, and after their conquest they made strenuous efforts to stamp it out – efforts which culminated in a battle and massacre on Anglesey in AD 59. We must assume that the Druid religion described by Roman authors arose out of the diverse regional and tribal religions of the Middle Iron Age. This process of amalgamation would have been hastened by the conquest of Gaul by Julius Caesar between 60 and 50 BC. Conquest can provide a strong catalyst for political and other changes, and it would be a mistake to treat the Druidic religion of the half-centuries before and after Christ, as recorded by (hostile) Roman sources, as being wholly representative of what had gone before. Whatever else they originally might have been, the Druids of the Impact Period were highly politicised.

In pre- and post-Roman times we are not dealing with a free market economy as we understand the idea today. Goods that were bought from abroad would mostly have been acquired for purposes of display or conspicuous consumption. Fine wines from the Mediterranean region came to Britain in large ceramic vessels known as amphorae. This was a trade that continued throughout the Roman period and into post-Roman times, mainly in west and south-western Britain.

Does this trade indicate merely a continuing taste for wine, or something more significant? The *longue durée* argument might apply: the consumption of wine in western Britain lasted for so long because it was embedded within some social practice that mattered to people. Certainly wine was enjoyed by those who could afford it, but its public consumption, probably during feasts, was important, just as in medieval times it was important that the Lord and his family occupied the high table in a staged, artificial fashion. Medieval mealtimes in the great hall were about more than eating, just as wine was about more than merely status: both were reflections of the way society was organised; ultimately they played an important role in the maintenance of social stability and security. That was why they mattered.

The amphorae came from Italy, Spain and the Mediterranean region. They were large and robust containers that were in widespread use for trade in Roman times. They mainly held wine, but could also be used for olive oil and a fermented fish sauce much beloved of the Romans, known as *garum*.[16] Britons were trading with the Continental mainland for maybe three thousand years before Christ, but these contacts seem to have become more frequent, if not regular, during the Earlier Bronze Age (say from 1700 BC).[17] By the Iron Age, roughly a millennium later, cross-Channel contacts were more formalised and took place at specific ports of trade which initially were located in south-western Britain. The earliest such port we know about is at Mount Batten (Plymouth, in Devon); it was succeeded as the main port of trade by Hengistbury Head (on the south side of Christchurch Harbour, a few miles further along the south coast, on the Dorset–Hampshire border).[18] The switch from Mount Batten to Hengistbury Head took place around 100 BC.

Recent excavations at Hengistbury Head have shown that trade between Britain and Gaul covered a wide variety of goods.[19] In many respects the range of materials exchanged reflected trade patterns in the much later British Empire, with luxury goods coming in and raw materials going out: into Britain came wine, figs, glass and other luxuries that have left no archaeological trace; these were exchanged for corn (wheat and barley), hides, cattle and metals (copper, tin, lead and the tin/copper alloy, bronze). Roman authors also mention the export from Britain of slaves and top-quality hunting dogs.

Barry Cunliffe has demonstrated that trade on the south coast was effectively controlled by a Gaulish tribe known as the Veneti, who were based in Brittany and who probably had actual outposts – trading settlements – in the British ports of trade.[20] It was the Roman presence in southern France (Provence) from about 125 BC which hugely increased the penetration of Roman culture northwards into Gaul. At this stage the penetration was cultural and economic, but after Caesar's conquest of Gaul, trade with Britain changed its pattern, shifting eastwards towards the new centre of British tribal political influence, the areas around the Thames and the extreme south-east.

Wine was made in Britain during Roman times, but only on a limited scale, as varieties of early-maturing grapes had yet to be developed. Most wine consumed by high-status Britons or Romano-Britons was imported. Before the conquest it came first via the Mount

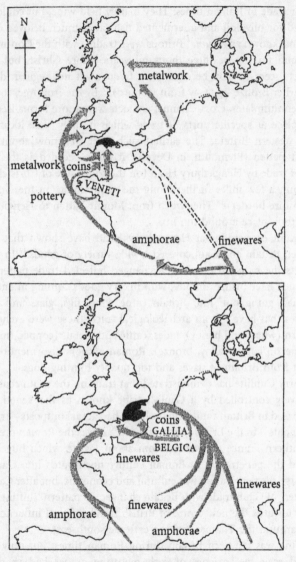

Patterns of trade between Britain and Continental Europe before (above) and after (below) Caesar's Gallic (French) campaigns of c.60 BC.

Batten/Hengistbury Head route, then through ports in the south-east; in Roman times amphorae are found in many places, but most probably entered the country through Londinium, or London, which was at the hub of the Roman road system. Large numbers of Spanish amphorae, mainly in the form of fragments, or sherds, are known from Britain in the first two centuries A D; thereafter political problems caused the British wine trade to shift north, towards France and southern Germany. Then, as now, stiff competition for imported wine was provided by British beer.[21]

I shall finish this rapid review of southern Britain before the Roman Conquest with two case studies of the landscape. The first is rural, the second is approaching urban.

Hillforts are a characteristically Iron Age class of site, consisting of one or more large ditches and banks placed around the crown of a hill. The up-cast from the ditches forms the banks which are positioned uphill of the ditch. Together the two form a wall-like defence, known as a rampart. Often the wall-like effect was heightened by strengthening the banks with an internal wood or stone framework which allowed the outer face to be vertical, or nearly so. The top of the bank would frequently be capped with a defensive wall, again in either wood or stone. Sometimes hillforts would have just one set of ramparts, but the larger examples nearly always had two or three.

Clearly the entranceways into a hillfort were a major point of weakness, and great efforts were made to render them more secure. Usually this involved the construction of additional ramparts and of baffles, walls and palisades to give the entranceway a maze-like configuration which included many positions from where the defenders could rain slingstones, spears and arrows down on any attacking force. Hillforts tended to be sited on prominent hills, and it is no coincidence that frequently their locations also happened to have been important in earlier times. Often, as for example in the case of Britain's best-known hillfort, at Maiden Castle in Dorset, the hilltop itself had been a religious and ceremonial centre for two or three millennia prior to the erection of the Iron Age ramparts.[22] These were special places with long histories. They would have been far more than mere refuges in times of trouble; indeed, the larger hillforts, such as Danebury on the chalk downs of Hampshire, would probably have been tribal capitals. Their initial construction and subsequent enlargement and elaboration were a major communal effort that must have been motivated by more than just fear for the future: they were important symbols of communal identity, and it is no accident that their presence usually dominates the surrounding landscape.

Hillforts and smaller defended settlements are very much a feature of Atlantic Europe, which of course includes Britain, but they are also found elsewhere on the Continent. Most were constructed in the Iron Age, although a significant proportion have roots extending into the Later Bronze Age. Large and elaborate hillforts are found on the hills and downs of south-west and central-southern England. Their construction seems to have begun in the late sixth and the fifth centuries BC. Barry Cunliffe sees this as a significant social change, probably brought about by population growth and competition between various communities for resources. At first there were many hillforts, each of which was surrounded by its own territory of fields or more open pasture. As time passed there was a process of consolidation, in which many of the smaller hillforts were incorporated within the enlarged landscapes that were now controlled by an emerging group of much bigger forts. Danebury is an example of such a large, successful hillfort. It was excavated by a team under Barry Cunliffe, and today we probably know more about Danebury and its hinterland than any comparable landscape in Iron Age Europe.[23]

Danebury was first occupied after about 550 BC, and almost came to an abrupt end around 100 BC, when the main fortified gate was burnt to the ground. Like all the larger hillforts in central-southern England, the defences of Danebury were massively elaborated every few generations, with particular attention being paid to the entranceways. Clearly the intention was to impress as much as to defend.

Having entered by the eastern gateway, the visitor to Danebury would find himself standing on a chalk road which ran in a gentle curve across the interior to the western entrance. This was Road 1. To the left were Roads 2 and 3, which were lined on both sides by a 'ribbon development' of post-built square granaries. At the centre of the enclosure was a temple or shrine which was reached via Road 4. Two further roads (5 and 6) serviced the main body of roundhouses which extended along the northern part of the interior. The organisa-

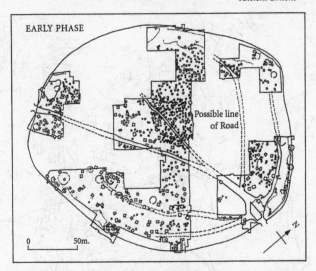

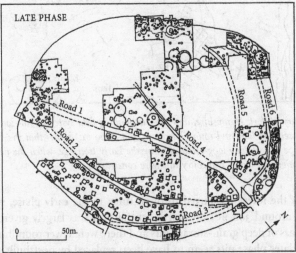

The interior of the Iron Age hillfort at Danebury, Hampshire, in its early phase, 550–300 BC (top), and late phase, 300–100 BC (bottom). The circular shapes are the foundations of roundhouses, the small squares are four-post grain stores, and the larger square structure towards the centre is a shrine or small temple.

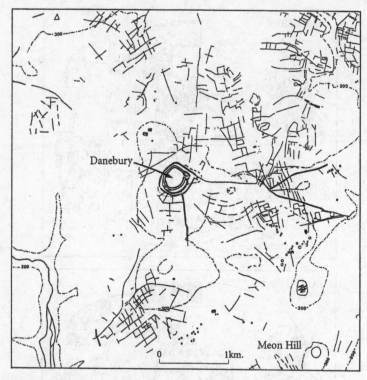

Danebury hillfort, Hampshire, and the surrounding field systems (550–100 BC).
The presence of long and round barrows (3500–2000 BC) shows that the
landscape was already long-established by the Early Iron Age, when the first
fortifications on top of Danebury hill were constructed.

tion of the interior changed through time: in the early phase, which
ended around 300 BC, the north-central area was largely given over
to a mass of deep grain-storage pits and there were fewer roundhouses.
In the later phase pits seem to have been replaced by post-built granaries, which were now far more common than in the early phase.
There were also many more roundhouses. The human population
would have been between three and five hundred at any single period.

The hillfort was clearly positioned at the hub of its landscape. By
the Iron Age many of the livestock-based economies of southern

Britain were being replaced by systems of farming that were more flexible and productive. These involved the keeping of livestock, but also the growing of cereals, such as wheat, oats and barley. Danebury was important for many reasons, but its role as a vast grain store must have been crucial to the region's economy. Many of the fields around the hillfort were used for livestock – air photos clearly show stockyards, handling areas and droveways. But they were also used to grow crops, many tons of which would have been processed and stored in the hillfort. So Danebury was not just an empty symbol of wealth and power – it actually contained and protected it in the real, physical form of grain.

We do not know for certain whether Danebury is typical of larger hillforts in the central-southern zone, but field surveys and more limited excavations at South Cadbury (Somerset), Chalbury and Maiden Castle (Dorset) suggest that it probably is.[24] This pattern of intensive settlement with roundhouses and numerous grain-storage pits seems to be a feature of larger hillforts in the central-southern region. Elsewhere in Britain, in Wales, northern England and Scotland, the interiors of Iron Age hillforts included very large open spaces; they never begin to resemble small towns, as Danebury does in its later phases of life.

Was Danebury ever a small town, or did it merely begin to resemble one? My feeling is that its population of five hundred people makes it too small to be considered truly urban. But there is more to it than that: the development of hillforts in Britain was a phenomenon that peaked before the Roman Conquest of AD 43. Had Julius Caesar invaded Britain successfully in 54 BC, the controversy surrounding hillforts and their urban status would be more clear-cut. As it is, we know that they were in decline as regional centres from the last century BC. Danebury, for example, effectively ceased to be a significant focus for settlement after 100 BC, although the landscape around it continued to prosper well into Roman times, most probably thanks to the effective politics of Cogidubnus, client king of the Atrebates, who was able to ward off some of the less friendly aspects of the new imperial regime. It would seem that the enlarged hillforts were a response to a particular set of social circumstances that prevailed in central-southern England in the Middle Iron Age – and as such they were relatively short-lived.

Whatever was happening on the hilltops, I suspect that the vast majority of the population actually lived in undefended farmsteads and villages on the lower-lying land surrounding the great hillforts. Today 'rescue' archaeology ahead of the construction of factories, roads and pipelines is revealing an extraordinary wealth of Iron Age settlement sites in southern Britain.[25] The landscape around Danebury was composed of fields, roads and trackways that were carefully and well laid out. The origins of this particular landscape, and hundreds like it across southern Britain, go back several millennia, to when the primeval forests were initially cleared to make way for crops and animals. What we see in the Iron Age is the culmination of a process that was already very ancient indeed.

We have seen how the focus of political and economic power shifted towards the south-eastern corner of Britain after the fall of Gaul to Caesar's forces. So this, if anywhere, is where we should expect to find evidence for *bona fide* urban life before the Roman Conquest of AD 43. So now I will turn my attention a little north and some distance east for my second case study, which centres on the north Chiltern Hills of Hertfordshire.[26]

As far as we know, most Roman towns were built either on or near significant centres of Later Iron Age trade and settlement. This in itself suggests a very considerable degree of continuity between pre- and post-conquest times. I want now to take a closer look at the way one of these places developed, and I have chosen a group of settlements in the northern part of the south-eastern region, around the gently rolling Chiltern Hills north of the Thames in my own county of Hertfordshire. This landscape lies within the part of Britain that began to grow in importance very rapidly in the Late Iron Age, and particularly after Caesar started his military campaigns across the Channel from about 60 BC. My case study will centre on the Late Iron Age settlements and the landscape around Verlamion, the British name for the subsequent Roman town of Verulamium, or St Albans.

London aside, only a small proportion of Roman towns and their Iron Age antecedents have been excavated to modern standards.[27] There were, it is true, larger-scale excavations in the nineteenth century, but these should be treated with some caution, as the archaeologists of the day did not possess the wealth of scientific techniques that are commonplace today. In some instances archaeologists, such as Professor Mike Fulford at Silchester, are re-excavating these old digs, and are finding important ancient deposits that still lie undisturbed. It would be a mistake to regard the pre-Roman towns of Britain as wattle-and-daub equivalents of their cement-and-stone Roman counterparts.* As we will shortly see, they were nothing of the sort.[28] So what were they like?

The short answer is that each one appears to have been different: there was no universal pattern to their layout, which instead would appear to have come about through a process of unplanned or organic development. Our case study, Verlamion, was positioned at the edge of the light, readily ploughed, loam terrains of south-eastern England. This change in soil marks a natural boundary between regions, and it is at such neutral, boundary areas that centres of exchange and trade spring up. The Later Iron Age saw quite a rapid expansion of population, and many areas once considered marginal were taken into agriculture. Verlamion was founded on such newly won farmland.[29]

There has been a lot of archaeological activity along the Chiltern Hills, and when this is combined with more recent aerial photographic surveys, it becomes clear that Verlamion did not sit on its own, but was part of a huge spread of Later Iron Age settlement with a number of major concentrations. Many of the more significant of these larger settlements have been excavated, and we now possess a remarkably complete picture of this important pre-Roman landscape.[30] If we look at these main concentrations closely we find that they consist of many earthworks bounding smaller individual territories, and there is also evidence for housing, much industry, various shrines, many cemeteries (often with high-status graves) and an élite or upper class of richer people. There is also an enormous amount of evidence for farming, both of crops and livestock. This is surprising, because the farming seems to have been integrated within the other activities in the densely settled areas. Farms and fields stood alongside houses and industry.

* Wattle-and-daub was the standard pre- and post-Roman building material. It consisted of a woven wattle (usually hazel) framework which was daubed (smeared) with a mixture of clay, cow dung and straw. This material (which in some parts of the country is known as 'cob') had to be kept dry, unlike true lime mortar, which was introduced to Britain by the Romans.

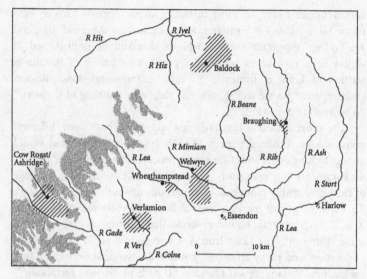

Major Late Iron Age settlements in Hertfordshire and the north Chiltern Hills.

It was a way of structuring social and economic life that worked: field systems and settlements grew steadily in size, and to judge from the amounts of rubbish they left behind them, people became better off.

The country around Baldock is a case in point,[31] and I have to admit a special fondness for it, having spent my youth and childhood on the chalk downs that overlook the town. This, however, is not dramatic country: there is no mighty bluff on which a Maiden Castle might be erected. But there are hills, albeit gentle ones, and there are two hillforts, at Arbury Banks and Wilbury Hill. These do not dominate the centre of the landscape so much as mark its periphery. Of course we cannot be certain that they are in fact on the boundaries of what the Iron Age inhabitants of Baldock would have regarded as their territory, but it seems quite possible. The hillforts aside, what strikes one most about Baldock and the other landscapes of the region is the general lack of defences: people were not at each other's throats, and raiders from outside were not expected. This was a peaceful landscape in which the residents felt confident of their personal security.

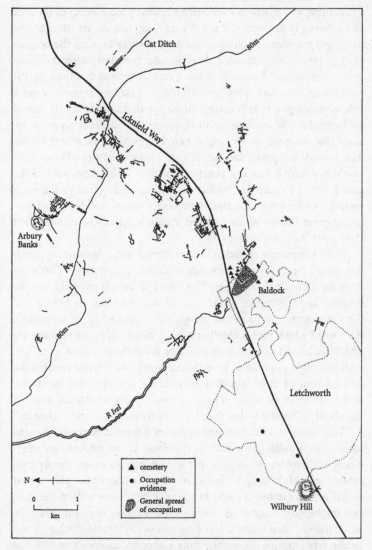

The main archaeological sites and features of the Baldock Iron Age complex.
The approximate extent of the Iron Age settlement and Roman small town of
Baldock is shaded.

Turning to Verlamion itself, with so many people living in the area and growing in prosperity, it is not surprising that earlier (Bronze and Iron Age) traditions of building great earthworks to mark the bounds of one's estate were rekindled. As time passed, doubtless too there was much competition for social status. I do not believe that these earthworks were defensive, pure and simple: it makes no sense to erect a defence through a heavily settled landscape that has previously shown no indications of internal, or intra-communal, strife. It seems more likely that what we are looking at here is something akin to the walls that bound the parks around British country houses. These walls would not have deterred a poacher, but they would have warned the casual visitor to keep out, and by following them round to the main entrance to the estate, the legitimate visitor would find his or her way to the great house. So they served a practical purpose of sorts, but their main role was to impress.

If the earthworks of Verlamion are plotted out, it becomes apparent how much larger was the Iron Age settlement, or *oppidum* (Latin for a town), than the Roman one. The term *oppidum* is generally used to describe large town-like settlements of Iron Age date in Britain and the Continent,[32] and I'm not altogether convinced of its usefulness. It's a word which lumps together a huge variety of very different sites which are united only by their size. Size is a reflection of other things, such as simple population growth combined with a trend towards the development of more stratified, hierarchical societies. But one factor that does seem to unite *oppida* in many parts of Britain and the mainland of Europe is that they were centres of trade and exchange.[33]

Verlamion was an Iron Age *oppidum* before it became a Roman town. What was life like within the *oppidum*? At face value the archaeological evidence would suggest that the various sites were merely concentrations of unusually intensive rural settlements, plus a fair sprinkling of earthworks and industry. If that were indeed the case, one might expect social life within them to have been organised on an essentially rural pattern, based on ties of family and kinship. It was family relationships – possibly quite elaborate, extended ones – that had provided the social 'glue' which held British rural society together for millennia. They were a way of uniting societies in regions which did not have a strong central or established hierarchical authority.

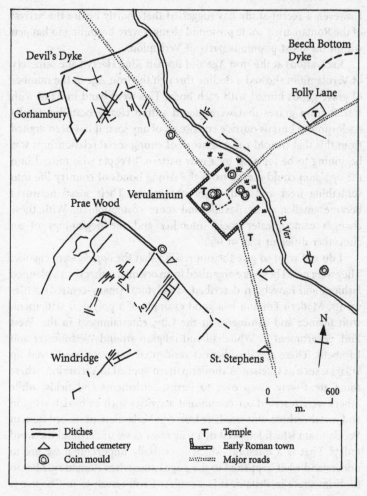

The Roman town of Verulamium (St Albans, Hertfordshire), surrounded by the earthworks and other features of the Late Iron Age settlement of Verlamion.

However, a recent study has suggested that shortly before the arrival of the Roman army some profound changes were beginning to happen within the most populous parts of Verlamion.

Excavations at the Iron Age and Roman King Harry Lane cemetery of Verulamium showed a decline through the Iron Age in the number of grave-goods buried with each body. This went hand in hand with a shift from graves that were placed within clearly bounded family enclosures to burials outside enclosures of any sort. It has been argued from this that the old rural network of strong social relationships was beginning to be replaced by a new pattern.[34] People who moved into the *oppidum* could escape from the strong bonds of country life into something freer and with fewer obligations. Their social networks became smaller, more flexible and more cosmopolitan. With these changes came greater social mobility and the beginnings of an altogether different way of life.

I do not want to give the impression that the *oppida* were chaotic. They were not. They were organised in an organic, rather than a planned fashion, and have been described as polyfocal (many-centred) settlements. Modern London is a good example of a polyfocal settlement, with finance and commerce in the City, entertainment in the West End, government in Whitehall and religion around Westminster and Lambeth. There are also distinct residential areas and swallowed-up villages, such as Chelsea. A similar pattern applied to Verlamion, where some areas were given over to farms, settlements and fields, while others were reserved for communal activities such as burial, religion and metalworking. But was Late Iron Age Verlamion, or indeed Roman Verulamium which followed it, a true *town* as we understand the word today? That is a question which is crucially important if we are to understand what happened to the population when Roman rule began to disintegrate in Britain. It is a subject I will return to in Chapter 7.

CHAPTER FOUR

My Roman Britain

IF THERE IS a big divide in my subject, it is between prehistory and Roman archaeology. Prehistorians like me deal with vast expanses of time, and rarely if ever see writing or inscriptions. Our approach to the past is usually deeply rooted in anthropology. Generally speaking, the repertoire of material we deal with is limited – there are, after all, not many things one can do with pieces of flint and relatively simple techniques of metalworking. Romanists, on the other hand, have to consider no more than a few centuries, but they make up for the short span of time by the breadth and depth of their erudition: for example, their ability to read obscure and invariably heavily abbreviated inscriptions can sometimes seem magical. They also need to understand coins and a vast array of intricate objects ranging from jewellery, locks and keys to imported items from the Mediterranean basin. Add to this the fact that their background will generally include ancient history, linguistics or classics rather than anthropology.

Rather than attempt a summary of Roman Britain in just one chapter, I will offer some thoughts on Roman and Late Roman Britain born of my own experiences as a field archaeologist.[1] The area in which I have spent my professional life is centred on the modern city of Peterborough, which is not just a region with a rich prehistoric past: it contains some of the most important Roman sites in England, and also lies near the heart of post-Roman Anglo-Saxon England. So it is ideally suited for an examination of what was happening during this fascinating period.

One thing that immediately struck me when I first encountered the evidence for so-called Anglo-Saxon incomers in the second of the two case studies I'll be discussing shortly, was the way they had instantly grasped how to live and farm in conditions and soils that can be agriculturally challenging. It was as if they had been doing it for years. Being a farmer myself, I know how hard it can be to come successfully to terms with new soils, land and drainage regimes. Those 'incomers' didn't seem to have put a foot wrong.

Early in my archaeological career, in 1970, I worked on a Saxon site at North Elmham in Norfolk, both because I admired its director, Peter Wade Martins, and because I believed I could learn more about prehistory by working on Saxon and early medieval settlements, where much of the evidence was very similar to what one would find on a pre-Roman site. One big difference, of course, was that sites of the later periods could benefit from written sources. In fact, I learned that although the written sources told one all sorts of useful things about the way parishes were laid out, where roads went and how people resolved tenurial disputes (i.e. over land or property), it was generally impossible to relate what they said to specific structures on the ground. The written accounts did not necessarily help one decide whether the pattern of post-holes known as building A was, say, a hall or a barn – to do that, one was forced to use one's archaeological judgement, just as on a pre-Roman site.

Before we go any further, I must pause to consider terminology. I will use the slightly long-winded term 'Romano-British' in the chapters that follow to describe aspects of Roman Britain. It is not a term I'm particularly fond of, but it is universally accepted, and besides, I cannot think of a better one to describe the people and the culture of Britain at the time. The term 'Roman' is used quite specifically by archaeologists to refer to the period of the Roman occupation from the Claudian conquest of AD 43 to the end of Roman rule, which is generally set at AD 410. This chapter will be about the Romano-British people of the Roman period in a part of Britain I know well.

Ask most people about life in rural Roman Britain and they will probably reply that it happened in villas. They may be a bit hazy about what actually went on in a villa, but columns, porticoes and bath houses with under-floor heating are usually mentioned. In fact there were not very many villas in Britain, and they occurred in quite specific parts of the country. Elsewhere, rural settlement continued much as it had done in Iron Age times.

In the 1970s and eighties I directed excavations of two small Roman hamlets in eastern England. As so often happened, they had started their lives as Iron Age settlements and continued into the Roman period. After the conquest of AD 43 they continued exactly as before, with 'native' or Iron Age-style roundhouses and with their farms and fields laid out as they had always been. The first archaeological indication of the Roman Conquest one comes across is the pottery. From the second half of the first century AD we find the local hand-made Iron Age domestic pots and pans being replaced by mass-produced Romano-British coarse wares. But there is no evidence to suggest that the people using the better, harder new pottery were different in any way from their Iron Age equivalents. In fact they were probably the same individuals, or their children.

The two Romano-British settlements I excavated were both close to Peterborough, and were typical of rural communities in one of the most prosperous parts of Roman Britain. I shall describe one of them in an attempt to show what life might have been like for an average Romano-British family in this area.[2] The name of the parish in which the site once lay, Maxey, comes from the Anglo-Saxon Macuseige, meaning Maccus's Island. I say 'once lay' because, like many other archaeological sites nearby, it has vanished into an enormous flooded hole left by the large gravel pits that border the southern parts of Maxey 'island'. I put the word 'island' in quotation marks because although the village is never flooded today, it lies on the floodplain of the River Welland, close to the point where the river enters the Fens. Consequently the land around it was subject to frequent floods in medieval and earlier times. One of the first Roman finds we made when we introduced fine-mesh sieving to our excavations in 1980 was a bone from a sprat, a fish which is at home in tidal waters.

In the past it has been suggested that the appearance of Anglo-Saxon place names like Macuseige signalled the establishment of new settlements by migrants from abroad. It is a theory that simply – and wrongly – links new names with new places. Archaeologically there can be little doubt that the good Saxon called Maccus was the last of a long line of people to link their names with this popular, flood-free place of settlement. Maxey had been a desirable area for at least four thousand years prior to the Saxon period. Occupation started there with the first clearances of the forest and the establishment of a Neolithic ceremonial site around 3800 BC, and continued, so far as we can tell, without any significant gaps until the present day.

The earliest site in Maxey Quarry was a Neolithic causewayed enclosure, a type of ceremonial and religious centre found widely across central and southern Britain. Causewayed enclosures were often located in marginal environments, presumably because they were believed to be in close proximity there to other worlds, such as the realms of the ancestors. Throughout the subsequent Bronze Age, the area continued to be revered as a special place for ceremonial and for the disposing of the dead, beneath a succession of barrows or burial mounds. Islands and water were important to the religious beliefs of both the Bronze and Iron Ages. Religion featured quite prominently in Roman and Saxon Maxey, and the fine parish church which sits atop a substantial and very intriguing mound still dominates the village. I do not believe that the selection of Maxey as a place to settle was ever just a simple matter of avoiding floods. There must also have been ideological and spiritual reasons why so many people chose to live there for so long.

What was life like in Roman Maxey? The first thing to realise is that it was never static or unchanging. Farms and houses may remain unchanged through time, but people are always altering their surroundings, often in little ways, and over the years these small changes accumulate – which is what happened at Maxey in Late Iron Age and Roman times. When we wrote up the excavations we distinguished ten distinct phases where the cumulative changes amounted to something distinctively different. For present purposes I will look at Phases 6 to 9 (late first century BC to early fourth century AD).

The first plan (Phases 6–7) shows the remains of a typical small Iron Age settlement lying above the abandoned ditches of Neolithic and Bronze Age ceremonial features, which are shown in outline. The large ditches would have served a dual purpose, both as drains and as field and property boundaries. Close to the larger ditches are the distinctive circular trenches (nos 1, 2 and 9) that acted as gutters around the outside of roundhouses. Known as eaves drip gullies, these circular features usually include a gap to allow people to cross into the main entranceway, which usually faces south-east, in the direction

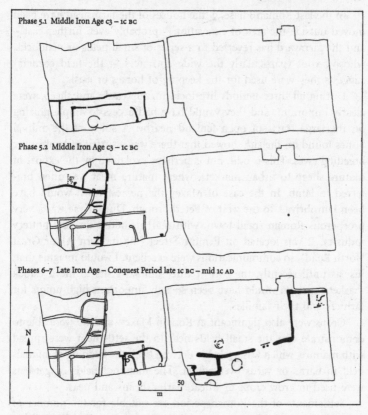

Phase 5.1 Middle Iron Age c3 – 1c BC

Phase 5.2 Middle Iron Age c3 – 1c BC

Phases 6–7 Late Iron Age – Conquest Period late 1c BC – mid 1c AD

N

0   50
        m

Three phases in the development of the Romano-British settlement at Maxey,
Cambridgeshire. Archaeological features shown in outline predate the phase
being illustrated (in black).

of the rising sun.[3] One tiny ring gully (no. 24) was probably dug to
surround a small stack of hay or straw.

In the next Phase, 8, the settlement shifts further east, and large
ditches are elaborated to form a series of small farmyards, probably
for the use of cattle and sheep. There is now evidence for three roundhouses (nos 3–5) in the new easterly farmyard, but one still remains
in the older yard to the west (no. 10). This phase also saw the construction of a small temple or shrine (12).

In the last Roman Phase, 9, the houses of the farmstead have been moved outside the area of excavation – probably even further east – and the farmyard has reverted to a series of small fields or paddocks, whose layout (particularly the wide entrances at the field corners) suggests they were used for the keeping of horses or cattle.

During all three periods livestock, mainly cattle and sheep, were clearly important, and they would have had access to ample grazing on the large tracts of open fenland nearby. A study of the animal bones found on the site showed that there was a surfeit of lambs over breeding ewes. This is odd, but is perhaps explained by the export of mature sheep to urban markets, where mature meat was often preferred to lamb. In the case of Maxey the nearest town would have been Durobrivae, to the west of Peterborough. Durobrivae was a very prosperous Roman small town, with markets and a thriving pottery industry. It was located on Ermine Street (the modern A1 or Great North Road), so communications were excellent. I would imagine that, just as until recently, the two or three annual visits to the livestock markets in town would have been socially important high points for farmers and their families.

Crops were also significant at Roman Maxey, and we were able to demonstrate that the small fields near to the settlement were spread with manure, which was probably derived from the bedding of animals held in barns or yards over winter. The manured fields or gardens were used to grow crops of wheat, barley, beans and peas.

Settlements of the Roman period are notable for the number of coins they reveal. There is so much information currently available that coin specialists have been able to predict what coins certain sites are likely to produce. I asked Dr Richard Reece of University College London to have a look at the five coins we found at Maxey. His first reaction was surprise verging on incredulity that we found so few, given the extent and thoroughness of our excavation techniques, which included the routine use of sieves and metal detectors – something that was still unusual back in 1979–81. He would have expected us to find coins known as radiates of the Gallic Empire (259–73) and issues struck between 330 and 348, during the reigns of Constantine I and his sons, but they were absent; instead we found an odd mix of coins which suggested, as he put it, 'the sporadic loss of irrelevant objects, rather than a sample of normal coin-loss, and hence coin use; it may be enough to question the relevance of coins to the practical economy of the site . . . It could lead to a most interesting future study, perhaps best entitled "The Pattern of Coin-Loss on Coin-Less Sites".[4]

Maxey represents a small settlement of a dozen or eighteen people in perhaps two or three households. We know of at least two other, somewhat larger, settlements in the modern parish whose Roman population may have amounted to as many as fifty to a hundred people. So far as we can tell, these hamlets or farmsteads were near the bottom of the social ladder: luxuries were rare, but not unknown, and most of the food produced seems to have been kept for local consumption. Although the inhabitants were far from wealthy, the half-dozen bodies we recovered were generally well-nourished and disease-free, apart from some minor arthritis and one case of osteoporosis, which could have been a diet-related problem.

All in all, the impression one gains from Maxey is of subsistence, but significantly above the poverty line. Rural life would not have been easy, but it would not have lacked its rewards either: there was evidence for pinkish-red Samian Ware, imported from Gaul and doubtless used 'for best', and we also found a number of bronze brooches, one of which had been mercury-gilded and included a jewel-like polished glass 'stone' setting. I have to admit that when I found it I thought it was Victorian and of little importance, so popped it into my pocket and then casually produced it in the pub that evening. When our finds specialist saw it lying on the bar, I was ordered home to put it safely under lock and key.

The archaeological world first heard about Maxey in 1960, when the huge numbers of wartime and post-war aerial photographs were assembled into a report, *A Matter of Time*, which showed how commercial quarrying of gravel was rapidly destroying swathes of ancient landscape in the river valleys of lowland England.[5] Most of the photos were of so-called 'cropmarks', ancient features such as field boundary ditches, farmyards, roads, burial mounds and trackways that have been levelled by centuries of ploughing. As a result of this agricultural smoothing they only show up in growing crops, usually between May and July. Viewed from the air, especially in a dry year, the cropmarks can be spectacular, but when you visit the site on the ground it is completely flat and featureless.

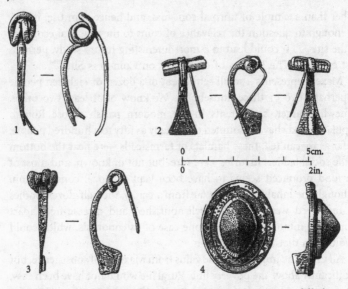

Four Romano-British bronze brooches from Maxey. Nos 1–3 are of fibula or safety-pin type; no. 4 is a mercury-gilded plate brooch with a black conical glass central inlay. Drawings by David Crowther.

I spent a great deal of time looking through the air photos of Maxey, and it gradually dawned on me that the Iron Age and Roman farms and fields that my team had excavated once formed part of a much larger system. Although the photos showed a spaghetti-like tangle of ditches, they did seem to make general sense. First, they appeared to form two distinct ribbons of development on either side of the wide, flat valley that bounds the River Welland to the south.* Second, most of the ditches ran either parallel, or at right angles to, the river. The only clear exceptions to this were two long, straight ditches at Maxey itself, which were diagonal to the general 'grain' of the landscape. These two ditches belonged to a very much earlier Neolithic monument, known as a cursus, and can be discounted from the present discussion.

The more I examined the aerial photographs, the more convinced

* At the time, aerial photographs of the area north of the river Welland were not readily available for study.

I became that most of the miles of cropmark ditches formed coherent patterns. Tracks and roadways seemed to fit in with the arrangement of fields, paddocks and farmyards. There was clear evidence too that some fields had been enlarged or subdivided, which is what one would expect from a living, growing landscape. It also accorded well with what we had observed in our excavations, where the fields were modified through time and the areas of domestic settlement drifted gradually eastwards.

It is very difficult to say precisely when this landscape came into being. One clue may be provided by a series of large Bronze Age burial mounds, often with multiple circular ditches surrounding them, which appear to be evenly spaced at roughly half-kilometre intervals along the southern part of this landscape. It's as if some time around 2500 BC people decided that the fertile pastures of the southern Welland Valley had to be parcelled up in an equitable fashion, and enlisted the help of their dead ancestors to ensure that that the arrangement was not abused. In the northern part of the valley the first ditched field boundaries appear around 1200 BC (i.e. the later Bronze Age), but in the south true fields are not defined until the middle of the Iron Age (around 300 BC).[6]

It would probably be unwise to regard the Welland Valley field boundary ditches as part of a true 'system', in which all parts must work together for it to be effective. In some areas fields were abandoned, in others they continued to flourish and new land was taken in. What we are looking at here is a coherent pattern of landscape which includes a number of individual field systems, rather than a single field system, *sensu stricto*.

The beginnings of any field system are always difficult to determine with any precision, for the simple reason that once they have gone to the effort of digging ditches around their fields, farmers then try to keep them clear of silt and rubbish – otherwise they would not work effectively as drains. In the Welland Valley, where flooding can still be a problem, most farmers dig out their ditches, or dykes as they are known, at least once every seven to ten years. Every routine cleaning-out of a ditch removes all the archaeological evidence that has accumulated in it since last it was dug. One is then left with a false impression of a field's true age.

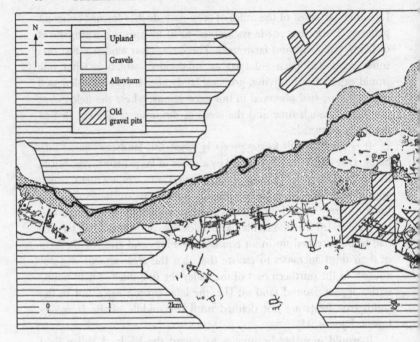

The main elements of the Welland Valley fields were, I think, in place by the end of the Iron Age, but the full flowering of the systems happened in Roman times.[7] There is plenty of evidence to suggest that these fields and farms thrived well into the fourth century; but what happened then? Again, it is difficult to date with any accuracy when a field is abandoned. If, for example, it changes its use from arable to pasture, the need to maintain its drainage becomes less pressing: grass can tolerate short periods of waterlogging, and on certain freely-draining gravel soils (which do exist in the Welland Valley) poor drainage is actually an advantage, especially in hot, dry summers. If ditches cease to be regularly maintained, the field can continue to function because of its hedges and fences – both of which leave little or no archaeological trace.

Once accompanying hedges have grown up alongside the ditches – a process that takes around five years – the need to retain a deep ditch as a feature of a field or farm boundary becomes less pressing.

Early field systems in the southern Welland Valley, as revealed on aerial photographs. Most were laid out in the Later Bronze and Iron Ages and continued in use throughout the Roman period.

These hedges can form features in the landscape in their own right, surviving as boundaries for many hundreds of years.[8] This may be one of the reasons why earlier field systems and their alignments can survive in the countryside for so long.

There is widespread evidence that conditions underfoot became wetter in the Fens towards the close of the Roman period. Certain regions, such as my own area of research around Flag Fen in eastern Peterborough, became uninhabitable in the fifth and sixth centuries, largely due to the fact that the River Nene regularly flooded the landscape round about. That does not mean, however, that people simply abandoned everything. They couldn't afford to. The fen margins are some of the richest grazing in Britain, and the Fens themselves are an abundant reserve of eels, fish and wildfowl: sources of the fat and protein that people must have if they are to survive the rigours of winter. There is no evidence to suggest that the inhabitants of Maxey abandoned the village at the end of the Roman period; instead they moved to somewhat higher ground, towards the centre of the 'island', closer to the church. What happened to the Romano-British landscape of Maxey at the close of the Roman period?

Work leading up to the publication of *A Matter of Time* led to a flurry of archaeological activity around the Maxey gravel quarries, and a few years ago I was given the job of editing and publishing one or two excavations that for various reasons had not made it into print.[9] This work set me thinking about Roman, post-Roman and even medieval Maxey. One of the reports in that volume is about a ditched settlement with a roundhouse at a place called Plant's Farm on what are now the western outskirts of the village. This site, which proved to be Roman, was part of the huge system or pattern of ditched fields and trackways that covered most of the southern Welland Valley. The Plant's Farm settlement lasted well into the fourth century, and like the Roman site we had excavated in the village further east, it seems to have reached its time of maximum prosperity in this, the last full century of Roman rule.

While I was working on the new report I had frequently to dip into a much earlier publication of excavations that took place in 1959 and 1960 a short distance north-east of the church. One of the excavators, Peter Addyman, went on to achieve fame both as the Director of the York Archaeological Trust and the inspiration behind the Yorvik Viking Centre. Peter and a local colleague, Ken Fennell, did a rescue excavation in 1959 and 1960 just across the road from the church. It was published in a national journal, with admirable promptness, in 1964, and it caused a huge stir.[10] At the time post-built rectangular timber buildings of the Middle Saxon period (650–800) were extremely rare, and they had found half a dozen. The site today is a flooded gravel pit.

So there was a substantial village at Maxey in Middle Saxon times, and it seems likely that its Early Saxon (450–650) predecessor lies just across the road, either in the churchyard or in the fields around it, which we know from air photos are extremely rich in archaeological features.[11] A shift of such a short distance would be entirely consistent with the type of 'settlement drift' that is commonly observed on sites of most archaeological periods in the area, and which we saw so clearly in our own Romano-British excavations at Maxey. As I worked on the publication of the earlier digs I became intrigued by the fact that both the Middle Saxon village and the possible site of its predecessor across the road were in areas that also included ditches of the Roman system. This raised the questions of whether the occupants of the first Saxon village were outsiders from abroad, and whether there was evidence for a clear break between the Roman system of fields and yards, and the appearance of the first post-Roman village.

My immediate instinct was that occupation had been continuous. Had I been looking at air photos showing a sequence of Bronze or Iron Age settlements, I would have had no doubt whatsoever: the arrangement of Addyman and Fennell's rectangular Middle Saxon houses precisely followed the alignment of the Roman boundary ditches. This could, of course, have been coincidence, but the excavators themselves noted that 'These two ditches seem effectively to define the northern limits of the site, and the aerial photographs show that most of the pits [of the Middle Saxon village] destroyed [by the quarry] before excavation were within the extension of Ditch A.'[12] Ditch A was a part of the Roman system and, most unusually, its bank survived up until the start of the excavation. This would strongly indicate that it served as a boundary, perhaps carrying an ancient hedge, throughout the Middle Ages.

So it would appear that earlier patterns of land allotment were influencing the shape of the Middle Saxon village. This in turn would suggest that the landscape at Maxey was still being managed by traditional rules and regulations of land ownership, which is not what one would expect to find if the population came to the area from abroad. Roman military engineers, for example, paid no heed to traditional British patterns of land tenure when they drove their long straight roads through the landscape; they had other, more pressing, concerns to worry about.

There is other evidence that the Roman and pre-Roman landscape continued to be respected in post-Roman and Saxon times. My predecessor in the Welland Valley, Gavin Simpson, also excavated extensively in the Maxey gravel pits. He quotes one example at Maxey where a Roman site probably continues into early medieval times.[13] However, his best-known site was in the main Maxey gravel quarry, at a spot known as Bardyke Field, where his excavations revealed a Late Iron

Age boundary ditch. 'This was completely filled by the mid-late second century AD, yet its bank must have survived for many centuries after and became known in the Middle Ages as the Bar Dik which gave its name to one of the open fields.'[14] I would attribute the survival of the earthwork to the presence along it of an ancient hedge. Gavin Simpson draws attention to other instances in the Maxey region where pre-Roman and Roman land-divisions 'determined the layout of medieval and recent landscapes'.

Are we witnessing here the survival, more or less intact, of entire Romano-British landscapes into Saxon and later times? The answer has to be no. Even in exceptional cases, such as the extraordinary buried landscapes of West Heslerton in East Yorkshire (which I will consider in more detail in Chapter 8), there was substantial modification through time, eventually leading to the replacement of one long-lived landscape by another. Generally speaking the alignment or 'grain' of the developing landscapes stayed similar through time and certain key features, such as roads, remained constant; but I find it difficult to believe that a millennium and a half ago people had the energy or the resources to obliterate old landscapes wholesale, and replace them with something altogether new. It simply does not make sense, and the available evidence indicates that it did not happen.

The survival of elements of the prehistoric and Romano-British landscape into later times is not unique to Maxey. In a paper by two leading authorities on ancient fields, Chris Taylor and Peter Fowler, Chris gave several examples of recently discovered sites where Romano-British fields and boundaries survived into Saxon and later times. Peter followed with a discussion of the implications of this, and provided a significant comment: 'Taylor ... offers two options to explain a direct link in Roman–Saxon field arrangements, both assuming an Anglo-Saxon takeover; but other alternatives come to mind, not least that of Britons continuing to farm their "ancient fields" well into the so-called Anglo-Saxon period.'[15]

A few years earlier Chris Taylor's *Fields in the English Landscape* (1975) gave many examples of Roman fields being taken over by incomers from abroad:

There is reason to believe that most medieval villages were occupied in Roman times and their fields subsequently taken over by the

Saxons. However, the basic problem of exactly how the Roman
fields ... became the medieval or open-strip fields still remains.
Can this difficulty be resolved? It must be, for the origin of the
medieval field system itself needs to be understood if its history is
to be seen clearly. Yet at this moment this cannot be done with
any certainty and only suggestions can be made about it.[16]

He went on to suggest a series of rather tortuous explanations for
something that at first glance seems both manifestly impossible and
patently absurd. Of course the simplest explanation of all would be
to do away with the idea of waves of invading Anglo-Saxons, but that
would have been inconceivable even in the mid-1970s. It was one thing
for prehistorians to debunk waves of nameless Iron Age immigrants
from the European mainland, as they had successfully done in the
previous decade; but the arrival of the mighty Anglo-Saxons on the
shores of Britain was something altogether different. In the public
perception, and in many archaeologists' minds, the coming of the
Anglo-Saxons changed Celtic southern Britain into England. To challenge that was to raise fundamentally important questions of national
identity and self-respect; it was a nest of hornets that any scholar
would hesitate to disturb. But it was the only plausible way to explain
how the use of Romano-British fields continued into the Early Saxon
period.

I now come to the time when my own belief in the large-scale folk
movements known as the Anglo-Saxon incursions began to wobble. It
happened that possibly the most important site of the Roman-Saxon
succession anywhere in England was being excavated on the western
side of Peterborough at precisely the same time that I was digging up
large tracts of the fen margins at Fengate, on the other side of the
city, to the east. That now-famous Roman to Saxon site is known in
the archaeological literature as Orton Hall Farm.

As I mentioned in my earlier book *Seahenge*, during the 1970s I
had a job in the Royal Ontario Museum which involved, among other
things, my coming to Peterborough each summer to excavate sites
along the edges of the Fens at Fengate, an industrial suburb on the
eastern fringes of the city. In those days the government believed that
many of London's problems of overcrowding could be sorted out by

the building of two rings of New Towns on green-field sites out in the country. Individual Development Corporations were set up for each New Town to receive direct funding from the Treasury. Luckily the board of Peterborough Development Corporation had a conscience, and realised that the new roads, housing estates and industrial areas would cause immense archaeological damage. As a response to this threat they decided to fund a full-time archaeologist, through an already existing archaeological body who decided, with every justification, that the New Town archaeologist should be a Romanist. This made sense, as the Romano-British remains in the area were of national importance. The outskirts of the New Town would probably impinge on the outskirts and satellite settlements of Roman Durobrivae, which was the largest, and one of the more successful, small towns in Roman Britain.

The appointment was duly made, and the successful applicant was Donald Mackreth. Don had had a highly distinguished career as an excavator, particularly at the pioneering urban excavations at Winchester, and he was also an excellent draftsman and an expert on Roman brooches.[17] As we have seen at Maxey, brooches occur commonly on Roman sites and can be a useful aid to dating, so Don's expertise would prove invaluable.

The site at Orton Hall Farm had been excavated by local enthusiasts since 1964, but in the late 1960s it was announced that a large part of it would be destroyed by the construction of an intersection on the proposed dual-carriageway ring road which today surrounds Peterborough. Shortly after his appointment Don assembled a team, and work began in 1973. It was completed in 1975, just as construction of the new road was about to commence. Originally the plan had been to excavate the site in a year, but that was before its true complexity had been revealed. Don and his team worked wonders to recover such a full record of so difficult a site in just three years.

In the first two years I made repeated visits to Orton Hall Farm, and as Don or one of his supervisors showed me around we would discuss what lay before us. I remember thinking how horribly complicated the succession of different features had become as the work progressed, and how glad I was not to be digging the site myself. I was also struck by the fact that different rules seemed to apply at each end of the Roman period. At the time I had just started work on an

Iron Age-to-Roman farmstead at Fengate, at the 'start' end of the period. Don was working on a Roman-to-Saxon farmstead, the 'finish' end. Yet a completely different set of interpretational criteria governed the two projects.

At my site, Fengate, there was no doubt that I was digging a prehistoric British farm occupied by Britons. After the Roman Conquest these same people decided to use a radically different type of mass-produced Roman-style of pottery, and sometimes to wear Roman-style brooches from the middle of the first century AD. They also ceased making old-style Iron Age pottery, which stopped quite abruptly when the first Romano-British mass-produced alternatives arrived on site.

Something very similar was happening on the other side of the city, at Orton Hall Farm, except this time the changes were the other way about: the pottery changed from mass-produced to hand-made, and ornaments changed from Roman to 'Anglo-Saxon', in particular a characteristic type of sleeve fastening known as a wrist-clasp, which works on the principle of the modern-day bra fastener, with a flattish hook and an elongated catch-plate or slot. It's a practical type of fastener that can easily be done up or undone single-handed. What I failed, and still fail, to understand was why the changes in archaeological artefacts, which were so similar at both sites, were attributed on the one hand to Roman 'influence', and on the other to Anglo-Saxon incoming 'settlers'? In other words, the changes observed at the earlier site involved the movement of ideas, and at the later of people. But why?

These thoughts troubled me for a while, but then I found myself busily engaged writing the academic report of my work at Fengate, and any ideas about what may or may not have happened in post-Roman Peterborough had to take a back seat. I thought no more about such things until 2001, when I set about writing *Britain BC*, a process that involved rereading various papers that debunked the Iron Age Celtic 'invasions'. As I read, all my doubts about the Anglo-Saxons re-emerged, but by now the archaeological climate had changed radically, and I found that my views were not only non-controversial, but quite widely accepted by leading authorities on the Anglo-Saxon period. It was quietly satisfying to know that I had come to them myself, independently, back in the early 1970s.

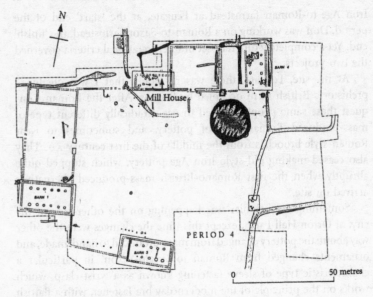

Orton Hall Farm, Peterborough: simplified plan of the Late Roman farm (Phase 4 c.225/250–c.375).

Let's have a closer look at Orton Hall Farm to see precisely how the Anglo-Saxon phenomenon affected the archaeology of an otherwise unexceptional Romano-British farmstead. As I have already noted, this area of Roman Britain was prosperous. Most of the wealth seems to have been based on the products of farming, and Roman Orton Hall Farm appears to have been a great deal more prosperous than either contemporary Maxey or Fengate. It's hard to suggest an obvious reason why this should have been so – distance from the regional centre, the market town of Durobrivae, may have been a factor, but the simplest explanation would be that the Romano-British rural landscape, like landscapes before and after it, included farms of many different shapes and sizes. Orton Hall Farm was one of the larger and more successful of them.

There is evidence for pre-Roman activity on the site, but it's pretty scrappy: a small pond which was shifted sideways and enlarged in Roman times, and a few ditches which may have formed parts of

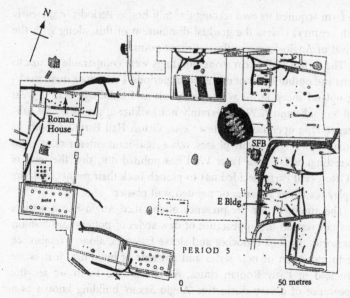

Orton Hall Farm, Peterborough: simplified plan of the Late Roman and 'Anglo-Saxon' farm (Phase 5: c.375–early sixth century).

fields, paddocks or even yards. Unlike Maxey or Fengate, there was no Iron Age farm or settlement directly beneath the Roman farm, although there was evidence for early settlement nearby. The farm gets going in earnest in the mid-first century AD, shortly after the Roman Conquest. Like most farms of the Early Roman period, it included a number – up to five or six – of roundhouses of traditional or 'native' Iron Age type. Donald Mackreth assigned the first Roman farm to Period 1, which ended around AD 175.

In Periods 2 and 3 (c.175–300/325) the farm becomes larger, and the space it occupies is transformed into a large ditched farmyard with a series of buildings around its periphery. Stone buildings appear for the first time in Period 3 (around 225/250), and the farm settles down: buildings cease to be shifted and become more static through time. By Period 4 (c.300/325–375), i.e. during the fourth century, which Guy de la Bédoyère christened the Golden Age of Roman Britain, Orton Hall Farm was having its own little Golden Age. During this period the farm acquired its own rectangular mill-house. Period 5 (c.375–early sixth century) covers the gradual diminution of this, along with the arrival of Anglo-Saxon settlers at some point.[18]

The Orton Hall Farm stone buildings were comparable in size to barns and outbuildings of more recent periods. I've visited small working upland sheep farms where the yards and buildings were a great deal less substantial. We're certainly not looking at a small-scale subsistence-type operation; whatever else, Orton Hall Farm, in both its Roman and 'Anglo-Saxon' phases, was a significant enterprise. It's also interesting, as Dr John Peter Wild has pointed out, that the owners of Orton Hall Farm decided not to plough back their profits in flashy display – such as mosaics or painted wall plaster.[19]

The argument for the presence of so-called Anglo-Saxon settlers does not rest on the appearance of new styles of pottery and fashion accessories, such as brooches and sleeve fasteners, alone. We also see the introduction of new styles and patterns of buildings, just as we witnessed in Early Roman times. At Orton Hall Farm we see the appearance of a very distinctive 'Anglo-Saxon' building known as a sunken feature building (SFB), or *Grubenhaus*, to use the German word (which rather instructively became the standard English term for these Continental-style 'pit dwellings'). A *Grubenhaus* is a small, squarish rectangular (the archaeological term is sub-rectangular) building which is characterised by a hollow or pit-like space beneath the floor. These pits can be half a metre or more deep. At either end of the pit is a hole for a post which supported the roof's ridge-pole. Similar buildings are found right across northern Europe in the fifth to seventh centuries AD, but they are particularly common in Britain.

I will discuss their function in Chapter 8, but here I want to note the presence of one within the bounds of a Late Roman farmyard, just outside a ditched yard which contained the post-holes of a small 'Anglo-Saxon' hall at Orton Hall Farm. Mackreth dates this SFB to the late fifth century at the earliest, and provides good evidence to suggest that it had fallen into disuse before the abandonment of the main farm in the early sixth century. The presence of a very early SFB is interesting, but its position outside what seems to have been a specifically domestic enclosed space suggests it was used as a farm building, not as a house.

The Romano-British house of Periods 3–4 was rectangular, made of stone and measured about twenty-five metres long by just over eight metres wide. Mackreth had problems defining its precise size because the walls had been 'robbed out' (an archaeological term to explain the removal – 'robbing' – of stone from an abandoned building for use elsewhere). But he was able to demonstrate clearly that the place of the Roman stone building had been taken by an 'Anglo-Saxon' hall-type rectangular building, made from timber.[20] As we saw in the Iron Age/Roman overlap, the introduction of stone to replace timber does not have to involve the replacement of the resident population. It is merely a change of building technique. With the decline of Roman influence and the breakdown of formal trading networks in the fifth century it is hardly to be wondered at that people reverted to a more traditional and readily available building material.

It is worth noting here that the most characteristic Anglo-Saxon domestic building, the so-called 'aisled hall', has interesting origins. We will see examples of these buildings later, at places as diverse as Maxey, near Peterborough, and Birdoswald Fort on Hadrian's Wall. Saxon aisled halls are traditionally believed to have been based on Continental buildings, but in fact aisled structures (i.e. buildings with two rows of roof-supporting posts in the interior) are probably the commonest form of building in rural Roman Britain. They usually occur in the form of a barn – as at Orton Hall Farm – or a house. In some instances the open-plan hall acquired partitioned-off spaces at one end, as also happened in medieval times, when the principal family began to feel the need for greater privacy. It seems to me far simpler to derive the Saxon aisled hall from the Romano-British aisled building than from parallels abroad. The only significant change is the shift from stone to wood – or from stone *back* to wood, if we bear in mind what was happening in pre-Roman times.

It might be supposed that the Roman to Anglo-Saxon sequence at Orton Hall Farm was a one-off, but it was not. As Don Mackreth noted in 1977:

> There was a time when it was thought that Saxons shunned Roman buildings as works of evil forces. This view was to a large extent based upon the apparent lack of Saxon finds on Late Roman sites.

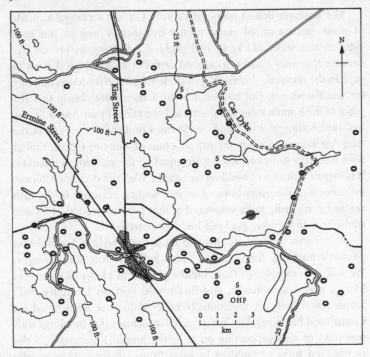

*Roman settlements in the lower Nene Valley around the town of Durobrivae.
The site at Orton Hall Farm is shown as 'OHF'; settlements that have
produced Roman and Anglo-Saxon pottery are marked 'S'.*

In recent years knowledge of Saxon domestic pottery has greatly
increased and many sites with a Saxon presence are now known.[21]

A large number of Romano-British settlements are known around
Durobrivae, and several include both Roman and Anglo-Saxon pottery.
One site currently being worked on at Haddon, close by the modern
A1, is producing quantities of Anglo-Saxon pottery that dwarf the
substantial assemblages found at Orton Hall Farm. It goes against
common sense to believe that the changes we are witnessing here
reflect the replacement of one population by another. Frankly, if I
were a prosperous Late Roman farmer living with my family in the
lower Nene Valley and I saw boatloads of settlers sailing up the river

with the express intent of taking over my farm, I'd put up a fight. I'd organise a militia with my neighbours. I'd do anything. But it would appear that they handed over their farms without a struggle.

Much of the phasing at Orton Hall Farm was worked out by Donald Mackreth in close collaboration with Rob Perrin, an authority on Romano-British pottery. Rob's report on his role in the detailed phasing of the site contains a revealing sentence: 'The phasing process was largely dependent on pottery dating, although the site showed a clear, logical development in layout and structure which provided a good framework into which the dating could be placed.'[22] That seems to me as clear-cut a statement as one could possibly wish: there is no mention of the disjunction, separation or misalignment that one would expect had the farm been taken over by an incoming population of new settlers. Quite the contrary, in fact. To my eyes the arrangement of the farm, in all its phases, seems consistent and logical, whether it is growing or decreasing in size. I know from my own experiences as a farmer that such development only comes from living and working in the same place over an extended period of time. When you move into a new place, things change: you see the farm through fresh eyes. Sometimes you get things right, sometimes wrong, but you never continue precisely where the previous owner had left off. People simply do not behave like that. It was good to have this feeling confirmed by someone so intimately associated with the day-to-day minutiae of the pottery phasing.

I will leave the final words on the Roman/Anglo-Saxon succession to Don Mackreth himself. Clearly he believes in the idea of an incursion of settlers, but he has trouble reconciling this concept with the evidence in the ground. Being a conscientious archaeologist, he expresses those doubts clearly, and I quote his words at some length because they sum up well the practical difficulties of pinning down those wraithlike, shadowy figures who were supposed to have swept across eastern England in the fifth and sixth centuries AD:

> The only tangible evidence [at Orton Hall Farm] for a direct inter-
> action between Roman and Anglo-Saxon is a sherd from a mor-
> tarium in an Anglo-Saxon fabric* ... There were Roman goods

---

* A mortarium is a kitchen mortar or grinding bowl. The term 'fabric' refers to the mix of clay used to form the mortarium. Pottery fabrics are a very reliable way of identifying different styles and traditions of pottery manufacture.

in use during undoubted Anglo-Saxon occupation, but no final evidence that these had not been gleaned from elsewhere. Otherwise, the argument for close association of the two cultures rests on a possible chronological overlap between latest Roman material and earliest Anglo-Saxon ... No feature sustains the view that the Anglo-Saxons used a Roman site in full working order, but the accumulation of detail ... leads inexorably towards that view.

There is no incontrovertible evidence that there had been a distinct break in occupation: too many of the proven Anglo-Saxon features only make sense if Roman structures were still standing. The impression is that the Romanised site had become debilitated before the Anglo-Saxon pottery arrived, but it was not possible to show that this must have happened before Anglo-Saxon occupation of all or part had become established.[23]

Mackreth's statement that 'the only tangible evidence for a direct interaction between Roman and Anglo-Saxon is a sherd from a mortarium in an Anglo-Saxon fabric' is important from two points of view. The first, rarely remarked upon by archaeologists who are sometimes more interested in dry fragments of pottery than in spicy food, is what one might term 'culinary continuity'. Roman cooking frequently involved the grinding of spices and condiments in a pottery mortar ('mortarium'), and it was a style of eating that the British rapidly took to, if we are to judge from the large numbers of worn-out mortarium fragments that occur on Romano-British domestic sites of even the humblest sort. One might suppose that an incoming Anglo-Saxon population, that had no Romanised traditions of its own, would have had quite different styles of cooking. But apparently not. It would seem that they liked the food of the people they overran so much that they went to the trouble of imitating a Roman mortar in their own pottery workshops. From a human, if not from a strictly archaeological, perspective, this strikes me as very odd.

If you remove the concept of the Anglo-Saxon settlers, the picture painted by Mackreth is of a Romano-British farm adapting to new economic circumstances brought about by changes in the political landscape of the late Western Empire. I do not believe that Mackreth is raising the point, but it has been suggested that farms like Orton Hall Farm became less economically efficient in late- and post-Roman times. Certainly there would have been changes: stone buildings were replaced by wood, and hard, factory-produced Romano-British pottery went out of use. There may also have been a move towards increased reliance on stock-raising. These changes may have reflected the fact that access to national distributional networks via markets at places like Durobrivae was starting to break down towards the end of the fourth century, but they do not suggest that the farm itself was in decline *as a farm*. The changes in what is today called the 'macro-economic climate' must have caused places like Orton Hall Farm to turn towards local trade, which initially would have been based more on barter than money. The farm, like the rural population of eastern England as a whole, had become rather less Roman and rather more Iron Age and self-reliant.

Recent excavations at Quarrington, an Early to Middle Saxon settlement near Sleaford, thirty-five miles north of Orton Hall Farm, have revealed some extraordinary results that challenge the idea that life in Early Saxon communities was as isolated and self-reliant as was once believed. The site revealed a large amount of Early and Middle Saxon pottery: over 2,330 fragments. The clay and other material added to the mix, or 'fabric', of the pottery was analysed and found to come from a wide range of sources: 'In the Early Saxon period, the fabrics at Quarrington are known to have come from southern, northern and central Lincolnshire as well as from Leicestershire.'[24] I suppose it would be too obvious to ask how these people, who we are told had only recently come to England, managed to establish such extensive trading networks so soon. I think it goes rather further than that. It is not just a question of 'trading networks', because we are dealing here with dispersed rural economies that were operating outside what we would regard today as a market economy.

Professor Martin Millett has concluded that even at the hub of the Empire, trade between Rome and the provinces 'was exchange demonstrably embedded within the social and political system'. He goes on to point out that much of the large-scale movement of goods, such as the provision of supplies to the army, was actually motivated by reasons that were more complex than free trade. 'These patterns develop in such a way as to demonstrate that the system was not simply a function of unbridled economic forces.'[25]

If the 'trade' that was so characteristic of the Roman monetary economy was not simple free trade, what was it likely to revert to when the Empire collapsed? One thing we do know about pre-Roman British economies is that they did not operate on the basis of trade at all. To use Martin Millett's phrase, it was 'exchange demonstrably embedded within the social and political system'. Only this time the political system *was* the social system.

I suspect that in post-Roman, as in pre-Roman, times, goods and commodities were given or exchanged as part of short- or long-term social obligations. Maybe one farmer paid another for the use of land by giving seed corn; the practice of giving 'bridewealth', or goods and services as part of a marriage agreement, would have knock-on 'trade' obligations that would continue for years. Powerful men would expect tribute in some form from their followers, and so on. The list is endless.

I believe that the operation of 'socially embedded' exchange networks continued throughout the Roman period and into post-Roman times, and may well help to explain the survival of certain traditional trading places into the fifth and sixth centuries (as we will see in Chapter 7). Such exchange networks take generations to build up, and Quarrington may not have been as exceptional as at first it appears. The expert on Anglo-Saxon pottery J.N.L. Myres, for example, produced convincing evidence for the existence of pottery workshops, whose cremation urn products appear in more than one cemetery.[26] Surely, of all things, the distribution of cremation urns *has* to be 'socially embedded'.

I would view the fourth to sixth centuries in eastern England as broadly similar to the first centuries BC and AD, with an essentially stable rural population existing in a political context that was changing quite rapidly. The population appears to have grown from Early to Middle Saxon times, to judge from the internal development of numerous rural sites like Quarrington.[27] 'Socially embedded' exchange networks, both in Britain and overseas, were certainly allowed to develop – indeed to thrive. All in all, I can see no convincing archaeological evidence for 'Dark Age' chaos, disruption and turmoil.

CHAPTER FIVE

Late- and Post-Roman Britain: The Situation in the South and East

SIR FRANK STENTON'S HISTORY of Anglo-Saxon England, first published in 1943, is a remarkable book that still sets the standard by which all other work is judged. The third edition of 1971 includes a few nods in the direction of archaeology, but it remains fairly and squarely based on documentary evidence. His first chapter, 'The Age of Migration', begins with these words:

> Between the end of Roman government in Britain and the emergence of the earliest English kingdoms [the early seventh century] there stretches a long period of which the history cannot be written ... The course of events may be indicated, but it is certainly not revealed, by the isolated or incidental references to Britain made by writers of this or the following age. For the first time in five centuries Britain was out of touch with the Continent.[1]

It's the last sentence that I want to query here. Archaeology shows that from the end of the fourth century there are clear signs of contact between Britain and the Continent – to take just one example, the *Grübenhaus* that we encountered in the previous chapter at Orton Hall Farm. During the fifth and sixth centuries the archaeological record of southern and eastern Britain is almost overwhelmed by new styles of pottery and other objects that have close parallels on the European mainland. Archaeology, if not history, shows that, far from being 'cut off', people in eastern Britain were probably more closely in touch with communities across the North Sea than they had ever been.

We spent the last chapter in the realms of field archaeology, and concluded with the thought that the developments observed at Orton Hall Farm, and doubtless at Maxey too, were ultimately caused by changes, to use that horrid cliché, in the macro-economic climate. At the grassroots level, to use another, the structure, if not the organisation, of rural society probably remained largely unaffected by these changes: families or lineages continued to grow and the bulk of the population still lived in the same places – a theme I will return to in more detail in Chapter 8. Now I want to take a broader, historical view of the political events that led to the end of Roman rule in Britain.

The first point to make is that there was no sudden and dramatic collapse in which the stability of the *Pax Romana* (Roman Peace) broke down, as it were overnight, to be followed by chaos, anarchy and pillage. It would be a mistake to view the Roman period in Britain, or indeed elsewhere, as a time of absolute stability and order, when nothing changed, even if that is the impression one gets when visiting museums and tourist attractions such as villas and Roman towns. The Roman world could be a tumultuous place, with new emperors declaring themselves in charge, first to their troops and then to as many people as would listen. Consult any list of Roman emperors and it makes the English medieval monarchy, even during the Wars of the Roses, look remarkably stable. If, for example, we take the twenty emperors who reigned in the thirty-three years from 235 to 268, their average period in office works out at about nineteen months. If you leave out the eight-year reign of Gallienus, it is much less even than that.

It's all a question of degree. The macro-political system of the Later Roman Empire may have been unstable, but that instability was usually confined to a relatively small number of senior army officers and political heavyweights. It did not often spill over into fully-fledged civil war. And of course every so often a remarkable emperor, such as Constantine or Theodosius the Great, would arise and the system would function like clockwork once again. To put this instability into perspective: even in the fourth century, Roman citizens were forbidden from carrying arms – and so far as we know it was a rule that was actually applied.[2] That suggests a level of general stability within the Roman Empire that was not matched, even remotely, within barbarian Europe.

A list of the Roman emperors of the fourth and early fifth centuries

House of Constantius and their rivals:		House of Theodosius and their rivals:	
Constantius I (*Augustus*)	305–6	Theodosius I ('the Great')	379–95
Constantine I ('the Great')	306–37	Magnus Maximus	383–8
Constantine II	337–40	Eugenius	392–4
Constans (mainly in the west	337–50	*Following the death of Theodosius (395) the Empire is split into two:*	
Constantius II (mainly in the east)	337–61	*In the West*	
Nepotian	350	Honorius	395–423
Vetranio	350	Marcus (in Britain)	406
Magnentius	350–3	Gratian (in Britain)	407
Silvanus	355 (in Gaul)		
Julian II ('the Apostate')	360–3	Constantine III	407–11
Jovian	363–4	*In the East*	
House of Valentinian and their rivals:		Arcadius	395–408
		Theodosius II	408–50
Valentinian I	364–75	*Emperors continue in the East until the fall of Constantinople in 1453*	
Valens	364–78		
Procopius	365–6		
Valentinian II	375–92		

AD shows that, with certain notable exceptions such Constantine the Great (306–37), Constantius II (337–61), Theodosius the Great (379–95) and, in the Western Empire, Honorius (395–423), the reigns were also short, and sometimes nasty and brutish to boot.[3]

It would be a mistake to see Britain as a place of little consequence in the Roman Empire. Britain was one of the most garrisoned of all Roman provinces, with about sixteen thousand legionaries and a fluctuating but often equal number of auxiliary troops; there was also a huge array of dependants, plus supply and support services.[4] Not only does this reflect the fact that the native British population was large, well organised and certainly capable of resistance, it also suggests that Rome needed what Britain had to offer, and was prepared to pay the necessary price. But it should also be borne in mind that Britain was a useful place to 'store' troops.[5]

It has already been noted that Roman Britain was not a static society, and we will see that changes, for example in the organisation of towns and of the army, were well under way before the final years of Roman occupation. Later Roman Britain has a distinct character from the more Imperial or Classical Empire of the first and second centuries AD. This is not necessarily due to a process of disintegration, but of adaptation to broader political changes that were taking place elsewhere in the Roman world.[6]

One of the most important events of the Later Roman Empire, the official adoption of Christianity, had strong links with Britain. In the year 306, following the death of his father Constantius I, Constantine the Great was proclaimed emperor in York, by the army. In Guy de la Bédoyère's words this was an act of usurpation 'which had unimaginable consequences for the history of the Western world, but much of what followed took place beyond Britain'.[7] There was then a protracted power struggle which ended with Constantine's defeat of his principal rival, Maxentius, at the Battle of Milvian Bridge in Italy in 312; many of Constantine's victorious troops had been raised in Britain. Milvian Bridge left Constantine in control of the Western Empire, but another rival, Licinius, was still in power in the east. Constantine did not defeat him until 324.

Constantine the Great lived up to his name, but the manner in which he achieved this – by simple military might – would ultimately prove one of the major flaws of the Western Roman Empire. The process by which a new emperor was chosen had long been a problem, but Constantine's example opened the gates to anyone who could muster sufficient military muscle. No longer did powerful or successful military leaders have any reason to curb their ambition – and the result was the instability of the state.

While the military and political leaders of the Empire were struggling for control, Christianity was rapidly growing in popularity among the population at large. One of its great strengths was its inbuilt organisation: if you accepted Christ, then you also accepted the Church and its hierarchy of priests and bishops. The Emperor Diocletian saw Christianity as a threat to the Empire, and ordered a great persecution in 303. Fortunately for them, the Christians of Britain and Gaul were not heavily affected by this purge, as their own 'sub-Emperor', Constantius I, was not anti-Christian, nor was his son Constantine the Great. It is ironic that Constantine, who seized power in such a ruthless fashion, was one of the more tolerant emperors. In 313 his Edict of Milan guaranteed total religious toleration throughout the Empire. Christianity was the favoured religion in the west, and after the defeat of Licinius in 324 Constantine extended the favour to the east.

Constantine's long reign ushered in a new age of stability in Britain, much of which seems to have been centred, not surprisingly, on his old power base of York, the military part of which was extensively enlarged and refurbished. York, although the most magnificent of the early-fourth-century civil and military works, was by no means alone. Many town walls were augmented with bastions during the fourth century; villas in the countryside, too, had additional yards and wings built onto them. There are many Roman villas in southern Britain, and they are best understood as buildings and workplaces that functioned within a working landscape. They were essential to its smooth operation, and can be seen as the Romano-British equivalents of Victorian country houses; they included comfortable rooms for the squire and his family, but provision was also made for estate workers.

I have already mentioned the Nene Valley pottery workshops.[8] They were well established by the end of the second century, and flourished throughout the third and fourth. It would appear that they were still in full production at the beginning of the fifth century, but died out when their products were replaced by so-called Anglo-Saxon wares, which we now know from sites like Haddon and Orton Hall Farm were being produced in substantial quantities, probably in local workshops; by now the market, if such there was, was regional rather than national.*

* The remarkable man who revealed many of the Roman sites in the Nene Valley was named Edmund Tyrell Artis. In the first part of the nineteenth century he was Agent to the Earl

I have focused on the countryside around Durobrivae because it was a prosperous and not atypical Romano-British landscape. It was a setting that could be matched elsewhere in southern and Midland Britain in the fourth century, around places like York, Lincoln, Oxford and the Thames Valley. The south-eastern corner of Britain, north and south of the Thames estuary, which rose to prominence in the final decades of the Iron Age following Caesar's campaigns in Gaul, continued to prosper.

Rural southern Britain in the third and fourth centuries was well populated, and criss-crossed with roads and trackways that kept the various farming settlements and larger estates in close touch both with each other and with the goings-on in town. It is my contention that a rural population that was by now well used to such sophisticated standards of communication would have accepted the macro-economic changes that were taking place elsewhere in the Roman world – largely, I suspect, because they had no option. But because the farms and communities in each region would have stayed in touch with each other they would have adapted to the changing circumstances *together*, which would have given them both strength and flexibility. It is misleading to see the changes of the late fourth and early fifth centuries through modern eyes: to us, Roman civilisation seems vastly preferable to the Dark Age peasant economy; but was this necessarily such a stark contrast in rural areas? One could also question whether something like the decline in the standard of tableware was actually that important to people. It is entirely possible that these changes towards a simpler style of life meant that communities no longer had to bear a punitive tax burden, and in the process discovered the freedoms of self-determination.

To sum up, rural Romanised Britons in areas like the Nene Valley would not readily have given way to waves of Anglo-Saxon settlers, because they had too much to lose: their lifestyles may have altered

Fitzwilliam, of Milton Hall, just outside Peterborough. He was a close friend of the great 'peasant' poet John Clare, who lived in the village of Helpston just south of Maxey. His consuming passion was Roman archaeology, and he mainly excavated on the estates of the Earl Fitzwilliam, publishing the results of his work in 1828. In the early 1970s I had the good fortune to spend a couple of years living in a flat within the former stable block at Milton Hall. I will never forget my surprise when one morning I stumbled across a magnificent Roman mosaic in the old dairy – moved there for safekeeping by Artis over a century earlier.

in certain not very important respects in the final years of the fourth and the start of the fifth centuries, but otherwise they lived much as before. Most important of all, their security lay amongst themselves. They hung together, and adapted themselves to the changing realities of the fifth century. Contrary to popular opinion, these new realities did not consist of social chaos and economic meltdown. If that were the case, how does one account for the large numbers of Romano-British sites which appear quite peacefully to have adopted new styles of pottery, dress and buildings? These are people who are making informed and rational decisions. They have been, and continue to be, in regular contact with each other, and are not being forced to do things that are antipathetic to them.

The peace and prosperity enjoyed by the Roman province of Brit-annia in the early to mid-fourth century can in large part be attributed to the long reign, the personality and the prestige of Constantine the Great. Constantine's death in 337 set in motion a chain of events that were to have great importance for Britain.[9] But not immediately, because we know from numerous excavations that economic con-ditions – and presumably this implies stability among the population at large – remained favourable in southern Britain until the second half of the century.

There is a danger in trying to identify specific political or historical events in the archaeological record. It is a notoriously difficult process, but when it seems that such a correlation has been successfully achieved it tends to sit there, unchallenged and seemingly immovable. The rebellion of the Icenian Queen Boudica in AD 60 and 61 is a good example. It left burnt destruction levels in Early Roman towns in East Anglia and London – but that does not mean that every mid-first-century fire in East Anglia should be labelled as Boudican. Bakeries and blacksmiths' shops can burn down without the help of a rebellion.

If there is a difference, culturally speaking, between prehistorians and Romanists, it is that the former tend to fight shy of assigning historical causes to layers of soil in their excavations, whereas the latter will seize the opportunity with both hands. This difference is readily explicable. Because there are so few historical events that can apply to prehistory, in the past we have sometimes forced our data to fit them. Then, when the misfit is pointed out – often with the independent assistance of radiocarbon dating – the proponents of the supposed correlation retreat in confusion. Either that, or they stick to their guns resolutely, which can be embarrassing or awkward.

The Roman period is replete with historical events of all sorts and sizes. These can often be linked, with greater or lesser reliability, to changes in coinage – and coins are found in excavations. So something as minor as the enlargement of a house can be linked, say, to the changes in the tax regime introduced by a particular governor. You may believe these correlations if you like, but they lead to a climate of thought which demands that such correspondences be made even when the known historical events start to fade away, as happened, of course, in the so-called Dark Ages. It is then that authors such as Gildas, who had their own reasons for writing and are widely accepted as being unreliable as historical sources, are treated like Caesar or Tacitus, whose reliability is far greater – although both those authors had their own agendas too.

Strained archaeological correlations, such as the sudden appearance of Anglo-Saxon 'settlers' in Late Roman farmhouses, are the result of habit. During the full Roman period, archaeological and historical tie-ins could be made credible. So a pattern was established. It was a pattern that suited a period where provincial administrative responsibilities were by and large well defined, and where dates could be pinned down with considerable precision. But in the fifth century the situation changed radically, and it was no longer 'safe' to attempt to answer historical questions with archaeological data. In that respect, if in no other, the 'Dark Ages' marked a return to prehistory.

We are into 'unsafe correlation territory' as we approach the latter part of the fourth century. What we do know is that Guy de la Bédoyère's 'Golden Age' of Roman Britain lasted well after Constantine's death in 337, and even beyond the midpoint of the century, when, in theory at least, political events within the Roman world at large and the Western Empire in particular ought to have led quite swiftly to instability in Britain. Those events were traumatic, and it would take more space than I have available even to sketch them.[10] Suffice it to say that following Constantine's death there was a brief period of chaos without an Emperor at all. Then Constantine's second son Constantine II was made senior emperor, with personal charge over Britain, Gaul and Spain. Another son, Constans, controlled Italy and Africa; a third son, Constantius II, held Constantinople (founded by their father) and the Eastern Empire.

Very few institutions in the Roman Empire were ever static for long, and the army was no exception. Extensive military reforms began under the Emperor Diocletian (AD 284–305). The army was divided into two groups: a mobile field army of fighting troops, and garrison forces stationed at places such as Hadrian's Wall. Control of the army became a military matter, and was largely removed from local civilian administrations. The purpose of these reforms, in Professor Sheppard Frere's words, was 'partly to ensure the growth of a professional class of officers and partly to promote greater mobility by the creation of a central field army distinct from the static troops on the frontier'.[11] Constantine I introduced further changes to the way the army was organised. The field armies were divided into regional forces, or *comitatenses*, and *palatini*, which were under direct imperial control from Rome. By the time of Constantine's death it was a remarkably flexible and effective military force. Each of the three emperors who succeeded him had his own field army, which he commanded absolutely. They also had smaller units which were intended for specific tasks. Sometimes these could be temporary forces, assembled for a particular project and then disbanded. In addition, there were also frontier or garrison forces which manned strategically important places.[12]

The partition of the Empire among Constantine's three sons was a recipe for disaster, and they promptly fell out. Constantine II, probably aided by British troops in his main field army, took on his brother Constans in Italy and was roundly defeated in 340. The victorious Constans paid a visit to Britain in the winter of 343. We don't know why he visited, but it may have been in response to barbarian attacks from north of Hadrian's Wall. His visit is supposed to be the reason why many cities in Britain were refortified at about this time – but this is approaching 'unsafe correlation territory'. What does seem probable is that Britain, Spain and Gaul were considered a separate province with their own leader, under Constans' general authority.

Constans was killed following a coup in 350, and after further power struggles Britain fell under the control of Magnentius, brother of the defeated Constantine II. Magnentius was a military man whose family background was ultimately Germanic – as was sometimes the case in the later Roman army. His short reign was not a success: he taxed the better-off heavily to pay for his military campaigns against Constantius II (of the eastern part of the Empire), and after two serious defeats he committed suicide in the year 353.

The Empire was now under the single authority of Constantius II. He was aggressively Christian. With calculated ruthlessness he made Christianity the sole religion of the Empire, and in the process subjected the Church to the authority of the state. When Magnentius had been in control of Britain he tolerated paganism, and had taken a field army which included British troops from there to fight against Constantius II. Constantius felt that Britain needed to be brought back into the fold, and he sent a particularly unpleasant man to carry out this task. He had earned a chilling nickname – 'Catena', which translates as 'the Chain' – by his ability to ensnare his victims. His unjust purge, which affected the upper echelons of society the most, even managed to destroy the official ruler (or *vicarius**) of Britain, one Martinus, a loyal supporter of Constantius II. Peter Salway sees the aftermath of the death of Magnentius in 353 as the end of the Golden Age of Roman Britain. Things would never be the same again.

Constantius II appointed his cousin Julian in charge of Britain and Gaul in 355. Julian had been brought up in the east, where he had acquired a deep interest in history and classical literature. He was also a great soldier, and waged a successful campaign against the barbarians who had invaded parts of Gaul from northern Europe. He drove them out and then began fresh military actions in Germany, which relied to a great extent on huge shipments of grain from Britain – one of the reasons for Rome's desire to maintain peace in the province.[13] Julian's re-establishment of the logistical connections between Britain and the Continental mainland in AD 359/60 was very important. Britain had always played a major part in the supply chain of both

---

* When I first dipped into Roman studies as a student I remember being surprised that Later Roman government and the political structure of the Empire seemed to have been modelled on the Church. Thus Britain itself is a *diocese*, and the person in charge of the diocese is the *vicarius* (hence 'vicar'). In fact, of course, in this instance the Church is following the terminology of the state, and not the other way around.

the army and the Empire, and Julian saw to it that these connections were restored.

Julian appointed a well-trusted aide, Alypius, as *vicarius* of Roman Britain. Alypius had barely taken office when news came in 360 that Picts and Scots were plundering northern parts of the province. Julian organised a massive response, sending four units of his field army to Britain under the command of Flavius Lupicinus. The troops reached London, but we know no more than that. Julian himself remained in Paris, where more pressing affairs detained him.

It would appear that Constantius II was growing jealous of Julian's successes, and he ordered him to send large numbers of his field army back east to serve him, the Emperor. The troops in the west had no desire to shift allegiance, and promptly proclaimed Julian emperor (or 'Augustus', as the senior emperor was termed). He was marching with his army towards Constantinople when, conveniently, Constantius II died of fever. Julian was now undisputed Augustus.

Julian's ambitions were cut short by his early death three years later, in 363. The army then elected one of their officers, Jovian, as Augustus, but he too died, and in 364 they selected Valentinian, a senior officer who had been opposed to Julian for various reasons, not the least being his own Christianity and his dislike of Julian's paganism. Valentinian I, a good soldier and an able administrator, was the last emperor to organise an extensive strengthening of the military defences of the Western Empire.

Meanwhile, back in Britain, unrest was growing. There is evidence that the barbarian incursions of 360 were followed by more in 364. But by far the most serious and concerted attacks happened in 367, when the so-called Barbarian Conspiracy (*barbarica conspiratio*) over-ran the entire island. This was far more concerted than anything that had happened previously. Up until 367 attacks on the Empire by 'barbarians' had been confined to raids, mainly around the frontiers. But in this instance the attacks by a number of different peoples and tribes were co-ordinated: Picts (from Scotland), Attacotti and Scots (both probably from Ireland and the Western Isles) attacked Britain; Franks and Saxons invaded the coasts of Gaul. Large areas of Gaul and Britain fell to these attackers. We do not know who led the conspiracy, but he must have been a remarkable man, both to keep his plans secret in advance of the action, and to hold the loose alliance of disparate forces together when the fighting began. The later fourth century was a time when the non-Roman barbarian peoples were producing leaders who would eventually, in the person of Alaric among others, prove capable of matching the best that Rome itself could produce.

What also helped to make the conspiracy so successful was the profound knowledge its leaders showed of Roman military organisation. By the late fourth century up to a quarter of the Roman army was composed of men from Germanic backgrounds, some of whom achieved ranks that today would be the equivalent of General. It's hardly surprising that knowledge of the Roman military system was widespread in so-called barbarian lands. They also had excellent intelligence, because the moment they chose to launch their attacks coincided with Valentinian going down with a serious illness. There is possible archaeological evidence for the success of the Barbarian Conspiracy: defences along Hadrian's Wall were altered and updated, civil settlements along the Wall were abandoned for good, and the walled military town of Corbridge in Northumberland showed evidence of destruction.

Valentinian sent four élite units from the field army to Britain under the command of Flavius Theodosius, father of Theodosius the Great, the last emperor of a united Roman Empire. The Romans' return to Britain was welcomed by the population at large, who had been traumatised by the looting and lawlessness of the barbarian incursions. Theodosius' forces did, however, encounter resistance, and his victory was a very substantial military achievement. Theodosius also used his authority wisely. Raiders were tracked down and army deserters, of whom there were many, were pardoned. Looted items were returned to their rightful owners, rather than being retained by the incoming troops, as would often be the case. In Britain the barbarians mainly came from north of Hadrian's Wall, and probably from across the Irish Sea as well. So far as we know, there were no significant numbers from the Anglo-Saxon lands along the eastern shores of the North Sea. Instead of Britain, these turned their attention to territories on the other side of the Channel, in Gaul.

By 368 or 369 Theodosius started a major programme of rebuilding and restoration in Britain. There is also some evidence that after about 370 a certain number of soldiers were positioned within walled civilian towns (previously they would have been stationed in military buildings, such as forts and barracks), both to protect the population and also doubtless to keep an eye on what they were doing. The Roman writer Ammianus Marcellinus, describing this reconstruction, tells how forts and civilian settlements had to be repaired or rebuilt; we also know from archaeology that some along Hadrian's Wall were abandoned altogether at about this time. This pattern of destruction suggests not only that the incursions had been of considerable scale and ferocity, but that certain of the Roman troops defending military installations did not remain loyal to the Empire.

Although the population at large welcomed Theodosius and his troops back to Britain, certain elements in the higher echelons of British society resented the rule of Rome, thanks to the efforts of men like 'the Chain'. Some of these may well have taken advantage of the lawlessness in 367 to further their own ends. It is also possible that the barbarian attacks in the north of Britain were echoed further south by an uprising, whether an orchestrated part of the wider Conspiracy or not we cannot tell, of essentially Romanised Britons against the lawful authority of Rome. This might help to explain why Theodosius was so measured in his actions after the Conspiracy had been put down. He knew that he could ill afford further to alienate the people whom he needed ultimately to run Roman Britain when order had been restored.

In 375 Valentinian I died and was succeeded in the west by his sons Gratian and Valentinian II. During the second part of the 370s the Roman Empire reeled from barbarian attacks by Goths from across the Danube frontier, who were eventually defeated by armies under the command of Theodosius, son of the Theodosius who had done so much to restore Britain after the depredations of the Barbarian Conspiracy. Theodosius the Great, as he is generally known, was a fervent Christian, but his main practical and administrative concerns were with the Eastern Empire, and during his long rule, which ended with his death in 395, Britain twice slipped beyond his direct control, the first time under the rule of Magnus Maximus (383–88), and then Eugenius (392–94).

To what extent was the diocese of Britain in practice a single, united population? A recent paper by Andrew Sargent has drawn attention to something with current resonances: the possible existence of a north–south divide. Sargent's work was based on data used to compile the recently republished Ordnance Survey Map of Roman Britain, which shows that villas, temples and shrines were largely confined to south of the Wash, with a scatter extending up the east side of England through Lincolnshire and Yorkshire; most of Wales and of England west of the Pennines, plus Devon and Cornwall, were devoid of them.[14] The distribution of various classes of military sites is almost a mirror image, with the vast majority extending across northern and west Britain; the far south-west seems to have been almost unaffected by the Roman presence. Sargent concludes that:

> The distribution of monument classes illustrates that there were two very different native cultures in Roman Britain, one of which was able to adopt and adapt Roman values and symbols, and one which apparently was not. These two cultural expressions had their roots in the tribal society of pre-Roman Britain ... and strong continuity has been identified from the Late Pre-Roman Iron Age among the native population: in the north and west this may have been more pronounced and have extended throughout society. Did these people 'become Roman' in their own way, or did they become Roman at all?[15]

In the light of Sargent's analyses it would appear that the Romanised élite was very much a southern and eastern phenomenon in Britain. We have seen in Chapter 3 that the processes of 'Romanisation' had begun in south-eastern Britain in the Late Iron Age, not because it was forced upon the élite, but rather because it was something they wanted to adopt. So they started to develop their own, southern British, style of Roman culture. New evidence is now starting to emerge that their culture was distinguished by mystical religious beliefs that might seem strange to us today. The beliefs in question are known as Gnostic, after the Ancient Greek word *gnosis*, knowledge.

Gnosticism had its origins in Greece, and was a mystical religious philosophy which placed great emphasis on the power of knowledge. Gnostics believed that through knowledge of spiritual truths man could escape the confines of mortal flesh and become one with God. It was a philosophy which emphasised the importance of intellectual and spiritual movement and development. Much was made of the pilgrimage or journey towards the ultimate unity with the Divine; it also laid stress on duality and opposition between conflicting visions of truth as the journey was undertaken. Baptism, a symbol of the journey's commencement, was a key element within Christian interpretations of Gnosticism.

Many people in the ancient world were affected by Gnosticism, including the writer of St John's Gospel (who probably was not the disciple of that name). This account seems to have been written later than the those of the three other Evangelists – quite possibly as late as the fourth century, when Gnosticism was flourishing. The Gospel opens with a mystical summary of the writer's own beliefs. This statement, when translated into the majestic language of the King James Bible, has to rank with the greatest poetry in English. 'The Word' is a reference to knowledge:

> In the beginning was the Word, and the Word was with God, and the Word was God. The same was in the beginning with God. All things were made by him; and without him was not any thing made that was made. In him was life; and the life was the light of men. And the light shineth in darkness; and the darkness comprehended it not.[16]

In a recently published account of Gnosticism in fourth-century Britain, Dominic Perring examines two mosaic floors in a house at Frampton in Dorset, one of a group of fourth-century villas surrounding the Roman town of Durnovaria (Dorchester).[17] He makes a persuasive case that the floors depict symbolic journeys that only make sense if they are seen through the eyes of a Gnostic. Most of the elements of Gnosticism are there, including the journey itself, the opposition or duality of pagan and Christian images, and the final achievement of divinity through knowledge by means of the Christian communion, or Eucharist. This service was celebrated by priests in a semi-circular or apsidal annexe that formed the focus of the second, and larger, of the two rooms given over to the Gnostic journey. A mosaic of the holy Chalice is at the focus of the annexe, where an altar might once have stood. Perring describes the purpose of the mosaics thus:

> The mosaics may ... have described the path to eternal life, and these rooms represented the ultimate ascent of privilege. It is reasonable to conclude that the goal of the quest described on the floor of the villa at Frampton was symbolised by the Eucharistic chalice, which here took on the attributes of a holy grail. Eternal life – the release of spirit – was the reward of this synthesis between soul and matter, divine and mortal, wine and water.[18]

He goes on to describe other mosaic floors, mostly laid between AD 320 and 360, in southern British villas which include motifs that are reminiscent of Frampton. He concludes that Gnostic and related forms of mystical Christianity were widespread among the ruling élite in southern Britain in the fourth century. It was in many respects a self-serving, exclusive form of worship, but it had some serious implications. To quote Perring again:

> The emphasis that Gnostic ritual gave to knowledge and initiation served to protect, not challenge, the existing basis of social power. This was a mystery religion accessible only to educated classes with the leisure to engage in its arcane secrets ... The Gnostics also rejected the structures of bishops and clergy, and relied on the 'wisdom of the brotherhood ... the spiritual fellowship of those united in communion'. These beliefs and structures were positively antithetical to the institutional Church. There are several reasons why such ideologies might have had a particular appeal to property-owning classes in the Romano-British countryside. This was a province where urban institutions remained comparatively under-developed, and where social power appears to have been exercised from aristocratic country houses.[19]

The Gnostic mosaics at Frampton and at Lullingstone in Kent can be dated to the period of Julian's rule. Julian ('the Apostate') was a pagan who tolerated mystical forms of Christianity such as Gnosticism, but the rulers and emperors who followed him (especially Gratian, Theodosius I and, in Britain, Magnus Maximus) were far less forbearing, and took particular exception to the fact that the Gnostics, in Perring's words, 'rejected the structures of bishops and clergy'. If the Church was becoming an institution over which the state had influence – and this was something that Theodosius the Great appreciated to the full – then it made sense to persecute the Gnostics, whose teachings undermined that relationship at a fundamental level.

Julian died in 363, and from about 370 – it is hard to be more precise – there are archaeologically visible changes that can quite reasonably be attributed to the new political climate in Britain (without, that is, running the risk of doubtful historical correlation).

Dominic Perring argues that if Christianity in southern Britain had been more Gnostic than orthodox, it would have been suppressed in the years 370–390. This suppression is likely to have involved the destruction of images, symbols and places that were thought to have Gnostic connections. Some of the specifically Gnostic images on the mosaic floors at Frampton and elsewhere were hacked away at about this time. At this time, too, we find the ritualised destruction and burial of church plate elsewhere in southern Britain. But for me the most vivid image of the suppression of Gnostic Christianity is provided by the deliberate destruction of some lead tanks carrying the so-called *chi-rho* symbol of the Early Christians. These tanks were probably fonts, connected of course with the ceremony of Baptism.

I will never forget the afternoon I came nose-to-nose with a Roman lead tank at the bottom of a deep well at Ashton, a substantial Romano-British settlement not far from Durobrivae, in Northamptonshire.[20] I had arranged to take a team of sixteen student diggers to the Ashton excavations for a site tour. Somehow we all managed to squash into my Land-Rover. We had lunch in a pub on the way, and arrived in excellent spirits. We were shown around, and were told about the well, at the bottom of which was a lead tank that had been found a couple of days previously. We were asked whether we wanted to go down. Several members of our team cried off, which I thought rather feeble until I took a look down it myself. It seemed very narrow and dark, and I was immediately gripped by a slight feeling of claustrophobia. Still, I felt it incumbent upon me to go down. So down I went.

The well was circular, lined with limestone and remarkably deep. It was a hot summer day, but as I descended into the shadow it was like clambering into a fridge. The stone walls looked remarkably fresh, and I was struck by the high quality of the workmanship, which would

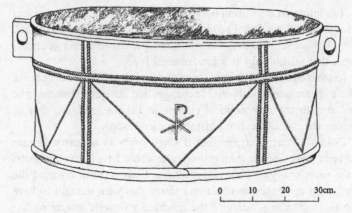

Circular Romano-British lead tank or font from Ashton, Northamptonshire, with the Christian chi-rho symbol prominent at the centre. The tank was made from three sheets of lead, about three millimetres thick, joined together and sealed with strips of lead; molten lead was added to make the joins watertight. The tank is thirty-eight centimetres high and eighty-four centimetres in diameter. When full its capacity was 220 litres, or forty-six gallons. Drawing by Maisie Taylor.

probably have been carried out by full-time professional well-diggers. As I descended I became increasingly gripped by a strange sensation that in retrospect I can only describe as the presence of the past. I became aware that everything around me, above me, below me, was ancient. Nothing had been restored. If I had been the Roman well-digger working 1,800 years ago, I would have seen precisely the same sights. Nothing had changed. I don't think I have ever been so completely in the grip of the past.

At the bottom there was not a great deal of space in which to stand, what with the ladder, the tank, and the clipboards, tools and buckets left by the archaeologists. The lead tank seemed to have been crushed by a giant foot, and its sides had been caved in. It looked most extraordinary. As I stared I realised that in Roman times I would have been underwater, and the tank before me could have served no possible practical purpose. I remember thinking that it made no sense whatsoever: why on earth would people dispose of a lead tank? Lead was a valuable commodity in Roman times; it could easily have been melted down and used to fix hundreds of roofs and leaky pipes, so why damage and then drop such a useful item down a well?

The Ashton tank (or tanks, as there were pieces from a second one down there too) is not the only example of a circular lead tank with a *chi-rho* symbol, or Christian associations, that appears to have been ritually destroyed. Several examples are known from East Anglia and the East Midlands, including no fewer than three from Icklingham in Suffolk.[21] One of these was found close to a small apsidal structure with obvious Christian and, bearing in mind the apsidal mosaic room at Frampton, possibly Gnostic Christian associations.

The ritualised destruction of these lead fonts is of interest in itself. Why destroy, bury or drown them? I think the association with water gives us a clue. I have already explained that water was an important symbol in pre-Roman times, and I believe something similar was happening at Ashton. At first sight the fonts had been destroyed, and that is how it might have appeared to a Roman soldier or official overseeing the operation. But to people who still shared vestiges of the old pagan religions, these rites would have had a different meaning: by being dropped into water, the tanks were being consigned to another realm or dimension, where they would continue to have life and purpose. To my mind, many people would have believed that the Ashton tank was not being destroyed at all when it was dropped into the water.*

There is now abundant evidence to suggest that pre-Roman religious rites were observed not just in rural settlements such as Ashton, but in towns throughout most of southern Britain – which makes one wonder to what extent the ordinary inhabitants of this, the most Romanised part of the province, had indeed become 'fully Romanised'. In a recent paper, Professor Mike Fulford draws attention to ritual practices that involved deposition and water in a number of Romano-British towns: at London, Silchester, Neatham (a small town on the Silchester–Chichester road), Baldock and Verulamium (St Albans).[22] Even the Later Roman fort at Portchester Castle on

* Dominic Perring has pointed out to me that many people in Rome also had a religious interest in wet, liminal places, so the idea of simple deception, although attractive, may not be valid. He agrees, however, that the placing of the tanks within water was indeed sending them to a new life in the Next World.

the south coast, where occupation did not begin until the late third century, has revealed examples of such rites, which seem – if we include the destruction of the Ashton lead tanks – to have persisted pretty well throughout the Roman period.

It follows that if 'Celtic' religious ideas survived though the Roman period, then other aspects of pre-Roman life must have survived too. If, as I believe, the post-Roman periods did not witness wholesale population change anywhere in Britain, then it is entirely reasonable to seek an Iron Age contribution – albeit a contribution significantly affected by three and a half centuries of Roman rule – in post-Roman times. We will see in Chapter 7 that prehistoric traditions demonstrably played an important part in the development of post-Roman culture in the west and south-west, but here I want briefly to examine the extent to which southern and eastern Britain became Romanised. This part of Britain adopted Roman ways more fully than communities elsewhere, but it is the way in which it became Romanised that interests me here. It is easy to see the adoption of Roman culture as a black-and-white process: off comes the woad face-paint and the hairy woven trousers, and on goes the toga. But it was not as simple as that.

There are increasing indications that the end of Roman rule in Britain may have been brought about by the British themselves. The same may apply to the Claudian conquest of AD 43. It has been known for some time that the immediate excuse for the invasion seems to have been to help an ageing expatriate British prince known as Verica, the son of Commius, who had been leader of the Atrebates, a British kingdom that covered parts of what is now Surrey, Berkshire and Hampshire. Verica appears to have been a successful and stable ruler. He probably reigned for thirty years between AD 10 and 40, which was a long spell by the standards of the early first century AD. His rule ended when his territory was overrun by forces of the Catuvellauni, a powerful tribe originally based in Hertfordshire and Essex, who were then being aggressively expansive under their similarly long-lived and successful leader Cunobelin.

Verica fled across the Channel and enlisted the support of the Emperor Claudius, who now had a 'legitimate' reason to invade Britain. From his perspective, Britain without Verica and Cunobelin, who had just died (some time around AD 40), was in a state of near-turmoil, and now he had a direct appeal for help. So in AD 43 he invaded. Like many others I have always believed that the Roman forces landed near Richborough in Kent.[23] Recently the only plausible alternative landing-place, near Chichester, in Sussex, has gained in favour. I suspect that we will be in a better position to know for sure in a few years' time, but if the Chichester alternative does indeed come to look more probable, then it could be argued with greater force that the Roman troops were coming to the aid of Verica's Atrebates, who would have welcomed them. Other tribal kingdoms were also friendly towards Rome.

Verica's successor as ruler of the Atrebates was a Romanised client king known as Tiberius Claudius Cogidubnus, and he ruled success-fully and for a long time, strongly supporting Rome until as late as the AD 70s or 80s. Dr Martin Henig of Oxford University points out that a client king 'is not the same as a puppet king; he is a ruler in client relationship to the emperor. There are obligations on both sides.'[24] So there is no reason to suppose that it was in the Roman interest to suppress tribal authorities in client kingdoms such as that of the Atrebates. Again, Martin Henig puts the situation well: 'Does an invasion need to be hostile to the inhabitants of a country being invaded? Modern experience of United Nations actions, for example, should tell us that such action can have an altruistic aim. The popular view of the Roman "invasion" of AD 43 was that the Italians took over and subdued the land of Britain for motives of profit and Empire. However, the reasons were far more complex.'[25] Life in the British client kingdoms would go on much as before, and Roman influences would be taken on because the presence of the Roman troops was generally welcomed. In such circumstances it is entirely natural that 'Romanisation' would very much reflect British traditions.

We see this sort of Iron Age/Romano-British continuity in the persistence of British or 'Celtic' sacred places such as the supposedly healing springs at Aqua Sulis, in Bath, and probably at the villa at Chedworth in Gloucestershire. We also see it at a number of more ordinary domestic sites that belonged to the Iron Age and Romano-British élites. One of these is in the same landscape as the Iron Age hillfort at Danebury, which incidentally is near Stockbridge on the western boundary of the kingdom of the Atrebates. Barry Cunliffe has

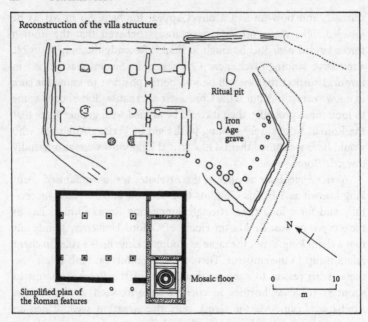

Plan of the aisled hall at Thruxton, near the hillfort of Danebury in
Hampshire. The hall was built in the late second or early third century AD.
A fine mosaic floor was added in the late fourth century. Outside the hall, to
the south, were two Late Iron Age features: the grave of a well-to-do person
and a deep 'ritual pit' filled with animal bones. Some time in the fourth
century AD the grave and the pit were included within the grounds of the
building by the construction of a stout post-built fence.

recently begun a project which aims to examine what happened in
and around Danebury in the Roman period. One of the sites he has
examined is a small villa at a place called Thruxton.[26]

The site is famous because it produced a superb mosaic floor
which was removed in 1899 and may now be seen on a wall of the
Roman Britain gallery at the British Museum. The mosaic depicts the
god Bacchus, and features a dedicatory inscription on behalf of a
Roman citizen called Natalinus, and also a Romanised Celtic family
name, 'Bodeni', presumably the name of the family that owned the
villa when the mosaic was laid down in the fourth century. The site

would be remarkable just for the survival of a Celtic name so late in the Roman period, but there is more to it than that.

The Roman building is of the aisled hall type (as discussed in Chapter 4), and was built in the late second or early third century A D. It was a comparatively modest structure, comprising just six roof trusses which were set on pairs of posts. At some point in the fourth century the end of the building was divided into three rooms, presumably because the owners required more privacy. Then in the late fourth century the Bacchus mosaic was laid in one of the rooms, which was now entered not through the hall as before, but directly from outside. This would suggest that the mosaic room was not part of the domestic house; it was not, for example, a formal dining room. It was most probably a shrine of some sort.

There are two clues as to the nature of the shrine. The first lies in the use of the family name Bodeni. This might suggest that the shrine had something to do with the ancestors. This idea was greatly strengthened by the discovery, outside the building, of the grave of a man wearing Late Iron Age brooches. These brooches suggest he was a person of some standing – an impression strengthened by the discovery nearby of a deep 'ritual pit' that had been carefully filled with animal bones, also in the Late Iron Age – and quite possibly during the funeral ceremonies that attended the man's burial. Normally one might feel that the presence of the Roman villa and shrine so close to an Iron Age burial was coincidental, but at Thruxton the grave and the ritual pit were united to the house by a fence of posts erected in the fourth century. There can be no doubt that the features outside the aisled hall belonged to the same settlement – and the same family.

Barry Cunliffe has summarised the situation both at Thruxton and at other Roman sites in the Danebury region:

It is abundantly clear that the Roman invasion of A D 43 was not a particularly significant event for the people farming the chalk downlands. There would, of course, have been new taxes to pay, a new range of consumer durables available in the distant market towns, and soon a new network of highways making travel much easier for those with time and inclination. But for the most part life was little changed. Farms continued to be owned and worked by

families whose ancestors may have broken the land many centuries
earlier – perhaps even before iron had come into general use.[27]

Bearing in mind that we still do not fully understand the extent to
which élites in southern and eastern Britain had become fully
'Romanised', it is worth returning to the way in which their religious
beliefs were handled by the Roman authorities on the Continental
mainland, particularly the destruction of objects with Christian iconography (symbols) in the decades between 370 and 390. Were these
official purges aimed primarily at Gnostic Christians and other perceived heretics by a civil authority that was keen to promote the
interests of the more orthodox Church establishment, or was something else going on? The old view was that it was caused by the turmoil
associated with the Barbarian Conspiracy of 367.[28] This supposedly
led to a breakdown of law and order and a return to paganism. In
this interpretation of events it was paganism, rather than orthodox
Christianity, which provided the motive for the ritualised destruction
of Christian symbols. This reading only works if Britain in the late
fourth century was indeed slipping into anarchy and chaos – for which,
as we have seen, there is precious little evidence. There is, however, a
rather extraordinary corollary if one accepts Dominic Perring's
interpretation of the events of 370–390; it has to do with the political
forces that may have been behind the termination of Roman rule in
Britain.

Perring suggests that one consequence of the repression of the
Gnostics and other heretical beliefs by the authorities was that the
ruling élite families of southern Britain became disaffected, because it
was their beliefs, their property and their identity that were being
attacked.[29] This suggests that the end of Roman rule was not just a
response to a build-up of large-scale barbarian raids, which as we have
seen usually came from north of Hadrian's Wall, and not from across
the North Sea or down the English Channel.

Whether or not the ruling southern British élite had indeed taken
part in the Barbarian Conspiracy, their excellent sources of intelligence
would have informed them that by the early fifth century the armies
of the Western Roman Empire were in no state to respond to a challenge
to their authority that came from within southern Britain itself. This is

important, because it suggests that the ruling classes in fifth-century southern Britain were not powerless straws in a barbarian breeze. In AD 367 there is every chance that they were a part of that wind. At all events, Dominic Perring's reinterpretation of the archaeological evidence suggests that during the final months of Roman rule the southern British élite may have exercised more control over events than has been hitherto supposed. It has even been suggested that the controlling élites may actually have revolted against Roman rule, because they had grown fed up with paying heavy taxes to a distant authority that was incapable of providing them with any protection.[30]

It does not surprise me that the southern élite could have behaved in this way: they had shown remarkable resilience in the face of orchestrated persecution, and we know that they possessed a strong sense not just of their own superiority, but of their unity as a ruling, civilised and Romanised aristocracy. I find it hard to accept that these were the men who were pleading to the Anglo-Saxons for help just thirty years later (in AD 449) – whatever Gildas might wish us to believe.

The Roman Empire enters its late phase with the death of Theodosius I ('the Great') in 395. Shortly before, he defeated more barbarian incursions and further attempts to reintroduce paganism. When he died the Empire was firmly Christian and the Church was in an assured and secure position. The army was winning victories, but these were gained with the help of large allied forces that were only loosely under Theodosius' direct control. This was a weakness in the system that would shortly have dire consequences. On the death of Theodosius the Empire was officially split into two, an Eastern and a Western Empire, ruled by his sons Arcadius and Honorius respectively.

After the death of Theodosius, the emperor was less powerful than before. He became more of a head of state than an active leader. Political and military leadership was provided by the chief minister, who in the west was almost always the senior military commander. The first of this new breed of chief minister in the west was Flavius Stilicho, a Vandal* by birth and married to Theodosius' niece, Serena.

Stilicho held power in the west for the first ten years after the death of Theodosius, and was widely supported by powerful factions

---

* A Germanic people, possibly originating in the Baltic region.

in the Church, the army and the senate in Rome. The Roman army in the early fifth century was not the force it had once been, and its commanders relied heavily on hired free mercenaries, or *foederati*. These barbarian forces within the army were always a source of weakness; furthermore, capricious but powerful allies such as Alaric, King of the Visigoths (who occupied southern Gaul and Spain in the fifth century), needed to be treated with the greatest possible caution. An idea of how difficult it must have been to command the Roman army in the fifth century is given by Stilicho's intention, in 408, to use barbarian forces to quell a mutiny among his Roman units.

There is as yet little reliable archaeological evidence for the employment of mercenaries in the Roman army in the late fourth and early fifth centuries in southern Britain.* This is odd, given what we know about Roman military history at this date. It is almost certain that British troops were employed in some numbers across the Channel, and it seems highly unlikely that that there were no reciprocal movements from the Continent to Britain. Given the large number of developer-funded excavations currently being undertaken, I would be most surprised if evidence for the employment of foreign mercenaries in the Late Roman army in Britain does not come to light. If this does happen, I confidently predict, first, that it will be greeted as 'incontrovertible evidence for a substantial Anglo-Saxon presence in Late Roman Britain', and, second, that any foreign mercenary who did not come from what is now northern Germany will be ignored, as somehow irrelevant.

The only contemporary source that covers the end of Roman Britain is the court poet Claudian (*d*.404), whose principal purpose was to praise the achievements of the emperor and his army. His reliability is therefore rather doubtful. Apart from him, there is of course Gildas, who also had his own agenda, and who was writing well over a hundred years after the events in question. Gildas mentions three Pictish wars before the middle of the fifth century. The first of these was extended, and did not end until about 390. Based on Claudian and Gildas, Peter Salway reckons that the second took place

---

* A Roman cemetery at Lankhills, on the outskirts of Winchester, has produced possible evidence for the employment of a few mercenaries from the Danube valley in Hungary, but this is a matter of hot debate.

in 398; it mainly involved the manning of sea defences against the Saxons and Irish Scots. It is not clear whether the Picts came by land or sea, but they were denied access to Britain. Claudian writes about further successful defensive actions against barbarian incursions of Picts, Irish Scots and Saxons into Britain in the year 400.

After the movement of troops into Britain for the first of the Pictish wars, from about 398 Stilicho was obliged, by a series of barbarian attacks on the Continental mainland, to start a process of gradual troop withdrawal from Britain. Archaeologically we see the decline in the Roman military presence reflected in the coinage. The last coins to be imported into Britain in substantial numbers were issues of Arcadius and Honorius of AD 402.* Presumably these were required to pay the troops; after that year troop numbers were too small to require the importation of coins in bulk.

While Roman troops were being moved around western Europe, barbarian attacks on Britain continued. There seems to have been an incursion of Irish under Niall of the Nine Hostages in 405; meanwhile on the Continent there were major Gothic wars in 402–3 and 404–5. By now Italy itself was under threat, and Stilicho was closely involved with the organisation of her defences. At this point the Roman troops in Britain revolted, and eventually proclaimed an upper-class, civilian Briton named Gratian as their emperor in 407 – a most unusual choice. He lasted four months before he was murdered. The army in Britain feared an attack from overseas, and had little confidence that they would be supported by Roman forces on the Continent, who had more than enough to deal with. So this time they proclaimed a man with an illustrious name, Constantine III.

Given the parlous state of affairs in the early fifth century, it seems odd that Constantine III and his forces should attempt to take over the Western Empire. This ambition says much about the army in Britain, and much too about their opinion of their former leaders. Constantine and his forces crossed the Channel to Gaul, and after a struggle Gaul fell to them by the end of 407. In the following year Spain fell to troops of the Constantine cause under the command of

---

* The minting of coins in Britain had ceased during the reign of Magnus Maximus, AD 383–88.

his son, Constans. Then, in 409, Honorius (Emperor, or Augustus, of the Western Empire) declared Constantine his co-Augustus. He was given control of the Gallic prefecture, which included Britain, Gaul and Spain. Unfortunately, however, his administrative capital had been moved from its traditional home at Trier, in northern France, to Arles, on the Mediterranean coast, fifty miles west of Marseilles.[31] This was a very long way indeed from Britain. As Peter Salway put it, the centre of gravity of the Gallic prefecture was now Mediterranean rather than northern.[32]

By now even the Mediterranean world was under barbarian threat. In 410 Rome was famously sacked by Alaric, King of the Visigoths, and in the previous year pressures were mounting on Constantine III's Gallic prefecture in both Spain and Gaul. He was now besieged in his capital, which meant that taxes and money for the troops could not find their way north. In 409 more barbarian actions, and the threat of further attacks, caused the population and troops stationed in Britain to revolt against the Empire. Constantine was in no position to suppress this, the third revolt in Britain, which was now officially outside the Empire. For Britain, the Roman interlude had come to an end.

CHAPTER SIX

The 'Anglo-Saxon' Origins of England

THE TIME OF THE ANGLO-SAXONS is commonly seen, in the words of the great historian of the period Sir David Wilson, as 'a no-man's-land, across which flit insubstantial, semi-legendary figures – Hengist and Horsa, Arthur, Alfred and Offa'.[1] That air of mystery, through which move the shrouded figures, has allowed people to take their eyes off the archaeological ball. After all, there is something wonderfully romantic and exciting about 'semi-legendary figures' with strange-sounding names who perform heroic deeds. I would not wish Hengist and Horsa to be banished from the centre stage of British history, but they have occupied it for a very long time. We should allow some of those in the wings their share of the limelight. In other words, let's look at the archaeology, because today we know a surprising amount not only about Early Saxon times, but about the last years of Roman Britain. Our principal new sources of information on the origins of the Anglo-Saxon phenomenon are not historical, but almost entirely archaeological.[2] We must briefly set the likes of Gildas and even Bede temporarily to one side.

I have heard it said that the only Saxon immigrants we can really be sure of are the three boatloads that Gildas mentions:

> Then a pack of cubs burst forth from the lair of the barbarian lioness, coming in three keels, as they call warships in their language. The winds were favourable, favourable too the omens and auguries, which prophesied, according to a sure portent among them, that they would live for three hundred years in the land towards which their prows were directed, and that for half the time, a hundred and fifty years, they would repeatedly lay it waste.[3]

Personally, I would query the 'three keels' too. The number three has a symbolic importance all its own – it could have been a nod in the direction of the Holy Trinity – but as a literal indication of quantity it seems doubtful. It must have been intended to have been read as a metaphor, together with the three hundred and half three hundred years that are also mentioned. This is not to suggest that there were no incomers from overseas, because of course there were. New scientific techniques are showing that the population of Britain and Europe was far more mobile than has been hitherto imagined. But that mobility did not manifest itself in simple waves of migrants who swept all before them. That sort of folk movement is the stuff of allegory: it's a way of painting a metaphorical picture that carries a particular message.

Metaphor and allegory were methods of popular communication that had roots in the Bible – after all, what could be a more memorable way to describe the Creation than the fable of Adam and Eve? The writings of Gildas and Bede are suffused with Biblical allusions, and both authors would have been skilled in the use of that particular technique of storytelling. I believe the 'three keels' in Gildas are akin to the three ships in the old Christmas carol that came sailing by 'on Christmas Day in the morning'.

In this chapter I want to examine the archaeological and historical evidence for the arrival of Anglo-Saxon migrants in eastern Britain.[4] The establishment of their settlements within the landscape is still generally considered to signal the birth of a new nation called England. In the popular perception it is the presence of substantial numbers of Anglo-Saxons that makes England different from the other nations of the British Isles. England is Anglo-Saxon, the others are Celtic or Gaelic. These are important issues to do with identity, and over the years they have attracted attention from historians and archaeologists. They have also acquired a huge number of self-sustaining myths* which are based on a circular argument that goes something like this: we know for a fact that the folk movements happened, so we will interpret all new evidence in the light of that knowledge.

---

* By 'self-sustaining myths' I mean, for example, the hundreds, possibly thousands, of excavation reports which routinely attribute the appearance of Early Saxon pottery to the arrival of settlers.

Let us begin with a summary of the archaeological evidence in favour of large-scale Anglo-Saxon migrations in the fifth and sixth centuries AD. As has been noted, the Anglo-Saxons are believed to have brought with them an entirely new set of objects that differ markedly from the Romano-British items previously in use. These include hand-made pottery, brooches and other fashion accessories, new styles of clothing and metalwork, such as knives, axes and weapons. They also introduced a new pagan religion, and with it a new way of disposing of the dead: cremation within urns in large cemeteries. The urns and fashion accessories are particularly important to the supporters of the invasion hypothesis, because they can be closely paralleled on the Continent, especially in parts of northern Germany.

Further evidence for influxes of new people is provided by the houses in which the Anglo-Saxons lived. A new style of house with a sunken floor, or alternatively a cellar-like space beneath the floor, the *Grubenhaus* or sunken feature building (SFB), is seen as particularly characteristic of the new migrants. These buildings are well known on the Continent. Similarly, larger, post-built rectangular 'halls' are also seen as an Anglo-Saxon introduction. The Anglo-Saxons are supposed to have introduced large villages, often sited on land that had not been settled previously. This in turn supports the suggestion that they cleared substantial areas of forest and occupied a Britain that was underpopulated and suffering from social and economic chaos following the withdrawal of the Roman legions.

It is argued that changes as profound as a new religion and rites of burial, not to mention new styles of houses and artefacts, when taken together amount to the presence of a new group of people. This argument is reinforced by the appearance of a new language, Anglo-Saxon or Early English, and the manifest hostility that existed between the 'incomers' and the Romanised 'native' British population of the north, the west and the south-west. I do not feel competent to enter into the controversy surrounding the origins of the English language. All I will note is that language is not necessarily a defining attribute of a particular ethnic group, and that the words and grammar of what was to become the English language were not solely derived from Germanic sources. Moreover, the process was to take two to three centuries, the period between the end of the Roman period and the first written records in Early English, which appear late in the seventh century.[5]

It is probably fair to say that serious scholars who believe in large-scale Anglo-Saxon mass migrations are now in the minority. Most people, myself included, accept that there was a certain amount of movement in and out of Britain, just as there was in the Iron Age and the Roman period. We might well discover one day that certain Anglo-Saxon cemeteries in, say, East Yorkshire, contain the bodies of immigrant populations. I do not believe, however, that such discoveries will invalidate the consensus that the changes attributed to the arrival of Anglo-Saxons were usually caused by people changing their minds, rather than their places of residence.

Heinrich Härke of Reading University is a strong advocate of the mass-migration position, for all of the traditional reasons: rapid population decline in post-Roman Britain, textual sources (e.g. Gildas), new types of pottery and other artefacts, the new rite of cremation and the new language now known as Early English. He also subscribes to the more controversial view that many of the skeletal remains in the cemeteries are 'of a population which is different from native types, but shows close similarities to populations in northern and south-western Germany'.[6] There are serious problems with this idea, not the least being that the size and shape of our bodies are affected by factors other than genetics alone. If one is looking for direct evidence for an incoming population, I personally would choose some of the more reliable science-based techniques, such as stable isotope analysis (discussed further in Chapters 8 and 9).

Härke argues that the population of Britain declined in the fifth century from a Late Roman high of two to four million to a later-fifth-century low of one to two million. He suggests that somewhere between one and two hundred thousand Anglo-Saxon settlers arrived in eastern Britain: 'Their settlement would have been interspersed with that of the natives, who assumed the position of a lower-status population.'[7] This idea has been suggested by other scholars, including Nick Higham, who less contentiously saw the incomers as a small élite of perhaps less than ten thousand people.[8] The trouble with these otherwise plausible suggestions is that they are not supported by the results of excavation, which show, as yet, no clear evidence for two distinct cultural entities in the fifth century. One would expect, for example, to find distinct 'Anglo-Saxon' and British cemeteries close to the same settlements, but that does not happen. There is precious little evidence for a fifth-century élite of any sort, let alone a foreign one.

I also find the suggestion that the population of late-fourth- and fifth-century Britain declined so catastrophically hard to sustain. If there was such a massive collapse, it is more likely to have taken place in the early fourth century, when life in British towns seems quite suddenly to have declined. There is indeed evidence that agriculture in Dark Age southern Britain became less intensive, but this can be explained by the need no longer to supply the Continental Roman army, nor to produce substantial surpluses from which to pay hefty taxes.*

Being a prehistorian, I tend to take a longer view than most people. I am happier dealing with millennia rather than centuries. I incline to the view that nothing of long-term significance ever happened overnight. The Great War may have been triggered by an assassination in the Balkans, but the tensions behind that horrendous conflict had been building up for a very long time. I think something similar applies in the present instance.

So far I have mainly discussed the Romanised and 'Anglo-Saxon' south and east of Britain. In the chapters that follow I will cross the country to consider the 'British' or 'Celtic' north and west. A broadly similar divide probably existed throughout later prehistory, from about 2000 BC, possibly reflecting the fact that Britain is an island that faces east and west. These two faces are separated by uplands that run down most of the centre. As a result, rivers with their fertile valleys and floodplains also run east–west, and drain into the North Sea or the Atlantic. Britain's geography positively encourages communities on both sides of the country to face outwards, away from the centre.

In 1972, in his book *Britain and the Western Seaways*, Professor E.G. Bowen explained the cultures of western Britain and Ireland in essentially maritime terms.[9] He saw ties between those regions and neighbouring parts of Europe, especially Brittany, Spain and Portugal.

---

* See the discussion of East Anglian post-Roman landscapes in Chapter 8.

More recently Barry Cunliffe has arrived at much the same view, but with a wealth of new information from Britain and the Continent.[10] For my part I would stress the strong ties that unite east and south-east England to the Low Countries and north-western France, and north-eastern England and eastern Scotland to Scandinavia and the North Sea shores of Germany. The natural overseas communication routes of at least half of England and Scotland lie towards the east, to the shores of the North Sea and the hinterland of north-western Europe.[11]

The east–west division of Britain broadly coincides with the Lowland and Upland Zones that the great archaeologist Sir Cyril Fox saw as being fundamental to the development of British landscape and culture – something he referred to as the 'personality of Britain'.[12] I tend towards a less closely defined view of these two Zones. I do not see them as inward-looking; quite the opposite, in fact. The Atlantic/North Sea contrast is just that: it's a long-term cultural *contrast*, not a divide, and it is one of the main characteristics of the British Isles. We saw from Andrew Sargent's study in the previous chapter that this contrast continued throughout the Roman period. It is my contention that in post-Roman times the division between 'Anglo-Saxons' to the east and 'British' to the west is a continuation of this same old, or rather ancient, theme. It's a cultural, rather than an ethnic, distinction. Being human, we like to personify such things, so we conjure up Arthur on one side and the likes of Alfred, Hengist and Horsa on the other. Doubtless there were similar heroes in the Bronze Age.

Before we consider the Anglo-Saxons and other possible incomers to Britain, we should think briefly about the land to which they are supposed to have come. On present evidence it would seem more than possible that the end of Roman rule in Britain was something that the British southern élite may have wanted to achieve. They had little confidence in the military help on offer from the Gallic prefecture, and considered that, all things being equal, it would be better to go it alone. As we have seen, the southern Romano-British élite had an identity of their own, and they must have believed that they stood a chance of surviving independently.

We can only speculate about conditions in the second and third decades of the fifth century in Britain, as there is little reliably dated archaeological evidence to go on. In those regions where there is continuity of settlement, such as the area around Durobrivae, there are no obvious disjunctions or breaks in the archaeological record.[13] So we must assume that life in rural Britain continued, but without certain distinctively Romano-British items such as wheel-made pottery and coinage, both of which ceased to be used around 420/430. These changes probably reflected the collapse of a money-based market economy. As we have seen, people went back to earlier ways of doing things in the countryside: barter was important, but so was exchange based on other, largely social, obligations.

Peter Salway considers that by the 440s at the latest a distinctively 'post-Roman' society had emerged in Britain.[14] Although there are indications of fifth-century occupation in towns, the nature of that occupation is a matter of hot debate. We must assume that settlement in post-Roman and Early Saxon Britain was essentially rural, just as it had been in the Iron Age.

In its early days the Roman army was famous for the way it moved potentially aggressive young men of various nations to distant parts of the growing Empire, where they could let off steam without fomenting civilian revolt – largely because they were not familiar with local languages and customs. It was a clever policy, and it worked well. In the later Empire various barbarian allies were employed as mercenaries. This also had the effect of introducing young men to new regions, and as we saw in Chapter 1, this was the way Gildas and Bede believed that the first Anglo-Saxons arrived in Britain. The presence of numerous Anglo-Saxon *foederati* in Later Roman Britain is often assumed, but is notoriously hard to pin down with any certainty. The assumption that they were there may be based on Gildas and Bede, but it also follows the writings of an influential archaeologist.

Dr J.N.L. Myres' great work of synthesis, published in 1969, was *Anglo-Saxon Pottery and the Settlement of England*.[15] He based much of his research on the shape, style and decoration of pottery urns found in 'Anglo-Saxon' cremation cemeteries in eastern and south-central England, and drew close parallels with similar pottery that was being manufactured at approximately the same time on the Continent. He concluded that the earliest British pots were made by ethnic Anglo-Saxon potters who had arrived in Britain as settlers.

When I read Myres' books and articles for the first time I was wholly convinced by what he had to say. I now realise that this was as much due to the power of his conviction as to the strength of his argument. He greatly admired Gildas, whose flowery Latin prose informs much of his work. This is Myres on the British failure to repel further waves of invaders using mercenaries, following the *adventus Saxonum* (arrival of the Saxons) around AD 450:

> The failure is pictured by the early sources in dramatic terms with the general uprising of all the settled barbarians and their destruction of Roman culture in the cities and the Church, the replacement in an orgy of blood and flames of what remained of the old world by the tentative and barbaric beginnings of the new.
>
> It is to Gildas that we owe the essentials of this picture, and there can be no doubt that he was right. He was, after all, born less than fifty years later ... and his parents must have been in a position to tell him directly of what they had themselves seen and heard of the years of destruction.[16]

Myres caused something of a sensation when he suggested that the earliest Saxon settlers arrived in Britain during his first phase of 'over-lap and controlled settlement' (*c*.360–410). This is just a decade or so later than the height of Romano-British fourth-century prosperity. Myres' next phase, of 'transition' (*c*.410–50), sees limited settlement during the so-called 'sub-Roman' period;* but the main waves of immigration are in his next phase, of 'invasion and destruction' (450–500). This half-century was a period of 'massive and uncontrolled land-seizure by Anglo-Saxon and other barbarian peoples, and ... the accompanying destruction of Romano-British civilisation'. He completes this summary of the main events of his third phase of Anglo-Saxon settlement with a telling phrase which provides us with the motivation behind his study: 'The contemporary pottery should throw some light on the nature and range of these movements, and on the background of the principal groups of settlers in different parts.'[17] In other words, the information found in the field during excavation was explicitly to be used to amplify and flesh out the observations of writers such as Gildas.

---

* The term 'sub-Roman', has a pejorative ring which recalls 'sub-human'. It is still sometimes used to describe the period 410–500.

Somewhat later, in 1977, in the discussion chapters to his comprehensive catalogue of English Anglo-Saxon pottery, Myres turns to Bede, who was writing in the years prior to 731, and who used Gildas as his main source for these early events. Myres had been writing about the regions from where the early Anglo-Saxon settlers might have come, and had drawn extensively on Bede. This is what he wrote next:

> These assumptions are all amply confirmed by the pottery. Even if Bede had never written what he did, it would have been abundantly clear from their pottery that the bulk of the settlers must have come from precisely the regions to which he pointed as their homes.[18]

In that brief passage we again find the circular argument, but it was published at a time time when the archaeological climate had changed a great deal since 1969, when Myres wrote *Anglo-Saxon Pottery and the Settlement of England*. So now Myres gives a nod in the direction of circularity; but it is only a nod. If leading authorities such as Myres were writing with such certainty about the wholesale migration into Britain of many tens of thousands of Continental settlers, it is hardly surprising that few people actually digging and writing up sites in the field were going to depart from such dogma. It would be professional and academic suicide.

I'm aware that I'm writing with the advantage of hindsight, but it has always struck me as odd that it never seems to have occurred to Myres and his colleagues that the data so expensively obtained from the excavation of cremation cemeteries and other sites could have served as an independent test of the generally unreliable ancient sources. I still cannot understand how the dramatic increase in new discoveries that resulted from the enhanced archaeological activity of the late 1960s had had so little effect on the world of Anglo-Saxon studies. Work carried out during this period certainly transformed our understanding of prehistory. To my mind the failure to adapt to changing circumstances says much about the prevailing culture of Anglo-Saxon studies in Britain, which was often text-led and archaeologically conservative. It is ironic that such intellectual conservatism should be used to shore up an idea that has no parallel or precedent at any other time in British history. Even the archaeologically much better attested Viking raids of the eighth and ninth centuries did not involve such a vast incursion of new people as actually to create a new nation that was culturally and ethnically unrelated to the other countries of the British Isles.

As I reread Myres in the preparation of this book, I was gripped with an extraordinarily strong feeling of *déjà vu*: it was as if I were rereading his contemporary Professor Christopher Hawkes, also of Oxford University, defining in considerable chronological detail successive waves of Iron Age incursions that never actually happened.[19] Like Myres, Hawkes defined his phases almost solely on the basis of changing pottery styles and the way they resembled supposed Continental originals. Myres looked for his Continental homelands in the Anglo-Saxon territories of northern Germany; Hawkes towards the valley of the Marne in northern France. Both, I believe, were mistaken in thinking that the pots which they studied with such erudition and care came with large numbers of people attached. Having said that, it is entirely possible that Continental potters or merchants could have established workshops in Britain.

Returning to less controversial matters, some dress ornaments and military equipment found in fourth-century contexts in Britain and elsewhere were clearly German-inspired, but much of this was 'standard issue', made in state-owned workshops in the Danubian provinces. The military fashions of the time were favouring Germanic styles in fittings such as belt buckles, just as civilian dress was to do later. These objects do not suggest the presence of German *foederati* in mid-fourth-century Britain. As Salway notes, it is unlikely that soldiers wore different uniforms according to their national origins.[20] If we are to find independent non-ceramic (i.e. non-pottery) evidence for *foederati* or irregular Anglo-Saxon military allies in Britain, it is most likely to be in late-fourth-century contexts. So far, however, it is lacking; which is not to say that German *foederati* were never present in Britain, but does suggest that they may not have been as widespread or numerous across south-eastern Britain as Gildas implied, and as Myres asserted.

So far I have discussed the *foederati* as the most likely source of evidence for an Anglo-Saxon presence in Britain in Late Roman times. But there is one other, often quoted and spectacular group of monuments which are grouped together under a name which proclaims a strong message. I am referring to the eleven or so 'Saxon shore' forts of eastern and southern England. Surely, with a name like that, which itself is quite ancient, we are on firmer ground. Sadly not. The presence of the 'Saxon shore' forts has helped to perpetuate the myth that Late Roman Britain was gradually slipping into a state of siege, and that the breakdown of law and order was attended by widespread lawlessness and piracy. The trouble with this view is that it makes many assumptions, most of which are wrong.

Let's start with that name. It first appears in one of the main sources we possess on Later Roman Britain, a document known as the *Notitia Dignitatum* ('List of High Offices'), a late-fourth-century (*c*.395) inventory of military resources and garrisons. Essentially it's a series of lists of places and forces, with headings that relate to their command structure. It was not written as, nor was it ever intended to be, an accurate historical account, and it was subject to various alterations and additions before it reached its final version, which we have today, probably in the early fifth century. Various military installations on both sides of the Channel were listed as being under the command of the *comes litoris Saxonici*, or Count of the Saxon Shore. It should be noted that just because the forts were listed under the same heading in the *Notitia*, it does not mean that they were part of an integrated system of coastal defences across the Channel, as has been suggested.[21] The *Notitia* was probably made for army administrators. It is not a strategic military document as such. It does not consider rules of engagement, communication, strategy, tactics or contingency planning. In other words, it does not provide us with grounds to suppose that British 'Saxon shore' forts had counterparts in Gaul, and formed part of a cross-Channel system of defence, as has also been suggested.[22]

Had the forts of the 'Saxon shore' only been mentioned in the *Notitia*, it is possible that they might have been overlooked by the early antiquaries. But they were also mentioned by William Camden in his great work on the antiquities of Britain, *Britannia*, published in 1586 and subsequently in 1594 and 1607. As its publication history suggests, Camden's *Britannia* was immensely influential, and continued to be so throughout the eighteenth and nineteenth centuries, in editions brought out by other antiquarians. Camden, doubtless with Gildas and Bede in mind, wrote about the depredations and robberies of the Saxons who 'grievously infested' Britain.

We have seen how in Victorian times the Anglo-Saxons acquired their importance as the means whereby barbarian Britain was transformed into civilised England. Victorian antiquarians and historians, using Camden as a guide, believed that the 'Saxon shore' forts must have played a significant role in events which were ultimately to prove so important to the origin of England. Thus a link was established that would prove extremely hard to break. Again, circular arguments were involved: the forts were along the 'Saxon shore'; therefore, self-evidently, they were built to defend Britain from Saxon attacks.

Even today the forts of the 'Saxon shore' are seen as a Roman response to third-century brigands and pirates from across the North Sea.[23] They have accumulated their own body of literature, which includes much theory and interpretation. The conventional wisdom on the forts of the 'Saxon shore' is well summarised by Stephen Johnson in his book *Later Roman Britain* (1980).[24] Johnson saw the forts as forming part of an integrated cross-Channel system of defence against barbarians who included two marauding seafaring peoples, the Franks and the Saxons. Having discussed the construction of the first shore forts, he continues:

> These preliminary precautions, such as they were, were inadequate by the end of the third century, for by then our sources record that Franks and Saxons were infesting the seas. At about this time, the Roman military authorities began to develop a number of the existing harbours into full-scale defended bases, positioning strongly walled forts on the larger river estuaries and on the exposed coasts ... to block Frankish and Saxon access to the interior of the province. These forts, clearly intended to hold a military garrison of both soldiery and sailors, were later to be known as the 'Saxon shore' frontier, protecting Britain from assault in an area she had little expected to be at risk.[25]

I do not share this view of the situation around the southern North Sea in the third and fourth centuries. Other authorities, such as Peter Salway, have their doubts about the forts of the 'Saxon shore' too,[26] and Andrew Pearson has suggested some alternative roles for them in a series of recent studies.[27] This work has, I believe, broken the circular argument which has traditionally placed Anglo-Saxon archaeology at the service of history. Pearson has provided us with an explanation for these south-eastern shore forts that makes practical sense, and that fits well with what we now know about second- and third-century Roman Britain.

The eleven 'Saxon shore' forts owe their fame not just to their resounding name, but because they are, for the most part, very imposing buildings.* They extend along the south-eastern coast from Brancaster, near the Wash, to Portchester Castle, close by the Isle of Wight. Portchester is among the most spectacular and well-preserved Roman buildings in north-western Europe. Like those at the next fort to the east, Pevensey, the Roman walls of Portchester were built into a medieval castle whose tower-like keep provides an excellent view of the Roman defences. The forts often feature projecting towers or bastions, which are characteristic of Later Roman military architecture. Bastions allow archers a clear field of view to shoot at an enemy attacking the main walls, but they also look very imposing, especially when seen from the land – which may provide us with a clue as to how the forts were used.

Pearson examined each of the forts in detail. He was at pains to place them in their local context, because with a class of site such as these, it is all too easy to assume that they comprised part of a working system, and had less significance in their own right. We should not presuppose that the forts were part of an integrated system of defence, which has not been proven. Again, there is an obvious danger of circularity here: we assume that the 'Saxon shore' forts are part of a system both because they line the south-eastern coast, and because we believe what we think the *Notitia* tells us. We must not fall into the trap of using the archaeological evidence to 'confirm' this version of events.

Pearson's analysis led him to some unexpected conclusions not only about the integrity of the 'Saxon shore' forts as a military defensive system, but also regarding their original roles and purposes.[28] On

---

* A twelfth has been suggested at Clausentum, Bitterne, Southampton.

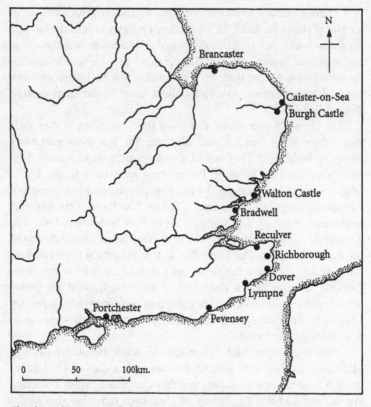

The eleven Roman so-called 'Saxon shore' forts built in the third century AD. These were probably fortified trading or distribution stations, rather than defences against attacking Saxon pirates, as is often assumed.

present evidence the forts were constructed in two distinct episodes, with Caister-on-Sea, Reculver and Brancaster being built in the first decades of the third century. Also at about this time the fort of the *classis Britannica* (British fleet) at Dover goes out of use, which firmly contradicts any suggestion that the forts formed part of a defensive system that integrated land and naval forces. The remaining forts were constructed later in the third century, between about AD 260 and 300.

Most Roman forts are jam-packed with military buildings and

installations, as we will see when we come to examine Birdoswald on Hadrian's Wall in Chapter 8. Often too, especially in the earlier years of the Empire's expansion, they were laid out on a standard plan, with barrack blocks, grain stores, parade ground and headquarters buildings in the same places. As one would expect of the finest army of antiquity, these forts were highly organised.

The strangest aspect of the 'Saxon shore' forts is the paucity of archaeological remains across their interiors. This is not the result of inadequate excavation (vanished timber buildings are not always easy to spot if one does not have the experience), as a large area within the walls of Portchester Castle was excavated by Barry Cunliffe, whose work at Danebury has shown that he and his team can locate even the most ephemeral of timber structures. What Cunliffe revealed, or rather did not reveal, at Portchester caused astonishment in the archaeological world.[29] He was able to divide the ancient features into a succession of phases. He proved that there was a Romano-British presence there in the third century, but that occupation was not at all what was expected: there were no barrack blocks, granaries or headquarters buildings. In fact, if one did not know that the excavations were within the massive walls that surrounded them, one would doubt whether Portchester was even a military site. It seemed to have most of the hallmarks of a civilian settlement, and not a very organised one at that. Certainly there was no evidence for the sort of gridiron street pattern one would encounter within a Roman military installation.

After a rather unexpected decade of abandonment directly after its construction in 285–290, Portchester was occupied throughout the fourth century and perhaps into the early part of the fifth. Most of the occupation was disorganised, to use Cunliffe's term, and there was only one period, between 345 and 364, when an attempt was made to impose a degree of order: timber buildings were reconstructed, roads and yard surfaces were cobbled, and coin loss declined – which indicates that rubbish would have been regularly removed and the place kept more clean and tidy. Thereafter disorganised, even 'squalid' occupation resumed.

As I have said, this does not sound like the usual style of Roman military occupation. Solid evidence for it being civilian was provided

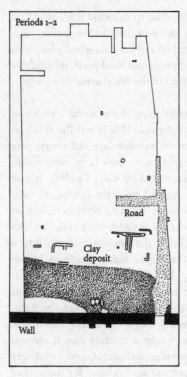

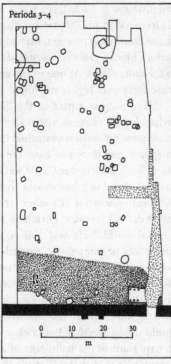

by the discovery of twenty-seven infant skeletons, which were buried throughout the third century. Other items, such as spinning and weaving equipment, attest to the presence of women. Women were in theory banned from Roman military facilities, relegated to the so-called *vici* (squatter-style informal settlements) outside the walls or ramparts.* But at Portchester family life clearly thrived within the walls.

Andrew Pearson has pointed out that the three early 'Saxon shore' forts at Caister-on-Sea, Reculver and Brancaster show evidence for substantial structures within their defences; Reculver was even laid out on a regular geometric plan. Where we have evidence for the internal layout of the later-third-century forts it is like that at Portchester:

* Simon James has pointed out to me that the ban on women within Roman forts was probably more theoretical than actual. The fort at Vindolanda on Hadrian's Wall, for example, has revealed the shoes of women and children.

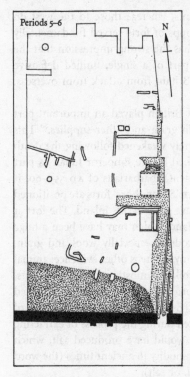

Three period plans showing the interior of the Roman shore fort at Portchester Castle, Hampshire, as revealed by Barry Cunliffe's excavations of 1961–72.

slight and irregular. Cunliffe's excavations were extensive. He stripped about an eighth of the area within the walls, so the absence of regularly-laid-out barrack blocks etc. cannot be the result of too small an excavated sample.

Pearson also says that the disposition of the three early forts makes no military sense, because they would have left Suffolk, Essex, southern Kent, Sussex and Hampshire undefended. This is particularly strange, because as we have seen, the area most threatened by Anglo-Saxon attack in the fourth century was the eastern end of the English Channel. He also pointed out that at least half of the 'Saxon shore' forts were abandoned before the end of Roman rule, at precisely the time when Gildas and Bede tell us that Saxon raids were becoming a problem.

There is another significant difficulty. The forts along the east coast, from Brancaster to Richborough, all have significant *vici*-type informal external civilian settlements, whereas those to the west do not. This suggests that the two groups of forts served fundamentally different purposes. All in all, one has the strong impression that the 'Saxon shore' forts never formed part of a single, unified defensive system that was set up to defend Britain from attack from overseas. So what were they intended for?

We saw in the last chapter that Britain played an important part in supplying the Roman army with grain and other supplies.[30] This logistical chain was broken or severely weakened following the death of Magnentius, but was re-established by the Emperor Julian as part of his campaign against the Continental barbarians of AD 359–60. It is noticeable how many of the eastern 'Saxon shore' forts are positioned near the mouths of rivers which have good access inland. The fort at Brancaster is very close to the Fenland, which may have been a huge imperial estate much of whose produce, especially wool and grain, might have been destined for the army. There is other evidence: animal bones from Burgh Castle in Norfolk are mostly of non-meat cuts, suggesting that the joints were exported elsewhere. Bradwell is located in the so-called 'red hills' area of Essex. 'Red hills' are mounds of burnt silt and sand that are produced during the process of extracting salt from seawater. The Fens, too, would have produced salt, which was an important and valuable commodity in ancient times (the word salary is derived from the Latin *sal*, or salt).

A close analysis of the exotic building stone used in the construction of Bradwell, and possibly other 'Saxon shore' forts, has suggested that these places were part of long-distance trading networks.[31] Pearson has pointed out that if the shore forts were indeed part of a trading system, it would explain why the first three were constructed before historical sources such as Gildas start to mention Saxon piracy. He also suggests that they might have served a secondary role following the collapse in value of Roman coinage from the middle of the third century. With money less able to retain its value, taxes would have been collected in kind – i.e. as goods or livestock. Shore forts would have served as fortified depots for the collection and redistribution of such taxes-in-kind.

If forts like Portchester were in effect secure stores, it might help to explain why their interiors were so free from obstruction. It might also account for the nature of the settlement there. Certainly soldiers would have been needed to provide a measure of security, but the main requirement was for a workforce that could move, maintain and keep an inventory of the goods under its care.

Pearson's reassessment of the 'Saxon shore' forts fits well with the picture of Later Roman Britain painted by writers such as Guy de la Bédoyère. It hardly seems likely that Britain could have enjoyed a 'Golden Age' in the fourth century if it was under constant threat from barbarian attack. Besides, as we have seen, most of the attacks that we know about and can pin down in the archaeological record seem to have emanated from north (and west) of Hadrian's Wall, rather than from across the North Sea. It makes far more sense to see the shore forts as symbols of prosperity than of paranoia.

If we have disposed of the 'Saxon shore' forts as a coherent defensive system, what was going on in the northern part of what was later to become England? This is the area where the threats from both north of Hadrian's Wall and from Ireland were becoming increasingly severe. It is here that we find convincing evidence for military refurbishment in the fourth century, at forts like Lancaster and Caernarfon in the west; and chains of new signal stations were established in the late fourth century along the Yorkshire coast and as far north as Sunderland. These last were clearly intended to counter a maritime threat from along the coast, further north.

To summarise the picture so far, it now seems probable that Gildas greatly exaggerated the severity of Anglo-Saxon piracy, which mainly seems to have been confined to Gaul and the southern side of the English Channel. Far from being cut off from the Continent, Britain would appear to be actively trading overseas throughout the fourth century, and perhaps later. Both the ex-Roman (but still Romanised) army and the ruling élite were well organised and seemingly secure within southern Britain. We have seen that they may have taken part in the great Barbarian Conspiracy of AD 367, but they also seem to have acquired a strong sense of identity, which included a significant religious dimension. From an anthropological perspective these people seem secure within themselves, and I cannot see why they should have crumpled after the official withdrawal of Roman forces, which in any case they may have instigated, in AD 409. The arrival of the Saxons, the *adventus Saxonum*, is supposed to have happened around AD 450. What caused a supposedly near-complete collapse in southern British élite and military circles in little more than a generation? If such a thing did happen, one would expect it to have left clear archaeological traces: massive war graves, settlement dislocation and 'knock-on' impacts in northern and western Britain. But so far they have not been found.

The conventional wisdom suggests that the later fifth century (from *c*.450 to 500) was when Anglo-Saxon settlers moved into Britain in large numbers. If that was indeed the case, the period of mass migration must have happened very suddenly indeed, and without the benefit of the 'overlap and controlled settlement' and 'transition' phases which Myres suggests must have happened if there was to be a period of 'invasion and destruction' from AD 450 to 500. Andrew Pearson does not quite grasp the nettle, but his implications are nonetheless clear:

> That the third and fourth centuries witnessed neither widespread piracy from the Continent, nor a fort-building response from the Romans, must have a bearing on our impressions of the state of the British province at this time. How the situation changed after the collapse of the Rhine frontier in 407 is a different matter, but by that point the majority of military bases around the British coast had long since ceased to function.[32]

I have mentioned that the ruling Romano-British élite in the south and east possessed a strong identity, which included a significant religious dimension. If Myres and the supporters of Gildas are correct, British culture in the south-east was completely displaced by Anglo-Saxon settlers. Britons from the south-east are supposed to have fled westwards into Wales and the south-west. (Incidentally, how that happened is anyone's guess: one would have thought that a million or so people on the move would have left a fairly strong archaeological trace.) But if Anglo-Saxon people and culture displaced 'native' practices, one would expect the latter to have vanished completely. They did not. If people were not moving around in great waves of migration, how and why did the archaeological changes of post-Roman times happen? What was going on when Britain became England?

Over the centuries Britain has produced its fair share of religious innovations, ranging from the Celtic Church to Quakerism. Generally speaking the official Church greeted them as one would welcome a scorpion to one's trousers. Pelagianism, or the Pelagian Heresy as it was rapidly dubbed by the Church at Rome, was a case in point. It was conceived by an early-fifth-century theologian named Pelagius who was probably born in Britain or Ireland, although it is not known when or where he died. Some time around AD 400 he travelled to Rome, where he was disillusioned by the moral standards he encountered there. This seems to have had a profound effect on him and the subsequent development of his theology. Clearly he held his views with much conviction, because during his career he was excommunicated twice.

Pelagius originally planned a legal career, which was probably why he visited Rome, where he encountered the established Church theology of Augustine, who taught that a person's capacity for good is most effective when that person wholly subjects his or her will to the will of God. Augustine also taught that human beings are too frail to achieve salvation without again submitting themselves to the will of God. Pelagius found these ideas abhorrent, because he believed that human beings were in control of their own destinies.[33] In effect, his 'heresy' denied original sin.

Pelagianism was particularly popular in Britain, especially among the ruling élite, and it is not very difficult to see why, given their erstwhile predilection for Gnosticism. Both 'heretical' views of Christianity stressed the importance of the individual as having free will, able to control his or her journey through life. Dominic Perring suggests that while there is nothing to indicate that Gnostic worship survived into fifth-century Britain, echoes of the dissent might have contributed to the intellectual formation of Pelagius and his followers.[34]

The persistence of certain religious beliefs has been a recurrent theme in this book. I have suggested that their longevity may owe something to the concept of the *longue durée*: they survive because they express sentiments that somehow lie behind the structure, the fabric of life. They are to do with cosmology, and also perhaps with the way that societies organised themselves. I view these fundamental principles as altogether more important than, say, language or a particular religious cult. Thus it is possible to see why elements of

Christianity, and indeed Gnosticism, would have appealed to people who once practised so-called Celtic rites, such as Druidism. Dominic Perring has speculated that there may have been general underlying similarities of outlook between the Gnostics and the followers of Pelagianism, but he goes further: 'Since the mosaics in the main room at Frampton described a form of grail quest, it is also possible to draw speculative connections between the allegories represented here and those subsequently incorporated in Arthurian legend.'[35]

Neither Perring nor I would suggest for one moment that the legend of the Holy Grail was added to the Arthurian canon by anyone other than Chrétien de Troyes. What we are suggesting is that the quest for the Grail was well received by its medieval audience because it appealed to them in much the same way that the Gnostic quests had struck a sympathetic chord, also with an élite audience, several centuries earlier. This is speculative territory, but it would seem odd that such similar quest stories would have appealed so strongly to two British élites if the later one was indeed wholly introduced.

I also find it hard to understand how religious beliefs such as Gnosticism and Pelagianism could have been espoused by an élite whose very existence was under threat from outside. According to Myres, by the mid-fifth century substantial numbers of immigrants were taking over a disintegrating society. What interests me is that both Gnosticism and Pelagianism were new theologies: they were innovative, and involved the acceptance of new concepts. We know from anthropology that a society that feels under threat from outside turns in on itself. In such circumstances the role of religion is to provide people with a core of stability in their lives; so beliefs tend to become more traditional, conservative, and perhaps even fundamentalist.[36] That is not what was happening in late-fourth- and fifth-century southern Britain. Certainly, if the archaeological record is any guide, society was indeed radically changing, but the incentive to change was mainly coming from within; it was not being imposed from without.

The Pelagian Heresy clearly troubled the British Church, who appealed for help to Rome. Their response was to send a powerful – charismatic we would call him today – preacher and ex-Roman general, Germanus, Bishop of Auxerre, who effectively countered the heresy at a mass meeting of Church leaders in St Albans in 429. He stayed on in Britain to win a battle against barbarian forces in Wales, during which he converted his army to Christianity. Germanus made a second visit to Britain around 446–47. These and other contacts between Britain, Gaul and Rome show clearly that the Church and organised Christianity played a major role in political life in the fifth century. As late as 455, for example, modifications to the date on which Easter was to be celebrated, made by Pope Leo I in Rome, were adopted by the Celtic Church in Britain.

At this point we should be clear that the famous Celtic Church of Britain and Ireland, with its beautiful carved crosses, isolated monks' cells and fabulous illuminated manuscripts was a direct descendant of the Christian Church of Roman Britain. It was not a phenomenon that was imported and adapted to the British Isles during the Dark Ages, the time when it flourished. It was something that was there already.

The eastern half of Britain was by no means as overwhelmingly pagan as is often supposed. According to the conventional wisdom, the waves of Anglo-Saxon migrants are supposed eventually to have caused Christian Britons either to migrate west or to reject their Christianity, which after all had only recently been acquired. Myres tells us that during his 'transition' phase (between about AD 410 and 450) it was 'abundantly clear that, whatever the relations between the two communities may have been, they remained rigidly distinct and no attempt whatever was made to weld them into one. This follows ... from the obstinate adherence of the German settlers to their ancestral practice of cremation, which implies ... that they were never converted to Christianity.'[37]

If there were 'German settlers', and if indeed incomers and natives were 'rigidly distinct', it makes no archaeological sense to find them using precisely the same settlements and buildings, as we saw at Orton Hall Farm. You cannot have it both ways: if the Anglo-Saxon settlers are new and different, they should inhabit sites that are new and different.

One striking aspect of Myres' work is the speed with which his phases flash by. Each is of about fifty years' duration. Such speed simply does not fit with what we know about the archaeology of social processes. By the late 1960s radiocarbon dates had begun to show that significant social change tends to be gradual. To a prehistorian, the phases that Myres was able to define – based, it will be recalled, largely on changing pottery styles – were essentially that: changing pottery styles, which can alter with remarkable rapidity.

Certain styles of pottery decoration and dress ornaments were subject to the whims of fashion, or had short-term or family significance. An example of such ephemeral decoration is the patterns still knitted into traditional fishermen's sweaters. I have long been struck by the similarity between patterns on nineteenth- and early-twentieth-century fishermen's sweaters, particularly from the Shetland Islands, and the decoration on early Bronze Age Beaker pottery. The fisherman's sweater is unique to that individual, and can be 'read' by those familiar with the patterning. Maybe the same applied to the pots, which were often buried with individuals. Both decorative styles, like Anglo-Saxon cremation urns, used a limited repertoire of decorative motifs that could be assembled in a huge variety of combinations. Anglo-Saxon urns and beakers relied heavily on stamped or impressed decoration that was arranged in clearly defined zones over the body of the vessel.[38] Detailed changes in decoration signify an individual's status and family relationships over short periods of time. That is the level at which they are most fruitfully studied; they are only indirectly about issues as broad as culture and ethnicity. In my opinion Myres overinterpreted his pottery because he was working at the wrong scale.

Whether or not Germans settled in Britain before or during the so-called 'Migration Period' of the fifth and sixth centuries, their culture had a profound effect on insular traditions of housing, fashion, burial and even language. I shall discuss the notion of a 'Migration Period' in the next chapter; here it is sufficient to note that Continental and British scholars believed – and many still believe – that the post-Roman period in Europe was a time of wholesale folk-movement. It was thought that the pressures released by the collapse of the frontiers of the Roman Empire gave rise to two centuries of social turmoil, which were characterised by migration.* But why should the social

---

* I too formerly subscribed to the idea of a 'Migration Period' – until, that is, I had to think about it closely for the preparation of this book. Sharp-eyed readers of *Britain BC* will have noticed that in the table of dates and periods I labelled the fifth and sixth centuries AD as the 'main period of folk movements from the Continent'.[39]

disruption brought about by the end of the Western Roman Empire cause people to wander aimlessly about? The usual response to drastic change is to 'dig in' and stay put. Migration simply imposes yet another form of stress at a time when people want stability above all else.

I believe that the changes in the archaeological record of eastern and south-eastern Britain are better explained by 'acculturation' than migration. Acculturation has been defined as the 'transference of ideas, beliefs and traditions . . . by long-term personal contact and interaction between communities or societies. Adoption through assimilation by prolonged contact'.[40] Acculturation (aided by the internet and other means) is the process behind, for example, the coming together of Britain and the United States today.

We saw in Chapter 3 that overseas contacts had been maintained since at least the Bronze Age, and they reached something of a peak in the Late Iron Age, when there is good evidence for quite extensive contact with places as far away as the Mediterranean.[41] During the Roman period London was a major centre of commerce, and in the next chapter we will see how trade and other contacts between Britain and south-eastern Europe continued throughout the Dark Ages. It seems to me that the creation of the distinctive insular culture that would later be termed England was in part the result of a persistent tradition of communication between Britain and the mainland of Europe. This was a complex process, that took time. It was not something that can be explained by a simple, single cause, such as mass migration.

Traditionally, southern Britain in Later Roman times has been seen as growing ever more insular, cowering behind its 'Saxon shore' defences before being driven to hire Anglo-Saxon mercenaries for protection against Anglo-Saxon 'pirates'. It will be clear by now that I do not believe that the southern Romano-British élites were that weak, or that stupid. By any standards, hiring Saxons to fend off Saxons would be reckless and short-sighted. Surely it would have been far better, and simpler, to hire Picts and Irish Scots, who had a proven record and were ready at hand.

We will see in the next chapter that concrete evidence for Germanic paganism is lacking in England, and that there is clear archaeological evidence to suggest that the supposedly new 'Anglo-Saxon' rites of cremation were by no means universally adopted, even in the so-called Anglo-Saxon heartlands of eastern England. There can be little doubt now that the changes that took place in burial rites in the fifth and sixth centuries were far more complex than had previously been supposed. To my mind it is inconceivable that the traditional economic heartland of Britain, in other words what was now becoming eastern and south-eastern England, should have been largely pagan – and therefore out of the religious and political picture – for most of the period between, say, 450 and 650. We know that Christianity continued to be a significant force in both western and eastern Britain, as we will see in the following two chapters.

It is ironic that the greatest support for the manifestly unreliable 'historical' version of 'Dark Age' Britain provided by Gildas actually comes from archaeology – and archaeology of a high class, technically speaking. Many excavations of Anglo-Saxon cemeteries and settlements have been superb, but with certain notable exceptions they take Anglo-Saxon incursions as given. As a student I spent two of the most miserable months of my life in December and January 1965–66 working on one of the key Early Saxon sites at Mucking, not far from Southend in Essex. The site was atop a gravel ridge overlooking the Thames estuary, and a cold, damp wind was our constant companion. The director, Margaret Jones, was one of the first archaeologists to realise that landscapes required excavation on a vast scale, and her team worked closely alongside a co-operative gravel quarry operator.

The discovery of the Mucking Saxon settlement and cremation cemetery caused an immense stir. Never before had so many distinctively Anglo-Saxon sunken floored huts or houses been found in England. Objects found within the graves were considered by Myres to be exceptionally early – dating to the decades on either side of AD 400, which would place their arrival to the Late Roman period. Myres suggested that they were probably introduced to Mucking by Germanic *foederati*, and he cited Gildas in support of this.[42] By 1974, after further seasons of work, I detected that Margaret Jones had become less attached to the idea of wholesale Saxon settlement, although she still paid lip-service to it in print. She found it hard, however, to deny that there was evidence for continuity: Mucking was, for example, 'the only site where Late Roman bronzes have been found in both Saxon graves and Saxon huts'.[43] The 'Saxon huts' were of the sunken feature building or *Grubenhaus* type. Sadly Margaret herself was unable to complete the gargantuan task of writing up Mucking, which still awaits full publication, but an excellent site atlas was prepared in 1993 by Ann Clark. In that report the discussion (by H. Hamerow) of the Early Saxon period still acknowledges the possibility of incoming settlers, although the conviction behind the words seems pretty thin:

> The evidence regarding the origins of the Anglo-Saxon settlement, and particularly for the presence of Germanic *foederati*, is inconclusive, though the hypothesis remains plausible. Despite apparent continuity of land-use from the Romano-British period, there is no clear evidence for socio-economic continuity or for the integration of the Romano-British and Anglo-Saxon communities.[44]

At this point I am tempted to enquire about those Late Roman bronzes that were found 'in both Saxon graves and Saxon huts' – they represent pretty good 'socio-economic continuity' to me. Instead, I shall offer one final thought about the Mucking landscape, which in many ways resembles that around Maxey.

Having both worked on the site and studied the detailed plans of Mucking, I am in little doubt that occupation was essentially continuous. Viewed as a landscape, rather than as a succession of separate archaeological features, it seems to show clear logical progression, first from Iron Age to Roman, and then from Roman to Anglo-Saxon. By and large Saxon features occur near Roman ones, and although Roman ditches may have partially silted up by the time Saxon settlement becomes evident, the alignments of later features, such as buildings and cemeteries, tends to follow that of Roman times. The fact that ditches had been allowed to silt up probably reflects a change in land-use, for example from arable to pasture. If there was discontinuity in the development of the Mucking landscape it certainly is not obvious to me.

Myres' two great studies of Anglo-Saxon pottery are detailed and comprehensive, but as happens from time to time in archaeology, their very size and exhaustive attention to detail conceal the fact that they have been used to bolster up some rather suspect ideas. Myres' erudition was overwhelming, and as Bodley's Librarian he had a vast repertoire of ancient material at his fingertips. Who on earth would have the temerity to take on such a formidable authority? Dr Sam Lucy did, in *The Anglo-Saxon Way of Death: Burial Rites in Ancient England* (2000), and to my mind she won hands down in a wonderful book that Professor Martin Carver, the excavator of Sutton Hoo, the well-known Early Saxon cemetery in Suffolk, described as 'one of the most important publishing events for twenty-five years – the clear, friendly and authoritative exposition of a subject that has long been shrouded in Masonic murk'.[45]

Lucy spends some time discussing the historiography of Anglo-Saxon studies in an effort to find what it was that started people on the circular chase to prove Anglo-Saxon ethnicity in England. Why were – and are – so many scholars so convinced that south and eastern Britain was colonised by settlers from abroad in the fifth and sixth centuries? It is almost as if they *wanted* to be persuaded of it.

The reason may lie in the nineteenth century. The Victorian era was a time when the previously separate strands of history and science came together in a form of both pseudo-history and pseudo-science which today we would simply label as racist. This doctrine held that human beings came in physically, mentally and intellectually distinct races, the 'purity' of which would be threatened by mixing with the blood of another race. This was of course a fundamentally flawed doctrine, which would have appalling consequences in the twentieth century.

Different races were ascribed different characteristics. Celts, for example, were hot-headed and emotional, while the German or Teutonic race, which included the English, thanks to those Anglo-Saxon migrations, was the best of the lot: rational, loyal, artistic, inventive, etc., etc. Sam Lucy quotes a passage from William Stubbs, Professor of Modern History at Oxford from 1866 to 1884. It was commonplace at the time to attribute English parliamentary democracy to Teutonic antecedents: 'The political institutions we find in the conquered land [England] . . . are the most purely German institutions that any branch of the German race has preserved.' Meanwhile in 1875 the historical novelist Charles Kingsley (Professor of Medieval History at Cambridge from 1860) maintained that Teutonic racial purity had given him 'a calm and steady brain, and a free and a loyal heart; the energy which springs from health; the self-respect which comes from self-restraint; and the spirit which shrinks from neither God nor man, and feels it light to die for wife and child, for people and for Queen'. Laying aside the stomach-turning smugness, it is strong emotional stuff, and one can understand why it persisted for so long.[46]

In 1895 the German prehistorian Gustaf Kossinna came up with a new 'culture-historical' approach to archaeology. This approach, which was to prove influential throughout the first half of the twentieth century, suggested that 'archaeology was capable of isolating cultural areas which could be identified with specific ethnic or national units and traced back into prehistory'.[47] Later he asserted that it could even isolate areas occupied by individual peoples or tribes.

It is easy, with hindsight, to rubbish the 'culture-historical' approach, but it did help take our understanding of prehistory forward, and it was based on certain useful observations. For example, burial rites are not easily changed, and the form of ordinary domestic items can indeed be linked with certain identifiable groups of people. But as an approach it was used poorly, and its principles were applied without much thought. This led to a multiplicity of invasions and migrations that were invented to account for even minor changes in the archaeological record. Prehistorians started to discard this approach in the 1960s, when the first generation of post-war archaeologists became more interested in the processes that lay behind the development of ancient societies than in their identification.

When Victorian ideas about the characteristics and purity of races were allied to the 'culture-historical' approach, archaeologists and historians believed they could provide a solid academic basis for English Teutonic origins. That is also why manifestly unreliable sources such as Gildas were pressed into service. Gildas' shortcomings were ignored because he was saying what people wanted to hear. These then were the forces that lay behind the circular argument that has bedevilled the study of fifth- and sixth-century Britain for over a century.

The 'Masonic murk' that Martin Carver referred to is probably at its most impenetrably dense when it comes to the study of cremation cemeteries and the objects found in them. It has generally been held that cremation was a new burial rite that was introduced to Britain by Anglo-Saxon incomers. In fact it had been well established in

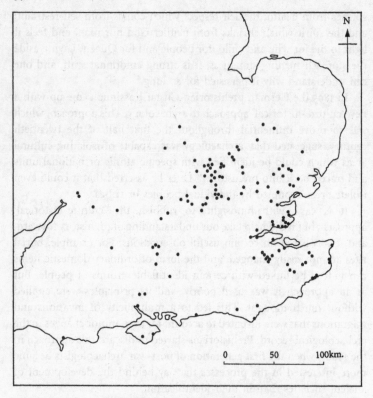

Distribution of Late Iron Age cremations. This should be compared with the southern distribution of 'Anglo-Saxon' cremations (see page 223).

pre-Roman Britain, and was the dominant rite in the Late Iron Age in Kent, where there are large cemeteries of what used to be called the 'Aylesford-Swarling Culture'. Generally speaking, Iron Age cremations are found along the eastern side of Britain; in my experience they often occur in small numbers in settlements rather than cemeteries.[48] By contrast, the dominant rite on the western side of Britain was inhumation within a small box or 'cist' made from stone slabs.[49] This is yet another example of the east–west divide that one finds so often in British prehistory.

Sam Lucy makes the important point that the presence of foreign objects on a British site does not mean that foreigners necessarily came with them – any more than there are German drivers in the many Volkswagens, BMWs and Mercedes-Benzes on British roads. She points out that it simply is not valid to jump from an object to observations about ethnicity. It is the way that objects were used that matters: grave-goods, such as brooches from Early Saxon graves, were used in Britain in ways that differed from Continental practices in the fifth century, and British versions of supposedly Continental originals are known from earliest times. Lucy suggests that the people buried in the Anglo-Saxon cemeteries may well have been British and, as we will see in Chapter 8, there is now scientific evidence to back this up. But why did they adopt these new objects and new rites in their funerary rituals and their daily lives?

The first answer to this question is that they wanted to. Maybe they preferred what they had seen, and possibly experienced, abroad. Maybe to the élites in south and eastern Britain the so-called 'barbarian' world north of the Roman frontier was more politically attractive than the Later Roman Empire, where taxation was an increasing burden and security could not be guaranteed. This exercise of free will is something that an archaeologist of the 'culture-historical' school would find hard to swallow. To such a person, people change their identities through folk-movement and conquest; his view of the ancient world is straightforward, verging on the mechanistic: pots equate with people, and influences spread or diffuse, rather like disease.[50] There is no allowance for invention and free will. Ancient cultures are not allowed to be unpredictable and human in the way they behave.

Sam Lucy is doubtful whether even cemeteries, with all their rich symbolic meaning, can yield reliable information on origins and ethnicity. But they can tell us much about what was going on at the time, what motivated people and gave meaning to their lives – and that is far more interesting than mere ethnicity. Writing about Anglo-Saxon cemeteries of the fifth to seventh centuries, Lucy states:

> They tell us little of migrants or invasions of people from the Continent and Scandinavia. Rather, they take us into a richer and more complex world, where we can encounter both the physical

reality of early medieval people, and something of their thoughts and aspirations. They also give indications of networks of influence which reached across the Channel and the North Sea ... People living in eastern Britain were integrally involved in these networks, which stretched from Norway to south-western France and probably beyond. They came into contact with a range of ideas, brought by merchants, travellers and others, and they selected those that were appropriate ... Perhaps the changes in burial rites seen from the fifth century are a result, to a certain extent, of this contact and appropriation of ideas – a process that allows for a certain dynamism in the people involved, rather than one-way traffic from the Continent to Britain.[51]

The exchange of influences and ideas that Sam Lucy writes about with regard to Saxon-period cemeteries has sometimes been referred to as a change in 'fashion', because dress, clothing and appearance were certainly a part of this new identity. Changes in female fashions required the wearing of brooches, both as decoration and to hold the new style of garments together. These brooches survive in graves and are very characteristic of the period: they are usually large, highly decorated, and to modern eyes seem rather overblown. Various items would be suspended from a belt around the waist. There was nothing new about such profound changes of personal identity. We saw in Chapter 3 that the final centuries of the Iron Age witnessed the adoption of new Continentally-inspired brooches, the so-called 'fibula event horizon' that J.D. Hill saw as 'the end of one kind of body and the beginning of another kind of body'. We can find further examples of such changes in personal appearance even earlier in prehistory: the 'ornament horizon' of the Middle Bronze Age in south-western Britain being a case in point.[52]

Sam Lucy is keen to point out that there was far more to these changes of appearance and identity than mere fashion. They were quite swiftly to lead to a new political orientation in the south and east, which from the sixth century onwards would find itself in opposition to different traditions in the north and west. It would be a mistake, however, to write 'fashion' off as necessarily trivial or ephemeral. It can be a symbol of more profound social changes, as in the 1960s, when mini-skirts were both a fashion and a token of young women's

Reconstruction of the Anglian style of female Anglo-Saxon dress. The shoulder straps of the outer gown were attached by a pair of small brooches; the large brooch on the bodice could also have been used to attach a cloak. The cuffs of the inner garment were joined by metal sleeve-clasps. From the belt hangs a knife and a pair of 'girdle-hangers' which were probably symbolic household keys and may have been worn as a form of amulet or protection.

newfound freedom, brought about by factors including the contraceptive pill and the emergence of the feminist movement.

If ever the Trustees of the British Museum decide to return the Elgin Marbles to Greece, the extraordinary finds from the royal ship burial at Sutton Hoo, in Suffolk, will probably become their most celebrated possessions.[53] Excavations in 1938 revealed the burial chamber, probably of a man (no bones were found), in an actual, probably seaworthy, wooden ship which superficially resembled a Viking longship. He was accompanied by fabulous gold jewellery and other items, such as a sword, shield, helmet, lyre, and a series of bronze Byzantine bowls from the eastern Mediterranean. The workmanship of the jewellery is probably British and is of the highest possible order; other items buried in the chamber were either made in, or show clear stylistic influences from, Scandinavia, 'Celtic' Britain, the Eastern Roman Empire (Byzantium) and beyond. Sutton Hoo was undoubtedly the burial of a pagan king – and most authorities now agree it was probably that of King Raedwald, an early ruler of the kingdom of Essex, who died in AD 625.

The Sutton Hoo burial was not a unique event. Martin Carver's excavations around the main mound have shown that there were more than fourteen barrows, and many graves that were not placed beneath mounds. Sam Lucy and Martin Carver see the flamboyance of Sutton Hoo as 'defiant paganism' in the face of Christianity, which was rapidly gaining influence in eastern England after AD 600. The finds from Sutton Hoo clearly demonstrate that East Anglia was an integral part of a larger North Sea community. The fact that the ship contained a king shows that by the early seventh century, social changes originally brought about by a process of 'acculturation' had developed their own momentum. They had become a real political force in the shaping of early England.

CHAPTER SEVEN

Arthurian Britain: The Situation in the West and South-West

WE HAVE SEEN how the southern élites may have played a significant role in the end of Roman Britain, and that their power had an economic base that was made possible by the stability and prosperity of the 'Golden Age' of Roman Britain in the early and mid-fourth century. I want to start this chapter with a brief look at the administration of fourth-century Roman Britain, and what it may have contributed to subsequent events.

Just as the organisation of the Roman army changed over time, so did that of the civil administration. Londinium (London) was the capital of the diocese of Britannia, which in turn belonged to the 'praetorian prefecture of the Gauls', which also included Gaul, parts of southern Germany and Spain. The capital of this prefecture was first at Trier in northern France and then, from the early fifth century, at Arles on the Mediterranean coast.

By the fourth century the diocese of Britain was divided into four provinces. Up until now we have concerned ourselves with the provinces of Maxima Caesarensis (provincial capital Londinium) and Flavia Caesarensis (provincial capital Lindum – Lincoln), together with south-easterly parts of the northern province Britannia Secunda (provincial capital Eboracum – York). In this chapter we will turn our attention to the less fully Romanised parts of Britannia Secunda and the most westerly province of Britannia Prima (provincial capital Corinium Dobunnorum – Cirencester). It should be recalled that significant parts of Wales and most of Devon and Cornwall were hardly affected by the Roman conquest at all.

BRITANNIA PRIMA Province name

⊙ Provincial capitals

▢ Bishoprics

● Civitas capitals or
main administrative centres

0   50m.
0   80km.

Hadrian's Wall
●Corbridge
●Carlisle

BRITANNIA
SECUNDA
●Aldborough
⊙York

Lincoln ⊙

●Chester

FLAVIA
CAESARIENSIS

R Trent

●Wroxeter

ICENI

●Leicester   Caistor ●

●Chesterton

R Severn

BRITANNIA PRIMA

MAXIMA
CAESARIENSIS   Colchester ●

●Carmarthen   ●Gloucester

●Caerwent   ●St Albans

⊙Cirencester   R Thames   ▢
                                                    London

●Silchester   ●Canterbury
●Winchester

●Chichester

●Exeter   ●Dorchester

Roman Britain in the fourth century.

The four main provinces were subdivided into smaller units known as *civitates* (singular *civitas*) or counties. The *civitas* capital was usually, but not always, the principal town and administrative centre of the province. Official administration was carried out in a large public building called a *basilica*; these usually formed a part of the official market and administrative centre of the town or city, known as the 'forum-basilica' complex. Below the *civitas* capitals was a tier of smaller towns which included places like Durobrivae, which was discussed in Chapter 4.[1] These smaller towns generally lacked an official 'forum-basilica' complex, but were nonetheless market centres for their regions.

Like all modern states, the Roman Empire depended on the collection of taxes to pay for civil administration and for military security. These taxes were collected by way of London. When Roman administration ceased, the official collection of taxes in Britain had already been creaking for some time, and it used to be thought that when the central authority of London petered out, everything came to a grinding halt. But we now know that a great deal of authority had already been transferred to the provincial capitals by the end of the fourth century. So when the official Roman presence came to an end, not a great deal changed: one layer of administration had been lost, and a huge burden of taxation had been removed. From the point of view of ordinary people these were positive advantages. Against them, however, should be set the collapse of the monetary system, and with it the trading and production of mass-produced goods such as pottery. The important point is that it was only the monetary market system that broke down: law and order did not. The Romanised élite saw to it that their relatively comfortable and stable existence continued throughout most of the fifth century.

The question of the demise of Romano-British towns is currently a matter of fervent debate among scholars of the Roman period. When I first learnt about British archaeology as a student, many things seemed simpler than they do today. Archaeology was on the brink of an intellectual revolt against the old 'culture-historical' school, a transformation from which it would never look back. Very often in situations where rapid change is about to happen, the people who will most be affected by that change seem completely unaware of the storm about to engulf them. That certainly applied in the Department of Archaeology at Cambridge, where many of the objectors to the then *status quo* were graduate students. They poured scorn on the idea of pots marching across Europe bearing culture-historical labels such as 'Beaker People'.

Nobody, however, was laughing at the Anglo-Saxons or the Romans, because these were taboo subjects, the province of historical archaeologists and classicists. When as a prehistorian one entered those particular academic worlds, one felt like a stranger. Here everything was calm and peaceful. Not so much as a breath of controversy was allowed to disturb the surface of their classical wine-dark sea. In the study of these later periods the 'culture-historical' school ruled absolutely, but very much at the behest of history: the purpose of archaeology was to confirm what historical sources suggested. I'm glad to say that the world of classical studies has since changed a great deal for the better. It's not perhaps quite as pleasantly anarchic as prehistoric archaeology, but it's tending in that direction.

Nowhere was the pervasive academic conformity more apparent thirty years ago than in Romano-British studies. In this conservative intellectual climate, towns did not exist in Britain before the Roman period, thrived during it, and collapsed at the end of it. Nobody gave a thought to the social implications of urban life: towns were treated as yet another technical innovation, like roads, masonry or factory-produced pottery. The fact that *people* had to live in them was not considered important. The towns appeared, almost it would seem by magic, and the population miraculously organised itself to live urban lives, having previously been rural. If that was what actually happened, it would rank as one of the most extraordinary social transformations in history – but at the time nobody seemed to think it even slightly peculiar.

The sudden transformation of a large part of the 'native' British population from rural to urban dwellers did worry prehistorians, who were more concerned about the social processes that lay behind historical events. Towns in Roman Britain were very much seen as 'historical events': their defensive walls survived, and the masonry and mosaic floors of their buildings had been revealed by excavation since Victorian times. Nobody but a madman could possibly doubt that they existed. So prehistorians sought precursors for towns in Iron Age Britain. Barry Cunliffe, as one of the few archaeologists who are equally at home excavating Roman and prehistoric sites, is uniquely qualified to judge whether any large Iron Age settlements could be considered as urban. He has come to the conclusion that some do show certain characteristics of towns: at Danebury, for example, there are lines of houses that face onto streets. But this of itself is not solely an urban feature: many villages and smaller settlements pack houses into a given area of land if for some reason space is at a premium – as it may be on the top of a hill. Cunliffe tends to use terms like 'proto-urban' to describe the situation in Iron Age Britain.

In recent years there has been renewed activity on some of the very large, dispersed Later Iron Age settlements of south-eastern England. In Chapter 3 I concluded that these areas were not so much towns as 'polyfocal settlements', with open countryside separating built-over areas. Maybe one day these settlement sprawls would develop into towns, but in the Iron Age they had yet to make this important step. They remained large, but essentially rural communities. What they lacked, and what a true town has to have in order to function at all, is some sort of local government. Without self-regulation settlement densities beyond a certain point become hazardous, due among other things to the spread of disease.

We saw in Chapter 3 that there are slight indications at the King Harry Lane cemetery at St Albans that a small proportion of the 'proto-urban' population in south-eastern Britain, may have been in the process of making the shift from a rural to a more fluid, urban style of life, but these are only hints, and they only seem to apply to a part of Britain that was under the strongest Roman influence prior to the conquest. I would be surprised if there were no indications of a shift of this sort, following almost a century of close contact with the Continental mainland with its many Roman influences. So, with the outside possibility of a tiny proportion of south-eastern Britain as an exception, it would appear that there is no good evidence for fully urbanised communities in the British pre-Roman Iron Age.

While prehistorians like Barry Cunliffe were addressing the problem of pre-Roman urban life, many Romanists were growing anxious about the status and nature of post-Roman towns. A famous conference was organised in Durham over Easter 1978 to consider 'The End of Roman Britain'. Richard Reece gave a controversial paper which suggested that Late Roman Britain actually ran from AD 400 to 700 in the western province of Britannia Prima, and did not come to a sharp halt in AD 410. He also pointed out that Romano-British towns went into a sharp decline in the late third century, and that after approximately AD 300 urban activity was very much reduced.

Some have suggested that there was a 'flight to the suburbs', but whatever happened, most are agreed that in the fourth century the Golden Age of Roman Britain was more a rural than an urban phenomenon.[2] The wealthiest members of society preferred to live out in the countryside in their increasingly luxurious villa estates. While new urban housing became rarer, places of public entertainment such as baths, temples and theatres were allowed to run down. The magnificent theatre at Verulamium, for example, 'became a public refuse tip. Standing, as it does, close to the forum and across the road from a still-functioning market building the theatre must have presented a dismal aspect.'[3] In the fourth century building within Romano-British towns almost came to a complete halt, and what work there was tended to be concentrated on the walls that surrounded them. This would suggest that if a threat was anticipated, people from the surrounding area would take refuge in what were, for the most part, ghost or skeleton towns.

Richard Reece's paper at the Durham conference caused a huge stir. When he offered it for publication it was accepted by the editor of the conference proceedings (and his advisers), but was refused by the publishers, who 'declined to print the volume if the paper were included'. So he offered it to the prestigious journal *World Archaeology*, which promptly published it in full.[4] The refusal of the first publisher to print such an important paper by a leading authority is an indication not just of how certain circles in Romano-British archaeology could be extremely conservative, but of how hard it was to alter entrenched academic attitudes. Some people would prefer no debate to real debate.

Richard Reece examined the supposed collapse of Romano-British towns from around AD 300.[5] This date was far too early to be attributed to Anglo-Saxon incursions (which he does not seem to believe in

anyway), and was on the very eve of Roman Britain's most prosperous century. He came to the conclusion that Roman towns in
Britain 'failed' because they had never truly existed. This is still a very
controversial suggestion, and is by no means accepted by everybody.
From the perspective of prehistory, though, it does seem to make good
sense.

Reece pointed out that towns around the Mediterranean basin
were true towns that were already in existence from the early first
millennium BC. So they were long-established when Rome included
them within her Empire. They had most of the characteristics of a
modern town: there were clearly defined cemetery areas, a system of
drains, water supplies, rubbish disposal sites and monumental administrative buildings. For reasons that are probably due to the
different way that societies were organised in the lands north of the
Mediterranean, the notion of true towns did not spread beyond
the south of France into Gaul north of the Alps. In northern Europe
those large, essentially rural settlements known as *oppida* were the
nearest equivalents, but they were hardly towns in the sense we would
understand the term today. They were more like enormously inflated
hillforts.

When the Romans conquered Britain, they set about establishing
a system of provincial and county administration. In the absence of
any true towns Reece suggested they established many of their *civitas*
capitals at places where people traditionally met to market and
exchange goods and produce. The Roman authorities formalised these
arrangements and built monumental administrative buildings and all
the other trappings of towns, including streets, walls and so forth.
The idea seemed to catch on, and these elaborated trading stations
grew in size and population. To Richard Reece 'this suggests a view
of the town in Roman Britain as a trading settlement within a classical
façade'.[6]

It follows from this that it is not necessary to explain why they
went into a decline at the end of the third century, because they had
never really got going as towns. The first parts to go were what Richard
Reece calls the 'trappings' of a classical town: the forum, the basilica
and the theatre. After the initial short period of enthusiasm they ceased
to be relevant, largely, I suspect, because society had not yet adapted

itself to be urban; it was an idea ahead of its time. You cannot have towns without townspeople, and if the population of Britain remained essentially rural, it is not to be wondered at that the Golden Age of Roman Britain was also a rural age.

I find Reece's ideas attractive, because they take into account the long-term development of British societies. They are not based on an assessment of the status of bricks and mortar alone, removed from their wider social context. He does not say that such-and-such a range of buildings are so large and complex that they therefore *have* to be part of a true town. Instead he looks at the people (and how they organised themselves) first, and the buildings second – which is how a prehistorian likes to work.

Starting in the later fourth and fifth centuries, first eastern and then western Britain underwent a process of de-Romanisation. True towns – and this time they were indeed truly urban – only came into existence from the beginning of the eighth century, some three hundred years after Roman rule. These urban settlements began as trading posts around the coast, at places like Hamwic, the Saxon name for Southampton. The fact that true towns began as trading centres supports Richard Reece's view that despite the Romans' intentions, the Britons were not yet ready for them. Incidentally, when Hamwic did get going, it did so with impressive speed: it covered about a hundred acres and boasted a population of two to three thousand people in the eighth century.[7] Most of the trade seems to have been with France, Germany and the Low Countries, together with other parts of Britain. Hamwic and other English trading ports went into sharp decline in the mid-ninth century, probably due to Viking raids which disrupted long-distance trade.

While Romano-British towns may have declined during the fourth century, there is now some evidence that some of them continued into the fifth. If one takes Richard Reece's view that in Roman Britain there was 'life in towns', rather than 'town life' in the sense that we understand it today, then the later occupation of the fourth, fifth and even sixth centuries (at Wroxeter, near modern Telford) was not truly urban. But on the other hand it was not 'squatter settlement', as I have heard it described, either. These places had been trading centres in pre-Roman times, and that is probably what they returned to being in the fourth and fifth centuries. I am sure that a proportion of the surplus produced at a wealthy site such as Orton Hall Farm would still have been taken to market in Durobrivae, only this time the 'buyers' would have bartered, and would have come from other farms and settlements in the neighbourhood.

The point is that the withdrawal of Roman troops did not signal the collapse of social organisation. London may have ceased to have been the centre of the diocese and the diocese itself ceased to have an identity, but the provinces and the counties still continued to exercise a degree of authority as they had done throughout the fourth century, despite the abandonment of many basilica buildings in the *civitas* capitals. The rural population was controlled from the large estates in the countryside. From the later fourth century villas may have been abandoned, but there is no evidence to suggest that civil order collapsed. Presumably the old élites still maintained a degree of control, perhaps aided by the Church, especially in and around towns. We have some evidence for such control at the Roman city of Viroconium Cornoviarum, or Wroxeter, in the province of Britannia Prima.

Wroxeter was the fourth-largest town in Roman Britain, and it is chiefly remarkable in archaeological circles because it survived for well over a century after the official end of the empire in Britain.[8] This is important because it proves that western Britain did not revert to 'Dark Age' chaos following the events of AD 410. Instead, there is evidence to suggest not only that people lived at Wroxeter, but that they lived what one might term ordered lives. These were certainly not squatters wearing rags and scavenging scraps of food among the ruins of former grandeur.

We owe the discovery of post-Roman Wroxeter largely to the painstaking excavation of Philip Barker, whose early death in 2001 came as a huge blow to everyone who knew him. Before Phil it is probably fair to say that most archaeologists had not spent a great deal of trouble systematically working through the deposits that lay above the Roman layers that interested them. In the early and middle twentieth century budgets were far smaller than they are today, and it made little sense to waste one's time and money carefully sifting through layers of material that were peripheral to one's main interest. No funding organisation would thank one for revealing the details of, say, a Victorian farmhouse, while leaving precious Roman deposits beneath it untouched.

Phil began his work at Wroxeter in 1966, and soon realised that the site was going to be different. For a start, it was a Roman city that had not been replaced by a Saxon and then a modern one, as happened, for example, at York, Lincoln and London. It was in fact a 'green-field' site, where cows were peacefully grazing. What damage there had been was largely accidental: the construction of a few cottages and farm buildings. Apart from that, the place had been abandoned in the seventh century when the powerful 'Anglo-Saxon' kingdom of Mercia overran the area from the Midlands. The history of the site meant that the latest Roman and post-Roman layers would still be there, largely undisturbed.

Phil had a shrewd suspicion that the 'Dark Age' buildings would have been made from timber, which would long since have rotted away. The buildings of the Roman town were made of masonry, and were not difficult to spot – in fact a two-storey-high wall of the main public building, the baths basilica, still survives, formerly as part of a barn but now part of a Scheduled Ancient Monument (to use the legal term). The upstanding wall is known as the 'Old Work', and it is well worth visiting.

The Old Work is now surrounded by the remains of the massive baths basilica, much of which was excavated in the nineteenth century. These earlier archaeologists had not found evidence of 'Dark Age' activity on site, but by modern standards their techniques were relatively crude. It was usual, for example, to employ workmen with picks and shovels. Thomas Wright, one of the main Victorian excavators at Wroxeter, was a freelance excavator and journalist, and he was plainly rather better at being the latter than the former. He does seem, however, to have had a genuine gift for publicising archaeology, which in the 1860s was becoming a subject of great public interest. This was a time when curiosity about origins and early history had been fuelled by Darwin's great work *On the Origin of Species*, published in 1859. Previous decades had witnessed the partition of prehistoric times into Ages of Stone, Bronze and Iron; public enthusiasm for archaeology was also greatly increased by the discovery of the Swiss 'Lake Villages' following the dry winter of 1853–54.[9]

Wright had written a book, *The Celt, the Roman and the Saxon*, which attempted unsuccessfully to pour scorn on the Three-Age system. Like almost everyone at the time, he accepted the Anglo-Saxon 'invasions' as fact, and like most archaeologists subsequently, he allowed that belief to colour his work. One example will suffice: it concerns 'the old man in the hypocaust'. This body was probably a post-Roman burial that had been inserted into the abandoned baths basilica hypocaust (under-floor heating system). But it was meat and drink to Wright, who 'saw the body as that of a poor unfortunate who crawled into the hypocaust to escape the Anglo-Saxon pillage of the city and who had died there alone and terrified'.[10] Not surprisingly, this tragic image haunted the public imagination for many years, and influenced poets and artists alike.

Phil Barker realised that the only way to identify the slight traces left by vanished timber buildings was to plot the precise position of every pebble.[11] It was an extraordinary undertaking, but it worked. I remember taking my own excavation team to visit Phil while he was digging some time in the early 1970s. We thought we were pretty good at working on geologically 'difficult' (i.e. variable) ground, where archaeological deposits were hard to distinguish from non-manmade features such as the filled-in fissures left by the freezing of old stream channels during the Ice Age; but that paled into insignificance when set alongside Wroxeter. I recall Phil trying to get us to see the faint traces left by a wall or path that ran across a patch of pebbly ground before us. All I could see were stones of different sizes. Then he showed us a plan of the area, and suddenly we could see what he meant. How on earth he and his supervisors spotted such things I will never know.

Phil Barker and his team concentrated on the area alongside the central official buildings of the baths basilica block, close by the Old Work. Like government or official buildings in other *civitas* capitals, the forum basilica building at Wroxeter experienced catastrophic problems at the end of the third century, when it burnt down and was abandoned as a building, if not as a site. The baths also declined: floors wore out and mosaics deteriorated. The damage to the baths building was made good, but in a more rugged, less lavish fashion, in the late third or the fourth century. There is evidence that trade

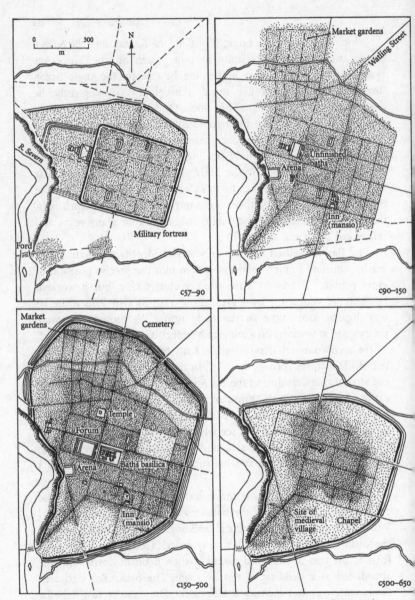

Scale: 0 — 300 m

N

c57–90

Military fortress
R. Severn
Ford

c90–150

Market gardens
Watling Street
Unfinished baths
Arena
Inn (mansio)

c150–500

Market gardens
Cemetery
Temple
Forum
Arena
Baths basilica
Inn (mansio)

c500–650

Site of medieval village
Chapel

The development of the Roman city of Viroconium Cornoviarum (Wroxeter) from its beginnings as a military fortress and civilian settlement to its final state as a small 'Dark Age' town. Areas of settlement are shown by stippling.

continued near the baths basilica, first with money and, after the collapse of the monetary system, using barter.

The 'Dark Age' buildings of the fifth and sixth centuries are remarkable, not just for their discovery in the first place, nor because they were made in a non-Roman technique, from timber, but because they were built in a Roman style and laid out using a Roman system of measurement (based on Roman feet).[12] This gives us a fascinating insight into the ways in which the post-Roman inhabitants of the town thought and acted. The process of de-Romanisation discussed by Reece may have begun, but evidently it was by no means complete.

There has been much discussion about whether the post-Roman use of Wroxeter was 'town life' at all. My own view is that it was probably something akin to what we saw at the very end of the Iron Age: intensive but essentially rural settlement around a market centre that was used by everyone in the locality. As any farmer will tell you, some form of market is essential to rural life. Very few farmers are fully self-sufficient, because they will always require new bloodlines when inbreeding becomes a problem, and sources of fresh seed when yields decline. Markets are also where they and their families can meet other people and escape from the confines of the farm. At Wroxeter the shell of the basilica, and doubtless the area around it too, had been made safe and was still used as a market. 'The conversion of a public building in this way reminded one of the staff of the excavation, who now lives in Warsaw, of the principal black market in communist Warsaw, held in the ruins of a burnt-out government building which had not been reconstructed after the Second World War.'[13] That is a telling image.

Some time roughly between AD 530 and 580 the centre of the old Roman city was transformed. The remains of the old basilica were demolished and the site was prepared to take a number of substantial new timber buildings, including one, known as Building 10, that was particularly grand. It is possible too that what had once been the cool room, or *frigidarium*, of the old Roman sauna-style bath building nearby was converted into a chapel. One reason for suggesting this was Thomas Wright's discovery of a dozen or so burials in the floor of the bath house surrounding the *frigidarium*; one of these was 'the old man in the hypocaust'.

This work has to have been organised in some way. It was not the unplanned activity of a group of squatters. The person in command may have been a local *tyrranus* (to use Gildas' term), or king, but if that were the case one might have expected him to have chosen a rural rather than an urban site for his headquarters, as it will be recalled that the Late Roman élites showed a marked preference for the country. If ever a place demanded an Arthur it is surely post-Roman Wroxeter, but his name has never been linked to it. Roger White and Philip Barker have, however, suggested a much more plausible controlling authority:

> If the *frigidarium* had indeed become Wroxeter's church then the likeliest occupant of Building 10, and for instigating the work in the first place, can perhaps be identified as a bishop. Such a conclusion may take some by surprise but in the context of the later and immediately post-Roman world this makes perfect sense. Bishoprics had been established by the emperors in the fourth century in every major town. Once established, they are likely to have become self-perpetuating, appointing and reappointing among themselves since there was no authority to answer to other than the emperor, the pope not yet having established primacy in the west.[14]

Wroxeter is not the only town in the province of Britannia Prima to show evidence for post-Roman occupation. The baths at Roman Bath, for example, were repaired and kept in use well into the fifth or even the sixth centuries. Chester too shows evidence for settlement after the Roman period, and also for a possible bishop, named Viventius. Elsewhere in the country there is evidence to suggest that the major decline in urban Roman Britain was around the beginning of the fourth century, rather than when one might have expected it, a hundred years later: there is evidence for fifth-century occupation near the crossing of the River Ouse at York.

One of the problems in recognising these late phases of settlement is that Roman pottery ceases to be used, and we still do not fully understand what immediately took its place. At Wroxeter, for example, Late Roman pots were frequently mended and maintained in (rather unhygienic) use. Recent research by Dr Mark Whyman of the York Archaeological Trust has shown that a form of rather unlovely, coarse, hand-made pottery known as calcite-gritted ware was made well into the fifth century, and was used by the inhabitants of 'Dark Age' York. Whyman's research gives us, almost for the first time, a means of accurately dating early post-Roman settlement in the York area. To judge from the buildings where these people lived and worked it was a smallish town-like settlement, in many ways comparable with fifth- and sixth-century Wroxeter.

Although less prosperous than in Earlier Roman times, fourth-century London does not seem to have been quite so run-down as other towns and cities of Roman Britain. Maybe this was because of the general wealth of the city's merchants and the value of their trade. Nevertheless, there is archaeological evidence that some properties in the city became open areas or yards at this time, so clearly not all was well. Matters became worse from the beginning of the fifth century, with the city disappearing in the space of a few years, the population presumably dispersing to the countryside.[15] Some of them probably took fancy mosaic floors with them, as there is evidence of them being cut up and removed.

In Colchester, or Camulodunum, in the heart of the Anglo-Saxon area, there are signs of Anglo-Saxon influences in Later Roman times, just as we saw at Mucking and elsewhere. If we assume that this is evidence for the spread of new ideas rather than mercenaries, it is interesting that two of the distinctively 'Anglo-Saxon' sunken feature buildings were found at Lion Walk, Colchester.[16] This famous site is located within the Roman walled town, and one of the 'Anglo-Saxon' buildings was built against the walls of an abandoned Romano-British house. Philip Crummy, who excavated the site, dates this occupation, which seems more akin to a 'squatters' camp' than anything more urban, to about AD 440–450.

Christianity was to have a strong influence on the development of western Europe in post-Roman times. Its roots lay, of course, in the Roman period, and the Church perpetuated not just the Latin language but many aspects of *Romanitas*, or Roman civilisation. The Church was also an institution that was capable of providing stability in unstable times. Maybe it was indeed the Church that lay behind the late occupation of Wroxeter – we cannot be certain. But even if it did not, it could have done, which is almost as important.

From a crudely historical perspective, we know that Christ was crucified in the first half of the first century AD.[17] A century later, Christian churches were to be found in many towns and cities around the Mediterranean. This was still a largely clandestine Church, which by its very nature is almost archaeologically undetectable, but it does not seem unreasonable to assume that it reached Britain at some point in the second century, given what we know about the efficiency of Roman communications. As we have seen, in Britain it became sufficiently well established to allow the development of two heresies and for there to have been a substantial backlash against them on behalf of the established (ultimately Celtic) Church.

So Christianity in Britain had probably already undergone over a century and a half of insular development before the withdrawal of Roman civil administration in AD 410. The next major event was the supposed 'introduction' of Christianity to Anglo-Saxon pagan Britain by St Augustine's missionaries, who arrived at Canterbury in AD 597 – or at least that is what most people over forty were taught at school. The only other thing I was taught about St Augustine's mission was the famous remark attributed to Pope Gregory the Great (590–604) after seeing two blond Anglo-Saxon youths in the market at Rome, that they were 'not Angles, but angels'.[18] The sight of them so moved him that he determined to send a mission to Britain. Bede goes on to tell us that, being Pope, he was not allowed to travel so far from Rome, which is why he entrusted the mission to St Augustine.

The notion that Augustine's mission was to pagans and new British converts is undermined by Bede himself. Dr David Howlett has described the situation Augustine encountered in Britain: 'According to Bede, before meeting Augustine the British bishops consulted a wise and holy hermit who advised them to follow Augustine, if he bore himself the yoke he wished them to bear. But when they approached Augustine he did the Roman diplomatic thing and stayed seated, which they interpreted as a mark of arrogance. Note that seven bishops turned up on this occasion, not the whole bench of bishops. That implies that more existed in the British Church.' Howlett added that the British were better Latinists than the Augustinian missionaries. All of this illustrates that sixth-century south-eastern Britain was far from a pagan wilderness. And we will shortly see that the Latin language and scholarship also flourished in the rest of Britain, especially Wales, the south-west and the north.

So south-eastern Britain was far less ignorant and pagan than the missionaries had been led to expect. We also know that in the seventy or so years that followed St Augustine's mission, the newly arrived Roman Church and the indigenous Celtic Churches developed their own liturgical practices, which reflected their different cultural backgrounds. It might seem odd to us today, but in the fifth and sixth centuries such matters as the means whereby the annual date of Easter Day was calculated actually mattered, because they were an integral part of the way people thought about life and the natural world.

We know that these calendrical debates were very important to people at the time, and I suspect that this is an indication of something ancient and profound. As I mentioned in the earlier discussion of pre-Roman Britain, religion and ideology were an expression of a person's cosmology or belief system. They were not distinct from normal, day-to-day life. The coming of Christianity started or hastened the process of such a separation, but in the fifth to seventh centuries AD, God, the Church and the mundane were still far more closely integrated than they are today. Religion was a real and powerful force in people's lives, and special days of celebration mattered to everyone. They had to be got right. The intricacy of the calculations that surrounded feast days was part of their mystery and magic. Just like the solsticial sunrise over Stonehenge, these liturgical calculations united the world of human ideology to a larger, natural order of things, which was now seen as the work of a supreme Creator.

The two Churches continued their separate patterns of development, and the submission of the Celtic to the Roman Church was not begun until a great assembly of senior clergy of both Churches met at Whitby on the Yorkshire coast in 664. After the famous Synod of Whitby, St Augustine's Roman Church would become the official Church of Britain. The Celtic Church, however, had been a powerful force in the land for perhaps three centuries, and its influence would continue to be felt for as long, or even longer.

Recently scholars of the Early Saxon period have grown dissatisfied with the notion that Britain was somehow different from the rest of the provinces that had once comprised the Western Roman Empire. In his recent book, *Britain and the End of the Roman Empire*, Ken Dark accepts the idea that Anglo-Saxon settlers arrived in Britain first as *foederati*, or mercenaries, but turned against their erstwhile masters in the Anglo-Saxon rebellion that Gildas writes about and which (if it happened) would have taken place some time around 490–500.[19] Before that cataclysmic event, he suggests that what had been Roman Britain remained firmly under British control. This is the period that would once have been dubbed the 'sub-Roman' period, but which Dark and others prefer to include within 'Late Antiquity', which broadly extends from the mid-third to the seventh centuries AD; it deliberately includes a significant part of the Roman period, because, as we have seen, changes in military and other institutions of the Later Roman Empire contributed to the changes that would affect not just the collapse of the formal Empire, but the continuation of civil life in the fifth and sixth centuries.

The idea of 'Late Antiquity' goes against the earlier view of life in post-Roman western Europe, where Roman order gave way to the so-called 'Migration Period', during which large numbers of people are supposed to have migrated hither and thither over the Continent, either settling down or passing through. Viewed from the perspective of prehistory, the very idea of a 'Migration Period' is absurd: why would people suddenly decide to move around in this peculiar and hyperactive fashion? What was in it for them, other than wholesale disruption?

With the exception of this one period, the lesson of the past is that as a rule human societies prefer to stay put, on land in which they have a personal, ideological and economic stake. Laws of marriage and other factors such as trade, exchange or persecution may lead to the movement of people, but that is quite distinct from wholesale migration. Similarly, raiding can eventually lead to more permanent settlements away from home. But even nomads restrict their movements to fixed routes which both follow seasonally available resources and are recognised by other groups living in the area. I know of no nomadic people that have wandered across the face of the earth unrestricted in any way.[20]

The picture of 'Dark Age' or 'Migration Period' Britain that is beginning to emerge bears little resemblance to the 'Pagan Saxon Period' as portrayed by Myres. Those terms themselves, with their heavily-charged, emotive words – 'Dark', 'Migration' and 'Pagan' – suggest a degree of pre-judgement, or prejudice. I do wish that those who study the post-Roman periods would come up with less loaded terminology: 'Stone Age', for example, carries with it no ethnic or cultural baggage in the way that 'Saxon', or even 'Early Christian', does.

Throughout his book Ken Dark writes about 'Anglo-Saxons' in inverted commas, as a token that he does not wish to assign them an ethnic identity. He takes a longer view of the period, tending to stress continuity rather than change, and makes a strong case for the survival of Christianity, even in the so-called Anglo-Saxon heartlands of eastern and southern Britain, throughout the fifth and sixth centuries. This undermines the old view that 'Dark Age' Britain was very different from the rest of what had once been the Western Roman Empire:

> In so far as most of Britain was different from other Late Antique western European societies at all . . . this was often because *more*, not less, of its Roman heritage survived and because the Britons were particularly effective in spreading their version of the Late Antique Romano-Christian culture to neighbouring peoples. What enabled these differences to occur was the ability of the Britons to retain their political independence longer than any of their Western provincial counterparts.[21]

The principal driving force behind Christianity in the fifth and sixth centuries was the Eastern Roman Empire, otherwise known as Byzantium. I have mentioned that the Sutton Hoo ship burial produced a set of Byzantine bronze bowls, and these are neither an outlying nor a unique find. A slightly different form of Byzantine bronze bowl has been found in the Thames Valley and in south-eastern Britain, along the Rhine Valley and into central Europe and the Adriatic Sea.[22] These bowls, which often stand on short feet, are known rather confusingly as 'Coptic' bowls, despite the fact that we know they were not made in Coptic Egypt.*

---

* I have chosen to describe these vessels as being made from 'bronze', as this will mean something to most readers. Technically speaking, Roman and post-Roman 'bronze' often contains small amounts of zinc, which makes it brass. To most people familiar with modern

We will see shortly that at least another possible trading route lay through the Mediterranean and thus to Spain, Portugal, Ireland and western Britain. Both Ken Dark and another authority on the period, Anthea Harris, argue persuasively that these connections played an active part in shaping the barbarian and ex-Roman west until at least the seventh century. I do not know the extent to which this was a deliberate political decision by leaders in the Eastern Roman Empire, now known as Byzantium. What I am convinced of, however, is that the so-called 'barbarian' west, which included Britain, was sufficiently sophisticated and well organised to be *worth* subjecting to such influence. This would certainly imply that paganism had not triumphed even in places like south-east England, which has quite a heavy distribution of bronze 'Coptic' vessels. It would seem probable that the Church was playing a significant and a growing role even in these easterly areas.

We have known for some time that the (Celtic) Church played an important part in the development of post-Roman society in the south-west. As Ken Dark puts it: 'We might see ... the fifth century as a turning point for the character of religious foci in western Britain. Whereas as late as the mid-fourth century the principal rural religious foci throughout the region were pagan temples, by 500 this situation had ceased. There is no trace of organised paganism in western Britain after the early fifth century, and the main religious foci are now monastic sites and churches.'[23]

Before Anthea Harris's *Byzantium, Britain and the West: The Archaeology of Cultural Identity* AD 400–650 (2003), the links between Britain and the Mediterranean world were best illustrated by finds from Wales and the West Country. The most famous of these finds have undoubtedly come from perhaps the best-known archaeological site in western Britain, the stunningly beautiful coastal site in north Cornwall known as Tintagel Castle. It's a place that cries out to have magic and legends attached to it – and not surprisingly, this is precisely what has happened.

If the archaeology of Britain has been bedevilled by the fact that

---

metal, brass is glistening and gold-like. The usual academic term 'copper alloy' is safe, but meaningless to non-specialists.

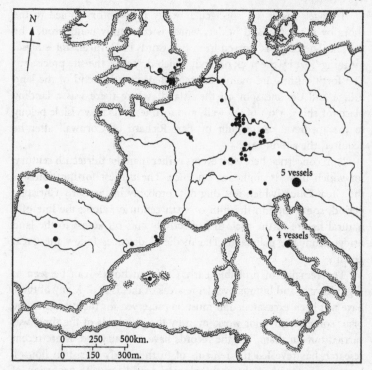

Distribution of so-called 'Coptic' bronze vessels produced in the Eastern Roman Empire (perhaps in and around Constantinople) during the late fifth and sixth centuries AD.

archaeologists tend to stick to their own time periods, one way around this sometimes rigid chronological compartmentalising is to become a specialist in a given region. There is one regional specialist who stands head and shoulders above the rest, and that is Professor Charles Thomas. He has researched Tintagel and written about its archaeology in a fine book.[24] He would certainly object strongly to the now old-fashioned term 'Dark Age' being applied to the south-west, and would prefer 'Early Christian'.*

* I was disappointed to see that 'Dark Age' is used throughout the otherwise excellent English Heritage guide to the castle. I suspect that this was not an authorial decision, but was made by an 'expert' in 'interpretation'.

Tintagel Castle is a spectacular rocky promontory joined to the shore by a narrow land bridge, which is constantly being eroded by the sea. The name is derived from two words in Cornish, *din + tagell*, meaning 'fort by the neck of land', which describes the site precisely.[25] The fortifications are mainly concentrated on either end of the land bridge and on one spot on the 'island', where there was a landing place for ships. Most of the walls and fortifications now visible belong to the medieval castle built by Earl Richard of Cornwall after he acquired the site in 1233.

I am concerned here with events earlier than the thirteenth century, for which there is abundant evidence. The earliest fortification was the Great Ditch, which was dug out, probably in the Early Christian period, some time in the fifth or sixth centuries, along the line of a natural fissure in the rock that effectively cuts off access to the land bridge from the mainland. The medieval defences follow the Great Ditch.

The remains of probable Early Christian houses can be seen as slight humps and bumps over large areas of the 'island'. Many of these have not been excavated, and must be preserved for the future. In the 1930s some rather poor work, even by the standards of the time, was carried out on them, but the records have not survived. More recent research has revealed the remains of further Early Christian houses, but what astonished the archaeological world was the profusion of finds from the Mediterranean that they revealed. No other fifth- and sixth-century site in Britain has yielded so much imported material as Tintagel.

The sheer quantity and variety of the Tintagel finds clearly show that we are not dealing here with, say, a chance shipwreck on a rocky shore. This has to be evidence of regular trading contact: the result of supply meeting demand. The demand for exotic things was certainly there: glassware from southern Spain, wine amphorae from Byzantium, oil jars and fine tableware from the north African coast. This is top-quality stuff, and it is moreover manifestly Roman in appearance. Arranged on an Early Christian prince's table, it would have proclaimed not only that he was rich and powerful, but that he espoused Roman values. He was telling the people who dined with him that he was a civilised Roman Briton. It was a potent message.

Tintagel was more than a temporary settlement. People lived and died there. Charles Thomas has revealed that some graves beneath low mounds in the churchyard of Tintagel church, above the cliffs that overlook the castle about half a mile to the south, probably date to the sixth century. This was the time that Tintagel may well have been the home of a powerful leader of Dumnonia, the ancient kingdom of what is now Devon and Cornwall. We first hear of Dumnonia in the Iron Age, and so far as we know it continued in existence throughout the Roman period, during which Roman rule barely affected the far south-west. It would seem probable that the adoption of Roman ways by the Early Christian British élites in Dumnonia was a way of express-ing their prestige, but also their identity. As we saw in Chapter 2, something similar happened in north Wales, but rather later, in the ninth century.

If Dark Age Wroxeter cried out for an Arthur figure, Tintagel makes an even louder plea, and Geoffrey of Monmouth, ever eager to please, provided one in his *Historia Regum Britanniae* (c.1136). In fact he generously provided posterity with the real thing: he suggested that Arthur was conceived there, following some morally dubious magic by Merlin, who transformed Arthur's father, King Uther Pendragon, to look exactly like Duke Gorlois of Cornwall. In this guise Uther then bedded the beautiful Igraine, the Duke's lawful wife, and the result was Arthur. It's an excellent, if unlikely, story, and the inhabitants of Tintagel have been dining out on it ever since.

In 1998 the press became over-excited by the discovery at Tintagel of the so-called 'Artognou' stone by a team of archaeologists from Glasgow University under Dr Chris Morris. This slate had been reused to cover a sixth-century drain, and it bore a scratched inscription with the name 'Artognou' on it. Artognou is not the same as Arthur, although both names come from the Welsh word for a bear. It was not, as the media screamed, conclusive evidence that Arthur was ever actually at Tintagel.

There is abundant evidence for a revival of trade between western and south-western Britain, north Africa and the Byzantine realms of the eastern Mediterranean in the fifth and sixth centuries. Tintagel was by no means the only place where such trade in luxury goods has been recorded, but by far the majority of find spots are in south Wales

Distribution of imported Byzantine pottery of late-fifth- and sixth-century date in Britain. Small dots, 1–4 finds; medium dots, 10–20 finds; large dot, 60+ finds; Tintagel, 80+ finds.

and the south-west. Apart from any other considerations, sea trade would have been encouraged by the political fragmentation of the Western Empire, which inevitably led to a deterioration of the originally Roman road network.

The small harbour at Tintagel is known as the Haven. It consists of a small sandy beach on the north side of the land bridge. Here the sea is relatively calm. Ships could be beached at the Haven or perhaps moored a couple of hundred metres further along the 'island' at a place which was converted into a defended wharf in medieval times. On the other side of the land bridge the shore is rocky and the seas fiercer. Tintagel would not have been a port as such, but a stop-off point for trading vessels that were 'leapfrogging' along the coast, moving from one small community to another. It was a pattern of trade that we know was popular in pre-Roman times.

Charles Thomas is of the opinion that the trade between Britain and the Byzantine world would have been carried out by merchant captains who sailed their ships around the Mediterranean, collecting what they knew would sell in Britain. (He is unpersuaded by the currently fashionable idea, espoused by Ken Dark and others, that this trade had broader political implications to do with the foreign policy of Byzantium.) The 'currency' used in exchange for the luxury items was probably mainly Cornish tin, which was shipped out of Britain in the form of ingots.

The recent find of a coastal settlement amongst the dunes at Bantham Ham on the south coast of Devon is particularly exciting. The site, at the mouth of the Devon River Avon, is a naturally sheltered sandy haven on an otherwise rocky coast. There were two episodes of Dark Age settlement, which included imported table wares from North Africa and large fragments of eastern Mediterranean amphorae. The size of these pieces is most unusual, and might suggest they may have been broken during the process of unloading a vessel. A few miles to the north-west of Bantham Ham the discovery of a wreck site in Bigbury Bay revealed over forty tin ingots of Late Roman or Dark Age date.[26] To me, this looks more like organised trade than the casual peddling of wares by adventurous merchant-captains.

The Early Christian period in the west and south-west is fascinating to an archaeologist because it provides evidence of how people make use of the objects and even the landscape around them to express their identity. The west was comparatively unaffected by the end of the Roman Empire in Britain, because most of it was beyond the broadly southerly zone of Andrew Sargent's north/south divide. Richard Reece sees the end of the Roman period around Cirencester, the provincial capital of Britannia Prima, as essentially being a return to the pre-Roman status quo. In the Iron Age people in the area lived a rural life, for some reason without much pottery (which is irritating if you are an archaeologist), and this was the style of life they returned to in the fifth and sixth centuries. He sees no evidence for chaos or social collapse, because communities were resuming a pattern of life that had not died out and that was already well-established prior to the Roman interlude.

Further west we see a more conscious adoption of various symbols that expressed people's identity. We have already seen how the south-western élites used Roman objects as a way of expressing their high social status and their identity as Romanised Britons, and we will see shortly how in Wales this reinvention of *Romanitas* reached extraordinary levels of intellectual sophistication. But there was another, British, side to the coin. The post-Roman élite in the west needed to encourage links with the pre-Roman past. In current anthropological jargon, it was a means of 'legitimising their authority'. Leaders like to do this from time to time, especially if the political climate is at all turbulent, as it was in the fourth and fifth centuries.* It would shortly become even worse when the 'Anglo-Saxonised' people of the Midlands and east turned their attention on the Romanised people of the west.

In the fifth and sixth centuries British leaders in the west paid special attention to sites and monuments that had been important in pre-Roman times. Very often these were in locations that stood out

---

* We have recently witnessed something similar in our own time. The aftermath of the invasion of Iraq in March 2003 has been bloody, and at the time of writing, more than a year later, to many people the political justification for it seems doubtful. So what does President Bush do? He seeks legitimation by copying John F. Kennedy's announcement of a Space Race: Kennedy aimed for the moon, Bush for Mars. Bush needs public legitimation if he is to win the next election, and he seeks it by emulating a predecessor who is acknowledged as a great leader.

from and dominated the landscape. Just like the builders of the great medieval cathedrals who chose spectacular sites at places like Durham, Lincoln, Salisbury and Ely, their aim was to impress and to dominate. These places quite literally overshadowed people's lives. They were intended to be a constant reminder of who was on top and who was below. The message was crude, but effective.

We have come across one of these sites already. Leslie Alcock was convinced that South Cadbury was Arthur's Camelot. To my mind that is something of a red herring: what matters is that that particular Somerset hillfort dominated the surrounding countryside, and had been a place of great importance throughout the last millennium BC. Modern research has shown that in pre-Roman times it sat within a prosperous and settled landscape of fields and farms.[27] The recent discovery of a ceremonial Late Bronze Age bronze shield that had been placed in a ditch and then ritually destroyed by having a wooden stake driven through it suggests that the hill was also a religious centre by 1000 BC.[28] Then, shortly after the Roman Conquest, we find clear evidence that efforts were made to erase or destroy the site's continuing role as a focus for the community and as a symbol of local people's identity.

The Roman army marched in. Burials were disturbed, ditches were filled in and a new shrine, to Roman gods, was constructed which it was hoped would focus local beliefs in a more 'constructive' direction.[29] To my mind it is no surprise that South Cadbury became an important centre in early post-Roman times: the ramparts were enlarged and new buildings were constructed on the hilltop. I suspect that South Cadbury had stood as a symbol of local British identity throughout the Roman period. It was the natural place for new Dark Age leaders to seek legitimacy in the eyes of the community.

If you stand on top of the South Cadbury ramparts you can clearly see the steep hill of Glastonbury Tor in the distance to the north-west, across the marshes of the Somerset Levels. Today Glastonbury Tor attracts strange theories and peculiar views of the past, as I suspect it always has done. There is something about the place that seems unnatural, improbable and, dare I say it, magical. The terraces that make the hill look like a grass-covered ziggurat have a perfectly normal explanation (they are so-called 'strip lynchets' formed by medieval agriculture), but many people believe they form part of a mysterious maze.

Whatever your opinions on Glastonbury Tor, it is reasonable to suppose that people in the past would have seen it as a special place.[30] If we add the extra dimension of water, because both the Tor and the Abbey are at the edge of the Somerset Levels, the place assumes added religious significance. In the Bronze and Iron Ages wet places, and particularly unusual wet places, were often seen as being close to the next world; Glastonbury is so strange that I think we could assume it was a religious centre, or a special place of some sort, even without the numerous remarkable finds that have been made nearby in the Levels.[31]

Viewed as a piece of landscape, the Glastonbury area is completely dominated by the steep-sided hill known today as the Tor. The name Glastonbury may predate Roman times: 'the stronghold of the people living at Glaston', a Celtic name possibly meaning 'woad place'.[32] The Tor is where anyone wishing to draw strength from pre-Roman traditions would establish a presence, and that is where we find Early Christian remains.

In the 1960s Professor Philip Rhatz was commissioned by a group of American Glastonbury enthusiasts to investigate the top of the Tor. He found no evidence for Christ's presence there, nor yet an Ark, but he did find the remains of a fifth- or sixth-century settlement, including sherds of Mediterranean amphorae. There were also traces of timber buildings, and a large number of animal bones suggested that top-quality cuts of meat had been eaten there (they were butchered elsewhere, presumably at the bottom of the hill). We now know from other excavations that feasting formed a part of life in fifth- and sixth-century monastic sites. Add to that the discovery of two burials, and it would seem that the top of the Tor was indeed an Early Christian monastic settlement.

I have to say I was slightly disappointed when I first visited Glastonbury Abbey in the 1960s. It seemed a bit shabby, run-down and really not very old. To make matters worse, I had hitch-hiked across England to see Philip's dig on the Tor, and like a typical student I hadn't bothered to check the dates. After a long climb, I found the place windy and deserted. So I felt little enthusiasm when I revisited the site nearly forty years later, being in no rush to see again the site of that late-twelfth-century archaeologico-religious travesty known as the Discovery of Arthur's Tomb (see page 36). I was, however, impressed by the new Abbey Visitor Centre and its excellent displays.

I was in that Visitor Centre and it was raining outside. Somewhere above me the Tor lurked, hidden in the mist. I was sipping a mug of coffee when my eye was caught by a small case with a bronze vessel in it that superficially resembled one of those supposedly 'Coptic' bronze bowls I discussed earlier. It was indeed a Byzantine piece, not a 'Coptic' bowl but a censer with a chain – a vessel used to hold burning incense. It was found during roadworks in 1980 on Silver Street, just north of the Abbey precinct, and probably dates to the late sixth or seventh century. It is a very fine piece, and one which can only have been used in a church.

The distribution map of Dark Age settlements in the south-west includes a number of reused pre-Roman sites, of which perhaps the best-known are the Iron Age hillforts of Cadbury Congesbury, also in Somerset, and Dinas Powys, in south Wales. Both are classic examples of places where 'Dark Age' leaders have sought validation through extensive reuse of significant Iron Age hillforts. Both, too, have yielded examples of imported Mediterranean pottery.

I will close this chapter with a most remarkable example of literacy in a supposedly 'Dark Age'. It consists of a series of what at first glance appear to be rather crudely carved stones, each one of which carries several lines of Latin inscription. They are mainly found in Wales, but other examples are known from the south-west. These inscribed stones are at odds with the conventional wisdom, as succinctly expressed by Dr David Howlett, who has done more than his fair share to debunk it:

> Some books about the end of Roman Britain imply that after the departure of military and civil administrators in AD 410 the Roman way of life ended suddenly, with gentlemen farmers abandoning their villas to live in holes in the ground, and everyone becoming illiterate.[33]

The writing on the stones is not in the usual style, of capital letters, found on Roman inscriptions. Instead they are written in a form which

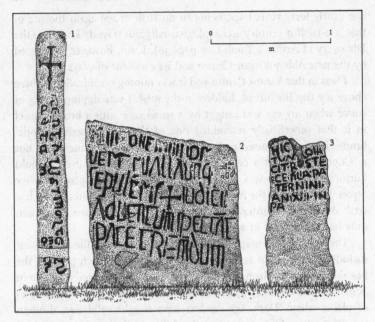

Examples of so-called 'Class-1' inscribed stones from Wales: (1) Towyn, (2) Llanleonfel and (3) Llanerfyl. Fifth–seventh centuries AD.

more resembles lower-case, or handwriting. Roman-style capital letters feature clean, straight lines which are well suited for carving in stone; the more cursive script of the Class-1 stones* looks clumsy and ill-executed, but in this case looks are deceptive.

They are memorial stones, each with an epitaph in Latin and/or Goidelic (an early form of Gaelic), sometimes written in a form of script involving a series of short strokes, known as Ogham. The inscriptions frequently employ Christian symbols, such as crosses. The stones are generally not much larger than a man, and where we know they are still *in situ* they appear to be sited with care, and occasionally in a way which seems deliberately to be mimicking the positioning of prehistoric standing stones – perhaps some kind of reference back to earlier traditions.

---

* They are known as Class-1 stones because they can be dated to the fifth–seventh centuries (Classes 2 and 4 run to the ninth and eleventh centuries respectively).

David Howlett and Charles Thomas have shown that the Latin language used in these inscriptions is literate and well-informed.[34] It is not the product of ignorant backwoodsmen grappling with an unfamiliar tongue, but spoken Latin of a high order, employing all sorts of clever word-play which was fashionable in the late- and post-Roman world: epitaphs could be read forwards and backwards, and would mean different things in the different directions.[35] Erudite tricks are also played with rhyme and with scansion. These stones are remarkable because they are quite common, and it seems reasonable to suppose that they could have been read by more than just the highest echelons of society.

Class-1 stones occur in areas of Britain that did not have a tradition of inscribed stones in Roman times. We must therefore assume that although some Latin may well have survived in certain households or in, for example, the Church, this was essentially a reintroduction or the introduction of a new tradition from outside. It was introduced because, like so-called 'Anglo-Saxon' culture in the east, people wanted to adopt it for their own reasons, which in Wales and the south-west included the notion of cultural identity, which would later come to stand for British identity. But where did this new tradition come from?

Leslie Alcock, like all great scholars, can be allowed to slip up occasionally, as he did with Camelot and South Cadbury; but on Class-1 stones his words still carry weight:

> Their overwhelming distribution pattern is away from the lowland heart of Roman Britain, and lies instead in the Irish Sea zone. This pattern reveals new influences, and some of the formulae of the inscriptions make it clear that these came from Gaul and the Mediterranean. In broad archaeological terms – but only in broad terms – they demonstrate the same contacts and the same routes as the imported pottery ... the distribution of [Class] I stones reflects the travels of the Celtic saints, both around the Irish Sea and beyond it to Gaul and the Mediterranean.[36]

The Celtic saints did more than just spread the word of God; they also took with them the important message that culture and learning mattered, and in the process they helped to inspire a sense of identity that would last for centuries. Their beliefs are growing in popularity even today. They must have been remarkably charismatic people. St Patrick, for example, lived in the fifth century and probably came from a family of Romanised Britons. When only sixteen he was abducted by Irish pirates and spent six years as a slave in Ireland, before he managed to escape in a ship bound for the Continent. We do not know how long he was away, but eventually, having acquired a Christian education, he was inspired by a vision to return to Ireland and spread the word, which he did with great success. For me St Patrick's life exemplifies the Dark Ages: there is erudition and literacy, travel and religion, but within a broader political context that is only slowly acquiring stability, following the enormous upheaval brought about by the end of the Western Roman Empire.

CHAPTER EIGHT

The Making of the English Landscape

ARCHAEOLOGISTS HAVE to read a lot. All too often the written style of what I have to read is dull, but the results of the research usually compensate for the stiff, jargon-ridden prose one has to wade through. Such reading is a duty, rather than a pleasure, and it has become a dreary fact of modern archaeological life. But there have been some notable exceptions – archaeologists who can really write – and of those my favourite is the late, great W.G. Hoskins, whose book *The Making of the English Landscape* (1955) is a masterpiece that changed the course of my archaeological life.[1]

Having read Hoskins, I knew that only one thing really mattered to me, and that was to understand what made ancient landscapes, and the people who lived in them, work. Hoskins saw the landscape as being inspired by past minds and imaginations; it was not merely a creation of hard labour influenced by practical considerations, such as the need to farm or to travel. He saw the influence of the Church in the development of the medieval landscape, and he sought evidence for social relationships, such as that of landlord and tenant, in the way, for example, that villages were arranged, fields enclosed or towns laid out. His landscape was a human phenomenon, and he wrote about it with extraordinary warmth, even when he was being analytical.

Hoskins wrote *The Making of the English Landscape* in the 1950s, and his views on the earliest landscapes are very much a reflection of that time. It was believed, for example, that there had been relatively little clearance of the forests that covered most of Britain before the Roman Conquest:

The clearance of the woodland was, indeed, the greatest single
form of change in the natural landscape, especially in the early
stages of the Old English [i.e. Anglo-Saxon] settlement before there
was any thought of draining the waterlogged fens and marshes.[2]

The notion that the Anglo-Saxon 'settlers' cleared the forests of eastern
Britain went hand in hand with the idea that these people were pioneers, reminiscent perhaps of those stout Englishmen who had settled
the woodlands of North America.[3] Unfortunately for that view, we
now know from numerous excavations and from surveys of past veg-
etation using pollen analysis that most of lowland Britain had been
cleared of tree cover by the end of the Bronze Age, around 1000 BC.[4]
While large tracts of forests undoubtedly remained, massive or wholesale clearance was not necessary after the Roman Conquest: it was
more a matter of eating away at the woodlands, a process known in
medieval times as 'assarting'.[5] The substantial areas of woodland in
post-Roman Britain were in places like the Forest of Dean. They
were less often found on the eastern side of the country where the
Anglo-Saxon 'settlers' were supposed to have hewn out their clearings
and established their homesteads. That work had been done for them
two millennia previously.

The ancient woodlands of Britain were an important resource that
did not necessarily need to be 'cleared'. It was they that provided the
timbers used in the construction not just of Britain's many churches
and great cathedrals, but her humbler houses and cottages too. Far
from being a subject for 'clearance', they had been managed with great
skill since at least the Neolithic period, five thousand years ago, to
provide forest products ranging from willow basketry to large poles
and heavy timbers.[6]

When reading accounts from the 1950s and before of how Anglo-
Saxon incomers cleared the forest cover that then cloaked large areas
of south-east Britain, it is hard to avoid the between-the-lines suggestion that these diligent, hard-working new arrivals did what the 'native'
Celtic communities ought to have done centuries earlier, were they
not so indolent by nature. Hoskins accepts the Anglo-Saxon invasions
as fact, but he clearly recognises that there are problems in reconciling
the received historical account with what he has observed in the field.

I suspect that were he still alive, he too would be a part of the anti-mass-migration tendency in the world of Anglo-Saxon studies. He starts his second chapter, on 'The English Settlement', with a statement of the then current view that 'the Old English swept all before them and built and planted afresh'. He then goes on to say: 'But this picture is far too simple and does not square with the facts ... hamlets and isolated farmsteads of great antiquity can be found dotted about the Midland[s] and the eastern counties.'

Hoskins even casts doubt on what was then the 'big idea' of Anglo-Saxon studies. It had been believed for some time that the thousands of villages that are today such a pleasant feature of the English country-side were a product of the Anglo-Saxon settlers. This notion was first put forward in a detailed and thorough country-wide study by the great nineteenth-century economic historian Frederic Seebohm. I was introduced to his work as a child, because the Seebohm family lived near the farm in Hertfordshire where I was brought up, and my best friend was also called Frederic Seebohm. Young Freddie showed me a copy of his august ancestor's great book *The English Village Community* (1883), which began with a study of the villages around Hitchin, our local town.[7] I found a copy in my grandfather's library, which I promptly 'borrowed' – and I have it beside me as I write. There is nothing like local and personal interest to fuel one's enthusiasm, and I spent many weekends on my bike visiting the places described by Seebohm, which were sometimes, but sadly not always, still there.

Both Seebohm's and Hoskins's books will continue to stand on their own merit as works of great scholarly insight, whether or not Anglo-Saxon invasions actually happened. But it is interesting to detect that Hoskins plainly had his doubts that villages were, of themselves, an indication of Anglo-Saxon settlement. To quote again from the first paragraph of Chapter 2, he notes that 'Even in Cornwall and Devon [both counties well outside the Anglo-Saxon area], in the far south-west, the large compact village can be found all over the map and is found at the time of the Norman Conquest.' In other words, Hoskins is plainly saying that large, compact ancient villages cannot be linked to 'Dark Age' incomers.

Hoskins was also of the then common opinion that Anglo-Saxon place names indicated new settlements established by incomers. He was by no means alone in this view. As late as 1991, A.D. Mills in the Introduction to his excellent *Dictionary of English Place Names* for Oxford University Press was able to write:

> The Anglo-Saxon conquest and settlement of Britain began in the fifth century AD, spreading slowly from the east to the west and culminating in the occupation of the whole of what is now England ... by the ninth century. These new settlers were the Angles, Saxons and Jutes, Germanic tribes from northern Europe whose language was Anglo-Saxon, now usually called Old English to emphasise its continuity with Middle and Modern English.[8]

It was even suggested that these new settlements could be given some sort of chronological sequence by the type of language employed. Names that included the elements 'ham' or 'inga' – Birmingham, for example – were thought to be early in the sequence, thus providing evidence that the incomers penetrated quite rapidly into the East Midlands.[9] In the last fifty years, however, archaeology has demonstrated that the new Anglo-Saxon names were actually given to places that had been in existence very much earlier (as we saw at Maxey in Chapter 4). The names are of interest in their own right, but should not be treated as reliable evidence for when a particular town or village was actually founded.

The traditional view of the 'Dark Age' British countryside is of a place where the landscape reverted to scrub and woodland following the collapse of the Roman Empire. But we have already seen that the fourth-century 'Golden Age' was essentially a rural phenomenon, and there is no evidence to suggest that the countryside 'collapsed'; indeed, if anything, rural settlement went from strength to strength. Similarly, the idea of living in large, close-knit (or 'nucleated') villages surrounded by the fields and pastures of what was to develop into the well-known Open Field system of the Middle Ages, had its origins in Late, not Early Saxon times.[10] Early Saxon villages, as we saw at Maxey, were essentially a continuation of Romano-British and Iron Age settlements. Nicholas Higham describes the situation clearly:

> This continuity of habitat and rural activity is a crucial component of our revised perception of the Romano-British/Saxon interface and is entirely incompatible with the notion of wholesale depopu-

lation on the eve of, or in the course of, Anglo-Saxon settlement. Nor did Germanic immigrants bring with them ready for use the ideas of living in a nucleated village or cultivating open fields ... The excavation of deserted medieval villages slowly revealed from the 1950s onwards that the process of settlement nucleation by which they came into existence was, at earliest, a late Anglo-Saxon phenomenon. Many instances post-dated the Norman Conquest.[11]

I recall the first time I came across solid scientific evidence that the end of the Roman period did not witness a collapse in the rural economy, even in those parts of eastern England which were supposed to have received the earliest Anglo-Saxon raids. It was in a paper published in 1994 by an old friend and colleague, Peter Murphy, with whom I had worked on a number of projects in and around the Fens. One would suppose that boatloads of Germanic warriors wielding their fearsome swords and those 'strong knives, commonly called *scramasaxes*, smeared with poison'[12] would have caused stalwart East Anglian farmers to pause momentarily from their labours. But apparently not.

Peter, who has been studying the changing environment of eastern England for many years, looked at sites of the Early Saxon period in Essex and East Anglia.[13] He was interested in testing the idea, current in the 1950s, that the more intensively farmed areas of the Romano-British landscape reverted to scrub and woodland after the Roman period. In theory at least the Anglo-Saxons then arrived and set about the task of felling the trees. He quotes Dorothy Whitelock (writing in 1952), a well-known authority on the Anglo-Saxons, who wrote that the Early Saxon landscape was 'heavily forested ... areas under cultivation were on the whole small, surrounded by woodland and waste'.[14] Why is it that the pejorative word 'waste' seems so inextricably attached to earlier views of the period? Personally, if I was part of a mass migration I would rather jump ship than farm a 'waste'.

In 1986 Oliver Rackham, the acknowledged expert on ancient woodlands, contested the idea that regrown (or secondary) woodland had established itself at the end of the Roman period.[15] His rebuttal of the traditional view was based on his knowledge of early maps and place names. Peter Murphy looked for solid scientific evidence to decide the matter finally. He chose three distinct types of landscape for his study: the coastal marshes of Essex, the river valleys of central Essex and the sandy Breckland of West Suffolk. His research was broadly based, and made use of plant remains (usually carbonised fragments from around ovens, hearths and bonfires), pollen grains and soil science. He took great pains to exclude any samples that might not derive from securely dated deposits. It was a model study of ancient environments.

Peter found no evidence for secondary woodland at any of the sites in his three areas. He did, however, find clear evidence that in some areas the intensive production of cereals, which had been a feature of the Romano-British economy in East Anglia, had given way to livestock farming in the fifth to sixth centuries. This would suggest a change in the rural economy from an intensive system in Roman times, intended to produce a surplus of grain to feed the urban population and the army both abroad and in Britain, to something much closer to subsistence farming. He noted, however, that the Iron Age and Roman field systems seemed to have continued in use, which might well suggest that the pastoral farming was larger in scale than mere subsistence. I strongly suspect that something very similar was also taking place further north, in the area around Maxey and Durobrivae.

One advantage of such a broadly based study is that it allows us to gain a glimpse of the way in which the Early Saxon landscape was managed in general. Peter concluded that Anglo-Saxon agriculture was very diverse: 'On the Essex coast an economy based on salt-marsh sheep-grazing may be inferred; in the Essex river valleys an economy in which oat cultivation on heavy soils seems to have been important; at Brandon [in the Breckland] an arable economy based on rye-growing ... with flax production in the river valley.'[16]

The point that arises from this is obvious, but needs making none-theless. This diversity of land use shows an extraordinary degree of adaptation to contrasting landscapes and soil conditions, at precisely the time when Anglo-Saxon settlers are supposed to have been colonising the landscape. I believe it would have been impossible for large numbers of migrants to have adapted so fast and so thoroughly to such diverse conditions; if there actually were any incomers, they must have been few in number, and have settled within existing communities.

It is also worth stating that secondary woodland will start to develop very rapidly once a farmed landscape ceases to be maintained – the process has already started in parts of upland Britain where sheep-farming is no longer possible. Within one or two years hawthorn and sloe bushes appear, followed swiftly by birch. Close on the heels of the birch trees come the true forest trees, oak and ash. If the process is rapid today, it would have been very much more so in the Early Saxon period, when introduced species such as grey squirrels, Muntjac deer and rabbits were not around to nip off growing shoots or ringbark young trees.[17] Once an arable field had been abandoned, scrub would have colonised it in about five years; secondary birch (or alder in wet areas) woodland would soon grow up through the briars and bushes. The field would have become an almost impenetrable thicket within a decade. The absence of such scrub and woodland regeneration is very significant for what it tells us about the East Anglian landscape in the early fifth century.

Peter Murphy's study was a pioneering piece of work, but today the evidence that disproves the idea that the post-Roman period witnessed a widespread rural economic and environmental 'collapse' is overwhelming. The technique of pollen analysis is particularly useful for reconstructing past environments, because the pollen present in, say, a long-abandoned well, ditch or pond reflects what was growing in the region as a whole. If there was woodland or pasture nearby, tree or grass pollen grains would be present. The trick (and it is not always easy to achieve) is accurately to date the layers from which the samples are taken. Pollen analysis is a very skilled business, and those who study the subject are known as palynologists. One of the best in the business is Petra Dark, and in her recent book *The Environment of Britain in the First Millennium* AD she has convincingly demonstrated that post-Roman England never reverted to anything even remotely comparable to a Dark Age 'waste'.[18]

So far I have largely confined my attention to the southern part of Britain, because that is where most of the 'Arthurian' and 'Anglo-Saxon' events are meant to have taken place, but the area of 'Anglian' settlement is supposed to have extended as far north as Yorkshire. I now want to examine what happened at the northern boundary of Roman Britain, at Hadrian's Wall. If the entire system did indeed collapse into chaos on the withdrawal of Roman troops, one might expect to find good evidence for it at the frontier. Put another way, did the Dark Ages start with a bang, in the north of what was later to be England?

I have to admit, as a slightly shamefaced Fenman, that I adore the wild landscape of the Borderland around Hadrian's Wall. It's hard to avoid a feeling of refreshing desolation as one gazes across the rocky fells where villages are absent and farms even today are few and far between, in contrast with the tamed landscapes of overcrowded, over-expensive southern England. This has always been the country of border raiding, cattle rustling and lawlessness. Or has it? New evidence would suggest that in Roman and Dark Age times the legendary wild behaviour of the Borders was controlled, with at least some success.

Hadrian's Wall, marking the northern frontier of Roman Britain, must rank alongside the Colosseum as one of the most remarkable monuments of the Roman Empire. It was constructed on the orders of the Emperor Hadrian (AD 117–138) during a visit he made to Britain around AD 122. Today, in company with sites like Stonehenge, it is classed as a World Heritage Site. It stretches seventy-three miles from coast to coast. But the Wall is not just a wall: along its length are a series of small 'milecastles' and much larger garrison forts. There is also a deep ditch, or *vallum*, which runs along the northern side of the Wall and which was a key part of the defences; with its various attachments and outworks, the Wall should be regarded as a sophisticated system of defence in depth.

When I first visited the Wall as a student, I had to dodge flying sheep and pursuing Border collies, not to mention irascible farmers and rusting barbed wire, to reach some of the more choice lengths of stonework. But today, thanks to an immense effort by English Heritage, farmers and various local organisations, one can walk the entire length of the Wall with no slavering collies, no barbed wire, just fabulous views.[19]

Hadrian's Wall is something of an icon. It stands as a symbol for the rule of Rome: to the north there was chaos and barbarians; to the south there was civilisation. It has also become symbolic of the way in which Romano-British studies have developed in recent years. In the past the Wall was seen almost exclusively through military eyes: great attention was paid to the way its defences developed and to the history of the army units that served there. Today our horizons have become broader, and while the military significance of this most extraordinary construction is still of great importance, we also want to understand both how it fitted into the local economy and what happened to it when the Roman Empire ended.

The conventional image of Hadrian's Wall is of a military work that was constructed across a barren landscape. To Roman military historians and archaeologists it was the first mark on an otherwise virgin canvas. But recent aerial photographic research has shown that the landscape on either side of the Wall was 'tamed' by being partitioned up into a series of fields and farms by drystone walls. These landscapes seem to have been first laid out in the Iron Age, but we know that farms were being enlarged or built from new at least as late as the mid-second century. We do not know to what extent these farms were allowed to continue in use after the construction of the Wall, but they would not have presented a direct threat to the Roman military, and they could have provided provisions for the thousands of garrison soldiers. Crops were grown in small fields near to the farm buildings, but the main fields were undoubtedly for livestock. Meat and milk, in contrast to grain, are commodities that do not travel well, and are best obtained locally. As the discoverer of these new landscapes, Tim Gates, puts it: 'We may have to think in terms of a more hospitable landscape around Hadrian's Wall than the one we have been accustomed to imagine.'[20]

The discovery of these extensive farmed landscapes in the corridor of land around the Wall shows how careful we must be not to apply hasty historical interpretations to the archaeological record. Analysis of pollen found in boreholes near the Wall has shown that the number of trees growing in the area declined quite sharply at about the time the Wall was constructed. This has traditionally been attributed to the felling of trees, to provide timber for the builders and a clear field of view for the defenders. That may indeed have been in part the case, but now we must also bear in mind that the farmers would have needed a deforested landscape for their crops, yards and livestock. That surely would provide a better explanation for tree-felling at a scale that registers at a significant level in the pollen record.

If the landscape around the Wall was not a barren waste, did the entire system collapse when the Roman troops pulled out? Indeed, *did* the Roman troops pull out? To answer these questions we again encounter the difficulty of recognising post-Roman or Dark Age timber buildings in the uppermost levels of a Roman stone-built site. At Wroxeter it took an inspired archaeologist, in Philip Barker, to perform this near-miracle. At Birdoswald (Latin name Banna), a large fort on the Wall in Cumbria, Phil's equivalent has been Tony Wilmott, who directed a most remarkable series of excavations for English Heritage, mainly between 1987 and 1992.[21]

The interior of Birdoswald, in common with the other major garrison forts of Hadrian's Wall, was packed full of buildings. In no way did it resemble those rather strange shell-like structures of the so-called Saxon shore. Outside the walls of the fort there was a considerable *vicus*, or civilian settlement. Immediately south of the fort there still is a high, partially wooded and spectacular cliff.

The fort was entered via six gateways through the walls. The main road, or *via principalis*, ran east–west and connected with roads in the *vicus* outside the walls. There were a number of important changes to the buildings within the fort in the fourth and fifth centuries. As originally laid out, it contained exercise areas, administrative and garrison buildings and granaries. One of Tony Wilmott's most spectacular finds was the remains of a complete granary roof which collapsed some time around AD 350, leaving a vast mass – Tony describes it as 'drifts' – of fallen stone roof tiles lying on the flagstone floor where the grain had once been stored. The fact that the fort's large granaries were abandoned in the mid-fourth century and never rebuilt suggests that the garrison was then supplied by local farmers, so that large quantities of grain no longer needed to be stored. It also suggests that the military contract supply system was beginning to encounter problems – of which the most likely was a shortage of money, itself the result of a failure to collect the ever-increasing Late Roman taxes.

There is some evidence that one building at Birdoswald may have been used as a church in the late fourth century, something for which there is much stronger evidence at two other forts on the Wall, at Housesteads and Vindolanda. The fort was improved after the Great Barbarian Conspiracy of AD 367, work that involved the building of a new barrack block and rebuilding parts of the main wall. By then

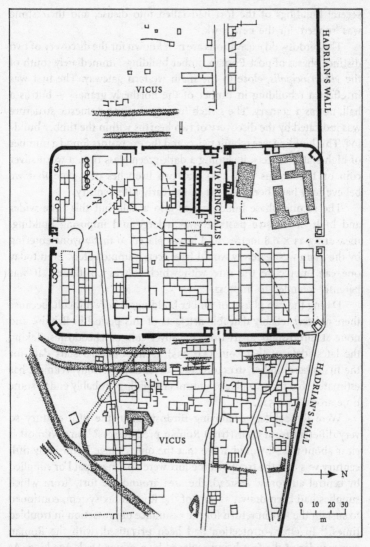

The main features around the Hadrian's Wall fort of Birdoswald, Cumbria. The features plotted here were revealed by means of a geophysical survey. Note the presence of a double ditch outside the fort walls.

several buildings of the fort had fallen into disuse, and their stone was 'robbed' for the new work.

The Birdoswald excavations are best known for the discovery of two distinct phases of post-Roman timber buildings, immediately south of the *via principalis*, close to the main western gateway. The first was in effect a rebuilding in timber of the northerly granary – but as a hall, not as a granary. The switch from granary to domestic structure was indicated by the discovery of two hearths within the timber building. This building was rebuilt twice, and the excavators found a number of high-status objects, including a dark-green glass ring, a worn silver coin of Theodosius (388–395) and two brooches of a type that we believe may have been current in the early fifth century.

The second-phase building was also a hall, but this time wider and built of massive posts. It was a large and imposing building, measuring 23 × 6.8 metres, and it was placed so that anyone entering by the main west gateway would have seen it immediately. Even today one can appreciate the care with which it was positioned. It was patently intended to impress.

Dating the two phases of timber buildings is very difficult, because there are few reliably dateable artefacts of this period in Britain, and none at Birdoswald, apart from the silver coin of Theodosius. Taking the latest date of that coin (AD 395) as the notional start date for the first-phase timber structure and its rebuilding, Tony Wilmott has estimated that the two phases of timber building probably ended some time around AD 520.

Were the soldiers occupying Birdoswald in the fifth century so very different from their (true) Roman predecessors? Tony Wilmott is clear about this: 'I would argue that the only change in the early fifth century was that the troops of the fort were no longer paid or supplied by central authority.' Instead, the area around the fort, 'from which supplies had been drawn as part of the Roman tax system, continued to sustain the fort in return for the assurance of protection in troubled times'.[22] In effect, protection had been privatised, with the Roman commander of the fort being replaced by a minor Dark Age king. As time passed maybe some of the *Romanitas* rubbed off, and the ruler and his soldiers became more like a warlord and his warriors. If one is looking for a job description for an early-fifth-century Arthur-like

A reconstruction of the main hall and service buildings of the second phase of post-Roman settlement at Birdoswald fort, Cumbria. In the background is the west wall of the fort and the double towered gatehouse of the main western gate. The principal road through the fort, the via principalis, *was narrowed to accommodate the new timber hall. The stonework foundations of two Roman granary buildings are shown below and to the left of the new hall.*

figure, the post-Roman commander of Birdoswald would be an almost perfect match. It is worth noting that Birdoswald was not alone in the north: we suspect that there was also fifth-century occupation south of the Wall, at Catterick and Corbridge, both, as Tony Wilmott suggests, 'the probable centres of petty kingdoms'.

Dominic Powlesland has devoted most of his professional life to the archaeology of a single parish and the land around it. In the process he has revealed an enormous amount about the history and prehistory of Britain as a whole. I would rate his research at West Heslerton in the East Riding of Yorkshire as one of the top landscape projects in modern Europe.[23]

I will never forget my first visit to Dominic's excavation at West Heslerton in the early 1980s. The wind was howling through the trees and the rain beating down on the roof of a building in which a small group of people were washing and marking finds. Looking through the incoming finds trays was a tall young man with wild hair and a vivid rainbow-coloured sweater. This was Dominic. I was struck by the fact that he had the broadest smile in archaeology.

A good field archaeologist develops a special attitude to wet or cold weather. You can't fight it, so you might as well enjoy it. Moaning will simply make you miserable, and that will soon spread to the rest of the team. For me, the worst thing about nasty weather is that it stops me from thinking clearly. What I remember best about Dominic's site tour is that he was wildly enthusiastic about every small pit, ditch and post-hole we encountered – and there must have been several hundred of them.

Most archaeologists require a bit of luck at some point in their career; the trick is first to recognise it, and then to turn it to one's advantage. Dominic's piece of good fortune was to be asked to examine some early Anglo-Saxon burials that had turned up in a sand quarry between the villages of East and West Heslerton in the autumn of 1977. He soon realised the potential of the site, and put together a research project, largely funded by English Heritage, that has been continuing ever since. There are two reasons why the West Heslerton project is so important. The first is the landscape in which it is located, and the second is the way it has been carried out by Dominic.

The Heslerton villages are located on the south side of the Vale of Pickering, which is sandwiched between the high Yorkshire Moors to the north and the gently rolling chalk hills of the Yorkshire Wolds to the south. The Vale of Pickering today resembles a flat dish with clearly defined and quite steep sides. The peaty soils in what are now flat fields were laid down when most of the area was occupied by a huge body of fresh water, some forty miles long, known to archaeologists as Lake Pickering. Lake Pickering formed at the end of the Ice Age, fourteen thousand years ago, when the River Derwent's outflow to the sea was blocked by 'moraine' – material that had been dumped across its path by a glacier. The edges of the lake have produced some of the best-known prehistoric sites in Britain, including the world-famous hunter/gatherer settlement of Star Carr.[24]

Over time, as peats grew and river-borne silts accumulated, Lake Pickering became a series of smaller lakes and marshes. The distinction between the peaty soils that were once wetland, and the drier sands and gravels around the edges of the now extinct lake, can clearly be seen from the air. Around the edges of the peats the familiar 'crop-marks' that we encountered at Maxey – the traces of ancient activity left in growing crops – are sometimes visible, but they are not always as distinct as one might wish. This is actually a good sign, because those places where the cropmarks vanish are in fact archaeologically more important. The reason for this is simple: the marks are not visible from the air because the crop plants' roots cannot reach down that far. And the reason they cannot do this is that they are prevented from doing so by layers of windblown sand. The sandy soils around West Heslerton are easily disturbed by the wind, and when they build up on the surface they preserve everything that lies below them. That is one of the main reasons that the archaeology of the site is so exciting.

Dominic realised that the only way to fill in the 'blanks' between the areas where he had good cropmarks was by using a combination of limited excavation and large-scale geophysical survey. Geophysical survey is a means of plotting ancient archaeological features that are buried beneath the surface and may not appear on aerial photographs; it is done electronically, either by measuring the soil's resistance to an electrical charge, or its magnetic properties, or even its ability to reflect a radar signal. It usually involves two people, one of whom moves the survey instrument over the surface of the ground, normally following a grid pattern. The second member of the team has the job of logging the results and checking the survey while it is underway. The geophysical surveys at West Heslerton had to be carried out on a truly enormous scale if they were to produce meaningful results. Dominic knew that this would produce a vast amount of data, but happily he is capable of writing highly sophisticated computer software which is able to manipulate graphics, such as maps, aerial photographs and the results of his massive geophysical surveys.

Dominic calls the most spectacular result of his work at West Heslerton 'the wallpaper'. It's a huge roll of computer printout about five metres long which we laid out on the floor of his sitting room. It was quite extraordinary, showing Neolithic and Bronze Age barrows, henges, fields and settlements; but the most remarkable thing was his so-called 'ladder settlement'. This was established around an Iron Age trackway which ran along the sandy edge of the wetland and remained in use for about a thousand years, throughout the Roman period and into the Dark Ages. The scale of this settlement is quite astonishing, and it is mirrored by another one on the other side of the Vale of Pickering. It was called a 'ladder settlement' because the transverse or cross-cutting ditches of a succession of fields, farms and yards resemble a crazy string or rope ladder that follows a sinuous path along the Vale, more or less on the line adopted today by the A64, York to Scarborough road.

The ladder settlement, which has so far been traced for a distance of about nine miles, consisted of large farmsteads, each of which possessed its own cemetery, every 250 metres. During the Iron Age, field systems developed on the up-slope or 'dry' side of the ladder settlement, but that does not mean that the wetter land would have been ignored, especially during the summer months when the wet meadows would have provided abundant free grazing for the sheep and goats that we know were kept there. For what it's worth, my own sheep would eat reeds in preference to grass any day.

The ladder settlement was abandoned some time during the fifth century. At first glance it might seem that this was a direct response to the end of the Roman Empire in Britain, but Dominic Powlesland points out that the decline had begun from the mid-fourth century, and probably owed as much to broader Romano-British 'macroeconomic' conditions as anything else. There is also good evidence that conditions underfoot were growing wetter towards the end of the fourth century, and this also must have played an important role, given the location of the ladder settlement alongside a wetland. As we saw at Mucking, so-called sunken feature buildings of *Grubenhaus* type first appear in Late Roman times, when the various elements of the ladder settlement were still in use. So they cannot be considered a reliable indicator of Anglo-Saxon (or Anglian, to be more specific) mass migration, which could not possibly have been underway at this early period. The idea of stationing *foederati* on farms in the Vale of Pickering is of course plainly absurd.

The next stage in the story of West Heslerton is the establishment of an Anglian village and its cemetery. So for the first time we have evidence for where the people in the graveyard actually lived. In death, they tell us a great deal about the way their lives were organised. The cemetery is on the landward side of the ladder settlement, and the village is south of that, towards the chalk slope leading up to the Wolds. The village was established towards the end of Roman administration, somewhere around AD 400. Had there been a gap in time between the abandonment of the ladder settlement and the establishment of the village, Dominic would have expected windblown sand to have accumulated between the last Roman and the first Anglian features; but none was present. The new settlement was actually located on top of a Roman site, but that was not a settlement. Instead it was a stone-built temple or shrine constructed after about AD 340, around a spring. The religious rites performed there seem to have taken place in the season of spring, probably in March or April. March was the start of the Roman New Year, and April was the month celebrating Ceres, the goddess of agriculture and fertility. The shrine produced over thirty thousand pieces of Roman pottery, which would suggest that it was visited by large numbers of people.

One might suppose that the new Anglian community was located close to the spring line for obvious reasons, but the shrine site seems to have been deliberately avoided throughout the life of the village, which would suggest that it was still respected in some way. The new village was laid out to cover an area of five hundred metres square. It was occupied for over four hundred years, and did not go out of use until after AD 850, by which time over 220 buildings had been built and used. The buildings consisted of *Grubenhäuser* (or 'pit dwellings') and post-built rectangular halls. Dominic is convinced that the *Grubenhäuser* were specialised structures used to provide dry storage. The wooden floor was raised above the ground on low turf walls, and the large pit below provided more space for air to circulate. A thatched roof rested on a simple A-frame that was supported by posts at each end of the large pit. It was a simple and effective structure. They are found dotted around the Heslerton landscape, and are not confined to the village. If they were indeed used to store grain (among other things), this would suggest that the countryside round about was law-abiding and free from bandits.

In the past the presence of *Grubenhäuser* has been used to suggest the extent to which post-Roman life slipped into a state of barbarism. Not even in pre-Roman times did people actually *live* in holes in the ground, although their pagan Saxon descendants were supposed to have done. The rectangular houses or halls in which we know that people actually did live were often quite elaborate post-built structures that combined both British and Continental traditions. While the pre-Roman, 'native' British tradition was to build round houses, rectangular buildings became more common on many sites during the Roman period, as we saw at Orton Hall Farm. Dominic has estimated that the Anglian village would have had a population at any one time of about ten extended families, or some seventy-five people.

As I have mentioned, the Anglian cemetery that went with the village has a great deal to tell us about the way society in the village was organised. The cemetery was used between the end of the fourth and the middle of the seventh centuries (say AD 650), when the villagers decided to bury their dead somewhere else – possibly in the grave-yard of an as-yet undiscovered church. There can be little doubt that the location for the cemetery was deliberately chosen to be near a very much older ceremonial and burial site of Late Neolithic and Bronze Age date (around 2000 BC). In Saxon times these barrows and other ceremonial sites would still have been clearly visible as earth-works. The earliest burials were cremations, and these were almost entirely restricted to within the area bounded by a prehistoric cere-monial enclosure and the external ring-ditches that surrounded Bronze Age barrows. Again, it would seem that the selection of these already ancient features for the earliest Anglian cremations was deliberate.

The arrangement of the non-cremated burials is of interest too. Dominic has convincingly shown that the cemetery grew from five separate centres, which subsequently spread out. He concludes that

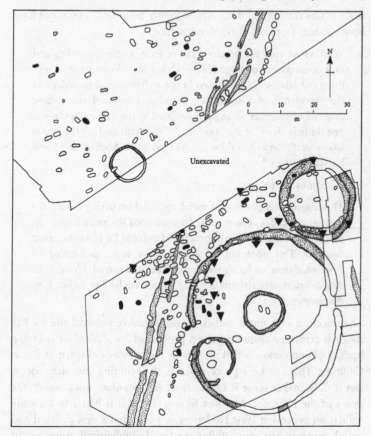

Graves in the Anglian cemetery at West Heslerton, Yorkshire. The circular features are ring-ditches that surrounded prehistoric barrows and 'henge'-like ceremonial monuments, dating to around 2000 BC. The triangles represent Anglian cremations of about AD 450–500. Other Anglian graves (shown in black) date between AD 450 and 650.

these represent five distinct lineages or families. The arrangement of the cemetery supports the view that the post-Roman changes at West Heslerton reflect a new social and political structure. The multi-centred arrangement must reflect a well-established resident population rather than a haphazard group of incomers, most of whom, being presumably male at this early stage of the Anglo-Saxon 'invasions', would not have been related. Dominic Powlesland writes:

> Whether we view the development of Early Anglo-Saxon England as a consequence of large-scale invasion and domination, something not adequately supported in the archaeological record, or as the emergence of a small new social and political élite whose material culture was willingly assimilated by the native population, one thing is clear: by the beginning of the sixth century the population of Eastern Yorkshire ... had adopted Anglian dress and burial practices.[25]

Later he goes on to say:

> The climatic, economic and social upheaval occurring during the declining decades of Roman Britain provided the perfect environment for the emergence of a new social order in Early Anglo-Saxon England. This need not be a new social order dominated by Anglian, Saxon or Jutish overlords. The widespread adoption of Anglo-Saxon material culture may reflect availability rather than dominance.[26]

The selection of a much earlier religious and ceremonial site for the Anglian cemetery again suggests a process of 'validation' or referring back, a phenomenon which we saw in the previous chapter, at South Cadbury. This can be a process which an incoming élite may adopt, but it only makes sense if the body of the populace understands the point of the reference. My own feeling is that it is better to view the validation process at West Heslerton as a sign that a new political and social *structure* had arisen following the de-Romanisation process of the late fourth and early fifth centuries. Dominic feels strongly too that there is no archaeological evidence for a powerful controlling élite, in either the cemetery or the Anglian settlement.

Reference back to earlier tradition is a recurrent theme in Anglo-Saxon northern Britain. At Old Yeavering in the hills of Northumberland a great Saxon period royal 'palace complex', which includes a unique timber grandstand or theatre, lies directly below the spectacular hill of Yeavering Bell, whose crown is occupied by a large prehistoric hillfort or *oppidum*, the ramparts of which are clearly visible from the valley below.[27] Further south, in the Yorkshire Wolds, a Saxon ecclesiastical site was placed alongside the largest single standing stone in Britain, known as the Rudston Monolith. The Saxon site was also positioned precisely at the point where three Neolithic so-called cursus ceremonial monuments converged.[28] In this instance it may be the Church rather than a civil authority that is claiming legitimation, but the underlying principle still holds good.

Archaeology has had its fair share of scientific techniques that have been greeted as the solution to all its problems. The most famous is radiocarbon dating. This was originally conceived in 1949, on the basis that the sun has been bombarding the earth's outer atmosphere with radiation at a constant rate. It was soon realised, however, that 'sun spots' and solar flares, among other factors, could cause solar radiation to fluctuate, and this in turn affected the calculations behind radio-carbon dates. At about the same time that this was appreciated, com-puters were becoming cheaper and more powerful, and scientists realised that it would be possible to compensate for the changing levels of radiation mathematically – a technique known as 'calibration' that one can now perform at home, using a programme downloaded from the internet. After about half a century of unreliability, the accuracy of radiocarbon dating is now accepted by everyone involved in archaeology.

It's important to keep the story of radiocarbon dating in mind when considering the new scientific techniques that are becoming available. They all have drawbacks, and they will all take some time to 'bed in'. None will solve all our problems instantly. I will touch on the problems to do with DNA and genetic research in the next chapter, but here I want to introduce a technique that at first glance seems to be relatively uncomplicated and to have enormous archaeological potential, although it requires very expensive equipment and highly trained scientists to carry out the laboratory procedures. It's known as stable isotope analysis.[29] When I visited the lab at Durham University of Dr Paul Budd, one of the pioneers of the technique in Britain, I had to put on overshoes, white overalls and a funny hat: all impurities must be excluded from the process.

The idea behind the archaeological application of stable isotope analysis is straightforward. It is based on the realisation that tooth enamel (the shiny, hard outer coating, not the softer dentine that forms the bulk of the tooth) is laid down in childhood and does not alter subsequently. In most children the adult teeth start to develop between three and four months after birth, and finish developing at about the age of twelve. Thereafter the enamel, but not the dentine, remains inert. As the enamel is forming, it takes up the chemicals that are in the child's environment by way of food and water. Certain elements are indicative of particular parts of the world. Levels of lead and strontium, for example, vary a great deal from one region to another. Oxygen is rather more complex: two of its isotopes, ^{16}O and ^{18}O, vary in response to climatic, geographical and meteorological conditions. So there will be a big difference, for example, in the composition of the stable oxygen isotopes found in tooth enamels that formed in Britain, with its warm, maritime climate, and the Alps, where conditions are more Continental.

I chose that example because this is precisely how we have come to believe that the rich Early Bronze Age burial close by Stonehenge known as the 'Amesbury archer' grew up in central Europe.[30] Stable isotope analysis does not tell us, of course, when he left central Europe and why he came to Britain: was he on a visit, or had he settled permanently in Wessex? These are archaeological questions that will need to be answered in other ways.

Paul Budd and his team looked at a selection of teeth from Anglian graves at West Heslerton. This cemetery is very early, and is likely therefore to contain the bodies of first-generation Anglian migrants. According to Myres, and others, these people would probably have been warriors from raiding parties or 'barbarian mercenaries'. The finds from the cemetery show close parallels with material from the Anglian European heartlands, around the Baltic coastal territories of Jutland (mainly in modern Denmark). So in theory we should know what to expect from the analysis of the tooth enamel.

Twenty-four samples were taken from the cemetery, and eight from prehistoric burials (of Early Bronze and Iron Age date). After analysis it was found, to nobody's great surprise, that the eight prehistoric people all came from the East Yorkshire area. Of the twenty-four samples from the Anglian cemetery, four most probably came from Scandinavia, possibly somewhat north of the true Anglian region; finds with parallels further north are known at West Heslerton, so that fitted the conventional model. But were the four individuals warriors?

Far from it. In fact they spanned the 250-year-long use of the cemetery, so they represent a series of events rather than a single large influx of new blood. What is particularly striking is the fact that all are female, and one is juvenile. Rather than being 'high status' graves, as one might expect, all four were among the poorest, in terms of grave-goods: none contained the fine brooches that are so character-istic of Anglian burials, and only one contained an artefact at all: a 'girdle hanger', a type of symbolic house key. Of the remaining twenty samples ten were local, but most unexpectedly the remainder came from west of the Pennines. This suggests that the infrastructure in the north of Britain was in a good state: roads were open, and people felt it was safe to travel not just in Britain, but further afield.

Maybe it is because we have tended to look at permanent struc-tures, such as great buildings, barrows, town walls and so forth, that archaeologists – and I include prehistorians in this – have generally underestimated the extent to which the population of Britain and western Europe moved around. We know that pottery and coins moved, and we also know that styles of art and decoration spread across Europe very rapidly. But we do not then go on to say that people themselves must have moved too. Just because pre-Roman roads have left little trace, some prehistorians seem to believe that they were not used. So distribution maps of the period are always based around river systems, the majority of which were untamed and would have provided a very precarious means of 'commercial' transport, especially in wet winters and dry summers. The people of the time *must* have had roads, if only to move their livestock. From the little we know, it would appear that these roads and droveways were laid out in an informal network that went from settlement to settlement; in general there seem to have been no major trunk routes. By the same token, we know that Roman roads survived into post-Roman times, and the presence of Saxon settlements at some distance from them should not indicate, as has been suggested, that the Saxons were somehow 'avoiding' them, but that they possessed their own system, which had probably developed from the pre-Roman informal network.

Communication became very much better in Roman times. One

striking example of this improved mobility was provided by the discovery in a well at Silchester of a memorial stone bearing an inscription in the Irish script known as Ogham. This stone dates to the Roman period, when the town was still in use, and it suggests not just that one Irish person lived there, but that there were people around who could read and understood the script. Who knows, maybe there was a local Irish community or enclave in the town.[31]

If West Heslerton is an example of the Anglian component of the 'Anglo-Saxons', its Saxon equivalent is in the Oxfordshire Thames Valley, in an area that has long been known as a region of Early Saxon settlement.[32] The presence of such an early area of settlement so far inland has troubled many authorities on the period, but most explain it by suggesting that the early colonists sailed up the river, preferring not to disembark in London or other suitable spots further downstream, which may not have been friendly territory. Susan Hughes is currently looking at the tooth enamel from bodies in Early Saxon graves at Berinsfield, in Oxfordshire. Her results provisionally suggest that this population did not in fact come from outside, but had grown up locally.[33] If this does reflect the ethnic composition of the local population, we must assume that the Thames was indeed a link to the outside world of the North Sea basin. For their own reasons – which we *must* allow them to have – the population of the middle Thames Valley possessed Early Saxon objects, so presumably they admired the way things were done across the North Sea. Doubtless there were people in Saxony who were influenced by tastes in post-Roman Oxfordshire.

Although the evidence of stable isotope analysis seems to support my contention that Anglo-Saxon mass migrations into Britain never happened, I still think we should be careful in the way we use this new technique. Take the seemingly open-and-shut case of Berinsfield. It is quite possible that the entire population could have migrated there a generation or two previously; if that were the case, their children or grandchildren's teeth would have formed locally. I would prefer to use stable isotope analysis as just one approach to the problems associated with proving or disproving mass migrations, or 'folk movements', as they are sometimes less contentiously labelled. We must look at all the strands of evidence together. I am aware that I have chosen to set the literary accounts to one side, but I have done this to redress a historical imbalance.

My final case study is also in the heart of Anglo-Saxon eastern England. This time we are further south, within clear sight of Lincoln Cathedral, one of the greatest masterpieces of medieval architecture. I do not believe that the position of the cathedral, high above the low-lying Fen-edge valley of the River Witham, happened by accident. I think its roots lie a very long way back in time indeed – maybe back to the start of the Bronze Age, over four thousand years ago.

Here I must declare a personal interest. For some time I have been working on the edges of the Fens around Peterborough, and a few years ago I was invited to be Chairman of the Witham Valley Archaeological Research Committee (WVARC). Normally such committees are tedious in the extreme, and the Chairman's main job is to try to keep members from nodding off. They meet in dusty rooms to discuss accounts, deadlines, grants, management plans, corporate or committee struc-tures – anything, that is, apart from archaeology. But so far the WVARC has been different. Yes, we have sometimes discussed money, but as we don't yet have very much, we actually spend our time talking about the archaeology of the Witham Valley.[34]

That archaeology is multi-period, which I love, because it allows me to meet and cross intellectual swords with specialists and colleagues who work outside my own field of Bronze Age studies. It's remarkable what one can learn from people like Paul Everson and David Stocker, who really know what they are talking about when it comes to the Middle Ages, or from a specialist in peat growth or Fenland flooding, finds conservation or monastic communities.

The floodplain of the Witham Valley is remarkably flat and low-lying. Even the valley sides tend to be undulations, rather than hills as most people would recognise them; until, that is, one approaches Lincoln, where the landscape becomes altogether more emphatic. The Witham Valley is in fact a lowland river valley that has become choked with a succession of deep fenland deposits. It forms a peat-filled spur which branches off the main Fenland basin northwards for some twenty-five kilometres. At its northern end it branches into two rivers, Barlings Eau and the main River Witham. It joins the great expanse of the Fens south and east of its junction with the Rivers Slea and Bain.

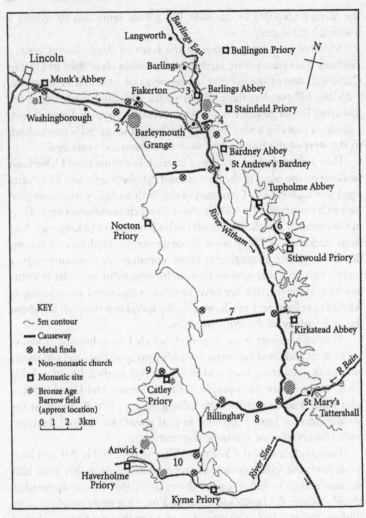

The River Witham Valley near Lincoln, showing the position of metalwork finds, the ten known causeways, Bronze Age barrow cemeteries, churches and monastic sites.

If one plots the distribution of important archaeological sites and finds in the valley, a remarkable pattern begins to emerge. We start with a series of Bronze Age barrow cemeteries which tend to be located away from the floodplain on slightly higher ground, often with a good prospect of the valley. They are regularly spaced, on both sides of the river, but with a gap at the centre which might well reflect a problem in 'archaeological visibility', rather than a real void or gap. The next thing to notice is the way the distribution of these cemeteries coincides with a series of ten causeways across the river. The dates when these causeways were constructed are still being established, but the one at Fiskerton (no. 2), arguably the best-known of them, was first built in the Early Iron Age, around 600 BC. There is no reason to think that the others are not of at least comparable antiquity.

There is something rather strange about these causeways, laying aside the fact that they seem in some way to be connected to ancient burial places. The Fiskerton causeway was built out of timber.[35] Like all wooden structures across a wetland it required regular repair, and tree-ring research shows that the people of Iron Age Fiskerton chose to do their structural repairs in years when there was a total lunar eclipse.[36] Even more exciting, it now seems that they were able to predict these events pretty reliably – which is extraordinary, as the calculations involved are by no means straightforward. What I'm saying here is that, like the barrow cemeteries, the causeways were more than mere functional landmarks. Yes, they helped people get across the floodplain, but they also served to divide the valley up into separate 'territories'. Not even that, though, is the full explanation of what may have been going on.

Whenever one finds a prehistoric site or feature that serves as a boundary of some sort, one usually discovers that people have made offerings there. In most cases those offerings reflect rank, status or the avoidance of conflict: they might include severed human or animal heads, shields, body armour and, most common of all, swords. Swords are symbols of rank and power, but they are also symbols of conflict, or alternatively conflict that has been avoided through some symbolic act. It all depends on the contexts of where they are found. The Witham causeways have revealed a large number of metalwork finds, including Iron Age swords and what is arguably the most famous archaeological find from the county of Lincolnshire, the Witham shield, now in the British Museum. My own site at Flag Fen near Peterborough has produced Bronze and Iron Age swords and shield fragments, but the finds from the Witham continue into Roman, Saxon, Viking and medieval times. The latest depositions are of complete swords that were placed in the water in the fourteenth century, or later.

We now come to the strangest aspect of this mysterious landscape. The final coincidence concerns the siting of what is probably the largest group of early (twelfth-century) monastic settlements anywhere in Britain. One might have expected them to have clustered around the edge of the Fens, as at Ely, Peterborough, Crowland, Thorny or Ramsey, further south in Cambridgeshire. Instead we find them extending up the Witham Valley, evenly spaced, and clearly respecting the distribution of the trackways and the metalwork finds grouped around them. So, viewed as a strictly archaeological exercise, the distribution of the Early Bronze Age barrow cemeteries played a part in determining the position of a series of Early Christian foundations. This is one of the reasons I think the great cathedral of Lincoln was placed where it was. Ultimately it is making the same statement as the church alongside the Rudston Monolith: it dominates the Witham Valley just as the parish church at Rudston towers above the Neolithic standing stone. Both are making reference back to earlier times and places.

There is another aspect to the story of the swords from the River Witham. The Arthurian legends make much of what are plainly very ancient themes such as Excalibur, the Sword in the Stone, and water itself (the Lady of the Lake). I am not saying that prehistoric religious beliefs survived intact, as an organised body of theological thought and ritual tradition. That would plainly be absurd. But something must have come through from pre-Roman times, otherwise it is hard to explain the fact that no less than 70 per cent of the known areas of ritual deposition in the Witham Valley survived into medieval times.[37] So rites involving the deposition of weapons in water are not just about making symbolic offerings of valuable objects. They also reflect the significance of the places where those offerings were made; that surely indicates more than a faint folk memory of some long-lost superstition. To me it suggests something altogether more potent, that was still important to influential people as late as the Middle Ages; these people were prepared to make substantial financial sacrifices to honour their beliefs, because many of the Witham offerings are fine items in their own right.

I cannot believe that the Witham was a unique late survival. Complete medieval, Roman, Iron and Bronze Age swords, daggers and other weapons have been dredged from many rivers in Britain, especially the Thames.[38] Sadly, the precise find spots are often unknown, and the shape of the countryside around the river has also been lost, so it would be impossible to attempt a Witham-style exercise in, say, London; nonetheless the balance of probability suggests that both ancient rites and patterns of land allotment were linked, and that in many places they survived into the Middle Ages.

We saw earlier how the story of the Holy Blood came to be associated with the Holy Grail. Richard Barber suggested that Sir Thomas Malory was aware of the cult of the Holy Blood, which attracted pilgrims to Hailes Abbey, near the village where he probably lived. Surely it is not unreasonable to suggest that many of the ancient themes that we find in the Arthurian tales could have been current for much longer than was once believed, and that they found their way into the literature in ways that recall Malory's adoption of the legend of the Holy Blood, which was already an old cult when he encountered it. Malory, Geoffrey of Monmouth and other contributors to the Arthurian tale were seeking to flavour their stories with an air of antiquity, so it would have made good sense to seek out customs that were known, or believed, to have had ancient roots. This must explain why authors as skilled as Geoffrey of Monmouth wove an elaborate myth around Caliburn, the sword which Arthur wore, and which was forged on the Isle of Avalon. It was a magical symbol of power, and not just in this world. Without realising it, they were telling us a great deal about the persistence of beliefs in their own time, and about rituals from the remote past too.

CHAPTER NINE

Continuity and Change

I SUSPECT THAT the most enduring legacy of Rome to Britain will not prove to be writing, Latin or even towns. It is something far less tangible, not unconnected with those famous straight roads. For various reasons, not the least being the need to collect taxes and for her armies to function effectively, Rome vastly improved communication throughout her Empire. This encouraged the spread of new ideas, including Christianity, first as a faith and then as a pan-national institutional Church. It was Christianity, as much as any other factor, that transformed the early medieval world, and made post-Roman Britain so different from what had gone before.

In Chapter 3 I wrote about the *longue durée*, or the persistence of certain ideas and practices over great periods of time. In the following chapters I also discussed how there were two Roman Britains, one to the south and east that was far more fully Romanised than the other to the north and west. I am not a great believer in archaeological distribution maps, which are often used by followers of the 'culture-historical' school to prove dubious points which cannot be supported in any other way. My principal objection to them is that often they wrench sites and other information out of their actual contexts. I feel that we should not treat our precious data in this way – somehow it seems disrespectful of antiquity. With these caveats in mind, I shall use two maps here. Neither is very specific, but they make a general point.

The distribution of Roman villas and other substantial buildings, which it may be recalled Andrew Sargent took to indicate the extent of the more fully Romanised part of Britain, coincides very closely with that of so-called 'Anglo-Saxon' cemeteries. What this tells me is that the Romanised British population was more ready to accept the new fashions, social and political ideas of post-Roman Britain than were the people to the north and west. It's not a question of invasion and takeover, but of attitude to life. On the side of the island where people had changed *less* during the Roman period, they resisted change *more* in post-Roman times. That seems to me to be both straightforward and self-explanatory.

I do not suppose we will ever know precisely why communities in eastern England decided to lean towards the Continent as strongly as they did, following the end of the Roman Empire. I suspect it was as much the continuation of a process that had been underway for some time as anything else. It is now quite widely accepted that supposedly 'Saxon' phenomena such as pottery, brooches and sunken feature buildings appeared on late-fourth-century Romano-British sites in eastern England. The *foederati* explanation has always been absurd; instead, I think we might be looking here at the start of a shift in political orientation towards the Continental mainland. I shall return to this theme shortly.

Modern archaeology owes an increasing debt to science. We saw in Chapter 8 how stable isotope analysis has thrown important new light on where supposed 'Anglian' and 'Saxon' people at West Heslerton in Yorkshire and Berinsfield in Oxfordshire actually came from. I was not surprised that neither site produced good evidence for actual (i.e. ethnic) Anglo-Saxons, but I was surprised at how mobile the West Heslerton population appears to have been. It was unexpected to find that almost half the sample analysed came from west of the Pennines.

I recently heard on Radio 4 that a team from London University had proved that modern populations in towns west of Offa's Dyke were genetically different from people in towns to the east. The report went on to say that the indigenous Celts were pushed west by a mass migration of Anglo-Saxons coming from the east. As a result, so we were told, the wholesale replacement of the British population by 'Anglo-Saxons' was proven.[1] When I read the paper that had caused all the fuss, I was immediately struck by two things: first, the certainty of its conclusions, which were even headlined in the title: 'Y Chromosome Evidence for Anglo-Saxon Mass Migration'.[2] The second was that the long list of references did not include a single excavation or survey

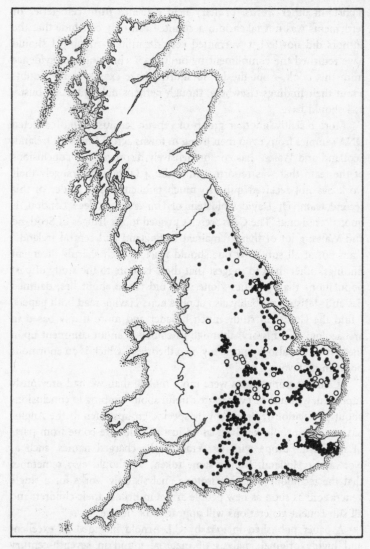

The distribution of Roman villas and their 'substantial buildings' (left), and 'Anglo-Saxon' cemeteries (filled circles, cremations; open circles, inhumations).

report. In other words, primary field evidence from cemeteries or settlements was not taken into account. I can only conclude that the authors did not feel it warranted consideration. I suppose I should have returned the compliment by omitting Y chromosomal evidence from this book – but life is too short. I have expressed my doubts about their findings elsewhere, though perhaps not quite as robustly as I should have.[3]

More recently, another group of genetic scientists, who collected DNA samples from 1,700 men living in towns across England, Ireland, Scotland and Wales,[4] has comprehensively disproved the conclusions of the team that was reported on Radio 4 (although strangely their work has not received quite so much publicity). The leader of this second team, Dr David Goldstein of University College London, is quoted as saying: 'The Celts weren't pushed to the fringes of Scotland and Wales; a lot of them remained in England and central Ireland.'[5] I am not at all sure how one should react to such sharply divergent findings, other than to suggest that there is more to the study of past populations than genetics alone. The old cliché about lies, damned lies and statistics probably also applies here. Having read both papers, I find the Goldstein study much broader and more firmly based in archaeology and history, although of course I cannot comment upon the genetics. It also supports my own theories – which is an enormous point in its favour.

If ancient populations were more mobile than we had previously supposed, we must be even more careful about jumping to conclusions about population replacement by specific groups, such as the Anglo-Saxons. The people involved could just as well have come from parts of northern Europe with less emotionally charged names, such as Norway or Holland. By the same token, we should also remember that the technique of stable isotope analysis only works for a single generation: as soon as new people arrive in Britain their children and all subsequent generations will appear to be 'native'.

A paper published in 1982 by C.J. Arnold included an excellent and highly original analysis of material found in seventh-century 'Anglo-Saxon' graves, of which Sutton Hoo is far and away the grandest.[6] It attributed the development of a hierarchical society to stress, caused initially by attack from abroad and latterly by internal strife in Britain. My reading of the evidence presented by the author is that the development of what one might term a 'warrior aristocracy' in the seventh century was not a response to stress at all – quite the contrary. Similar graves are found in the Earlier Bronze Age across most of southern Britain, but particularly in Wessex. In both cases – Saxon and Bronze Age – the social changes reflected by new burial rites involved military items such as swords and daggers; I would suggest that these were symbols of social status as much as weapons. I do not suppose for one moment that life in prehistoric times, or indeed the seventh century, was calm and peaceful; but it would seem that aggression, by and large, was *managed*. Societies could not afford to lose harvests or have their flocks dispersed by large-scale warfare. So raiding would have predominated over actual pitched battle – which is not to say that these raids would not have involved death and injury to dozens of people. Much of the fighting, too, would have been to do with social status within, rather than outside, a particular group.

So if the Bronze Age example is anything to go by, I would attribute the development of a more class-based society in the seventh century to growing *stability* rather than to stress. In the earlier second millennium BC there is evidence that communities were becoming less mobile, and that the landscape of Britain was beginning to 'set': territories were defined, and regional ceremonial centres, such as Stonehenge, were becoming established. This is precisely the time when we see the emergence of the so-called 'warrior aristocracy'.[7] The Bronze Age barrows were often grouped in cemeteries, as at Sutton Hoo, and it appears likely that each was controlled by a particular clan or lineage, which in turn may have been linked to particular holdings of land. This seems to parallel what was happening at the start of the West Heslerton Anglian village and cemetery.

The symbolism behind the building of a large burial mound or barrow is to do with altering the earth and placing a human spirit physically within the natural landscape, of which he or she then becomes a part. Being at one with the landscape, but residing in the realms of the ancestors, the being or beings within the barrow were believed to oversee, or maintain some influence or control, in the way that the landscape operated. It was not a passive or a submissive act to Divine Grace, in the way a Christian burial might be perceived.

Among other things, barrow burial is about territoriality and control of the landscape.[8]

Societies do not 'become' hierarchical for no good reason; there was a purpose behind the process, which may well have been connected with the control and management of resources, including land. Social stratification would therefore have been allied to changes in the way the landscape was operated, and perhaps even partitioned, which may help provide a general explanation for why landscapes at places like West Heslerton are substantially modified at the end of the Early Saxon period.

To return briefly to the centuries before the Early Bronze Age, around 2300 BC, this era was not marked by conflict and turmoil. Instead there is evidence that the farming societies of the preceding period, the Later Neolithic, were merely more mobile and more dispersed than those of the Earlier Bronze Age. So the building of the great Bronze Age monuments and the erection of so many barrows was in effect a symbol that the British landscape was beginning to be permanently parcelled up. Ultimately the process had to do with ownership and control. I suggest that something similar may have applied in the fifth to later sixth centuries in eastern Britain. Even before the collapse of the Roman monetary economy we find a shift away from towns, with perhaps greater reliance on livestock and local production.

In post-Roman times the provincial economy becomes a series of smaller economies with a far greater degree of self-reliance. During the fifth and sixth centuries these economies had coalesced into larger groupings that then emerged as the Anglo-Saxon kingdoms of people like King Raedwald of Essex. By then, societies in England had reached a degree of sophistication that gave sufficient long-term stability for jewellers and craftsmen to develop and practise their skills to a pitch that was without rival anywhere in Europe, outside Byzantium. Again, I cannot imagine that such skill 'popped up' as it were overnight, in the first two or so decades of the seventh century. We must be looking here at a tradition of craftsmanship that was handed on, probably from father to son, over several generations. None of this, it seems to me, could have happened in times of stress, instability and social meltdown.

To sum up, the situation we find in eastern England in the seventh century, with magnificent burials like Sutton Hoo, could not have come about if the preceding two centuries had been riven by strife. We know from prehistory that social change does not happen rapidly; the fifty-year phases proposed by Myres are manifestly absurd, but they are necessary if one accepts the 'cultural-historical' model of social change imposed through immigration. C.J. Arnold himself acknowledges that the social stress he uses to explain the changes he observed in seventh-century funerary rites may be more apparent than real: 'Aggression, recorded by chronicles and, *less directly, in the archaeological record*, was directed towards the most developed groups' [my italics].[9] Once again we find that the circular argument has returned: it seems to be the chronicles, rather than the archaeological evidence from the ground, that dictate the way in which we interpret 'Dark Age' processes of change.

I cannot leave this long-term view of the 'Anglo-Saxons' without returning to the subject of barrows. We saw in Chapter 6 that Sam Lucy pointed out that cremation was not a rite that had been introduced afresh, as it were, from across the North Sea. The same can be said of barrows. The 'Golden Age' of barrow burial was in the Neolithic and earlier Bronze Age, from around 3500 to 1500 BC. But the tradition persisted, especially along the eastern side of Britain. Hundreds, maybe thousands of Iron Age barrows are known from the so-called 'Arras Culture' of East Yorkshire (about which more presently), and recent aerial photography has revealed a liberal scattering extending south, through Lincolnshire and the East Midlands down into Cambridgeshire. I dug a couple at Maxey, where about ten are known to have existed.

At the very end of the Iron Age we know of a series of extremely rich burials, sometimes but not always beneath barrows, which extends from Snailwell in Cambridgeshire, via Welwyn in Hertfordshire, to Aylesford in Kent. As Barry Cunliffe points out, these burials drew upon a number of themes which could be combined in a variety of ways. Most included food and imported wine (in amphorae); cups and plates were provided for their consumption in the afterlife. Weaponry is notably absent, as if these Late Iron Age chieftains were making a deliberate statement to the effect that their status did not depend on

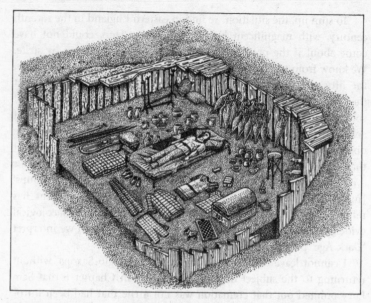

An artist's impression of the Late Iron Age (15–10 BC) 'royal' burial beneath the Lexden Tumulus, near Colchester, Essex. Many of the items within the chamber reflect the taste for exotic items such as wine, which was imported from the Mediterranean region, in the amphorae seen leaning against the wall beyond the king's head.

military prowess alone, and that they shared Roman values of civilisation. Whether they were as civilised in this respect as their grave furnishings would have us believe is of course another question entirely.

What is particularly interesting is what these rich, extremely high-status burials can tell us about contemporary attitudes to life. There are many echoes of Sutton Hoo, especially at the finest site of them all, a cremation burial beneath a large barrow on the outskirts of Colchester. The so-called Lexden Tumulus was excavated in the 1920s, and has never been fully written up.[10] A recent reassessment considers that the burial dates to 15–10 BC.[11] The burial was within a plank-built wooden chamber below a barrow mound of thirty metres diameter. Although the body was not found it was accompanied by a vast array

An artist's impression of the plank-built burial chamber below a barrow mound at Prittlewell, near Southend, Essex. The items in the chamber were still in place when they were excavated. The burial, which is pagan but contains Christian iconography, is of royal status and is closely comparable with Sutton Hoo and Lexden. Mid-seventh century AD.

of bronze objects and a suit of iron chain-mail with bronze and silver fittings that had been cut up and spread around the grave pit. There was a sheet of gold cloth and numerous other items in gold and silver. A folding stool and eighteen Italian wine amphorae were also found. The exotic items at Lexden suggest that the king – for surely this is what he must have been – looked beyond his immediate surroundings in his ostentatious display of wealth, but the deliberate destruction of his chain-mail recalls religious beliefs whose roots, as we saw at Flag Fen, were even older than the Iron Age.

Some of the finds from Sutton Hoo were already old when they were placed in the ground. The Lexden Tumulus most remarkably included a type of Middle Bronze Age axe known as a palstave, dating to around the thirteenth or fourteenth centuries BC.[12] This axe was well worn, in a way which does not suggest that it had been actually used as an axe, but rather as an ancient object of veneration. Its inclusion within the burial was clearly a deliberate act, and not the result of the grave disturbing an earlier archaeological feature. Surely the presence of this ancient object within a royal grave must indicate that people were aware of their history, and thought it important. Both the royal burials at Sutton Hoo and Lexden show an interest in the past that may be connected with rites surrounding the veneration of ancestors. Again, we might be seeing the continuance of a much earlier tradition at both sites.

An even more striking parallel with Lexden has recently been discovered twenty-five miles away, on the outskirts of Southend at Prittlewell.[13] This appears to be another seventh-century royal burial, perhaps two or three decades later than Sutton Hoo. In form the burial is pagan, because the body (which did not survive) was surrounded by a wealth of grave-goods, but it had been 'Christianised' by the addition of two gold foil crosses. What makes this discovery remarkable is that, like Lexden, it was a chamber grave. The chamber was square, measured about four by four metres, and was plank-built. Also like Lexden, it was sealed beneath a sandy barrow mound. The items buried with the king were all *in situ*. The inventory sounds strangely familiar, and shows yet again how wide the contacts were with other élites elsewhere in Europe. It includes glass bowls from Asia Minor, a folding throne (the Lexden example, also of probable Italian design, which is closely similar, was described as a folding 'stool'), decorated hanging bowls from Ireland, a solid gold belt buckle, gold coins from France, a sword and shield, a Byzantine flagon, folded textiles, a lyre and much more besides.

It would be foolish to suggest that Sutton Hoo and Prittlewell of the seventh century AD formed part of precisely the same religious tradition as Lexden of the early first century BC, but the persistence of many specific and general themes (for example, chamber burial within a barrow, carefully arranged containers for exotic drink, clothing/weapons and armour and thrones/stools) and the fact that the three sites occur so close together is remarkable. Doubtless diehard Anglo-Saxonists will write these things off as 'coincidence'. But it is not as if the tradition of barrow burial died out in Roman times in eastern England. I well recall, for example, passing by the Six Hills, six Romano-British barrows that were neatly arranged along the side of the Great North Road, on my way to school in Stevenage, Hertfordshire.[14] Sutton Hoo can thus be seen to form part of a long-lived local tradition. Of course it undoubtedly incorporates a wealth of new ideas gleaned from around the North Sea basin and Scandinavia in the fifth and sixth centuries, but the central concept, of rich kingly burial beneath a barrow, does not have to have been an idea introduced from outside. Such practices must have had resonances for people living in the area, who would have understood the complex symbolism underlying them.

At various points in this book I have made reference to the debunking of hypothetical 'invasions' or 'migrations' that were supposed to have happened in Britain before the Romans. I deliberately avoided discussing one particular example, because I wanted to leave the best until last. I have already covered this case study elsewhere, so I shall summarise the main points.[15]

The Yorkshire Wolds in the area around the small market town of Driffield have produced some of the most remarkable archaeological finds in Britain. In great measure this was due to an extraordinary Victorian antiquary/archaeologist named J.R. Mortimer, who was remarkable for the promptness and thoroughness with which he wrote up his excavations. His greatest contribution is undoubtedly his *Forty Years Researches in British and Saxon Burial Mounds of East Yorkshire* (1905).[16] His 'British' barrows are generally Bronze Age, but what is most striking is the fact that the Saxon and the British barrows very often occurred in the same places. It was as if the later sites had been deliberately positioned in the landscape, perhaps as a sort of homage to what had gone before. I need hardly add that this is not what one would expect of a recently arrived group of settlers.

Mortimer's barrows generally occurred on the higher land of the Wolds, but the burial grounds of the intervening Iron Age were often found down in the valleys. The Bronze Age barrows were round, but those of the so-called 'Arras Culture' of the Iron Age were square and surrounded by a ditch. Each barrow covered a central grave, often of a warrior with a sheathed sword, who is sometimes accompanied by a vehicle, known variously as a cart, wagon or chariot. Either way it was a light carriage, resembling perhaps a gig or pony trap. The Arras Culture came into being in the fourth, and lasted into the first century BC. Closely similar barrows to those of the Arras Culture are known from northern France, in the broad Marne Valley of the Champagne district – the presumed origin of the 'invasion'.[17] Some confusion has been caused by the fact that the 'culture' was in fact named after a small town in the East Riding of Yorkshire, and not after the better-known town and Great War battle site on the Somme.

Most archaeologists of the mid-twentieth century belonged to the 'culture-historical' school, in which, as we saw in Chapter 6, it was usual to ascribe change to invasion or migration. Most of these invasions were discounted in the 1960s and seventies, but the 'Arras Culture' hung on for longer because it did seem, even on close inspection, to be well-founded. Square barrows had not been found in Britain before their appearance in East Yorkshire, and chariot burials and the presence of distinctive 'anthropoid' swords* and joints of meat in the grave were also new. With these innovations went a new style of angular pottery, which was also found elsewhere in Britain. The pottery and the barrows had obvious parallels with a well-known group of square-ditched chariot burials in the Marne Valley. Up until the 1960s, nobody doubted that the Arras Culture of East Yorkshire came to Britain from overseas.

The book that was for many years to be the standard prehistory of Yorkshire was published in 1933. Its principal author, Frank Elgee, was an avid walker, and he personally visited and recorded most of the sites he writes about. This gave his work a credibility and personal touch that I find most appealing. Nevertheless, he was a man of his time, and by Chapter 8, when he starts to discuss the 'Arras Culture', he was on invasion number five, 'Gaulish charioteers' who 'overran East Yorkshire'. Incidentally, the people who were supposed to have invaded the Wolds belonged to the La Tène Culture; he was

---

* So called after their hilts, which were fashioned to resemble a man.

writing before the advent of radiocarbon dating, so his dates are a little recent:

> La Tène culture was undoubtedly introduced into Yorkshire by Gaulish invaders during the third century BC. Its characteristic chariot burials have their closest parallels in Champagne, the Marne region, and especially in the Seine Valley at Nanterre near Paris. The anthropoid swords are identical with French examples, the knobbed bronze armlets similar to those from Samsois, Marne.[18]

This could be Myres writing about Saxon cremation urns. Elgee and he share the judicious use of closely observed parallels to make points about population movement.

Dr Ian Stead, who excavated 250 Arras barrows between 1967 and 1978, is now firmly of the opinion that they do not represent an invasion or movement of people, because only the square barrows and carriage burials have clear parallels on the Continent.[19] Other essential aspects of Arras funerary rites, such as crouched burials and the grave-goods buried with them, are British. Similarly, local settlements of the period have recently been excavated, and these are typically British. No British prehistorian would today accept that the 'Arras Culture' originated in invasion. What they would say is that the Arras graves of Yorkshire, and the widespread introduction of angular styles of pottery, provide clear evidence that eastern Britain was in ever closer contact with communities not just in north-western France, but further afield around the North Sea basin and over Europe generally. It was an early stage of a process of communication between Britain and the Continental mainland that would continue without major interruptions until post-Roman times, and later.

I see communication between Britain and the Continent as an unstoppable process, because it depended on hundreds of thousands of individual contacts over huge periods of time. Gildas lacks all credibility to me when he suggests that cross-sea contact was a rare event: three boatfuls of Saxon warriors arrive on the coast and life in Britain, it would appear, is changed forever. He must be writing metaphorically: even in the Iron Age, the arrival of three boatloads of people from over the Channel would have caused no excitement at all. It would have been entirely routine.

It would not be particularly useful to debunk the various archaeological phenomena that have been linked to invading Anglo-Saxons. The distinctive sunken feature buildings, for example, are found at Mucking and West Heslerton (to mention just two of many sites) in Late Roman contexts, at a time when Anglo-Saxon invasions are not yet supposed to have begun. The 'culture-historical' response to this is to invent *foederati*, but what on earth mercenaries were doing at out-of-the-way places like Mucking is anyone's guess. Ultimately it boils down to a question of belief. Either you believe that England was founded by people from abroad, or you don't. To me the notion of Anglo-Saxon invasions is an archaeologically absurd idea. It also patronises the indigenous people, because it assumes that the post-Roman inhabitants of Britain would not have been capable of 'inventing' England themselves. Of course they did not do this either consciously or unaided, because they were in regular contact with a host of communities abroad. But they did it nonetheless.

Like J.R. Mortimer, I have spent rather too many decades researching the archaeology of eastern England, and I have observed the remarkable resourcefulness of the people whose remains and settlements I have excavated. I am in no doubt whatsoever that they were in regular touch with their friends and relatives overseas from at least 1600 BC – the date of the Bronze Age plank-built wooden boat, now in Dover Museum, which we know from an exhaustive series of tests and calculations would have been perfectly capable of crossing the Channel. Those contacts continued and intensified in the Iron Age. In the Roman period south-eastern Britain played a major part in feeding the Roman field army across the Channel. I cannot understand why archaeologists and historians have been so persistent in their belief that maritime traffic around the south-east of Britain was in one direction only: pirates, raiders and settlers entering Britain. Apart from ignoring the two-way maritime traffic of the previous two millennia, it is a view that defies both reason and common sense.

Conclusion

So Where Does that Leave Us?

THIS HAS BEEN a book about evolving identities, origin myths and the use or abuse of history and archaeology. The past continues to live in the way that we study, reconstruct and interpret it. We should treat it as a subject which has a life of its own. We should also recognise that part of its life exists within ourselves. If we take the trouble to think, write or talk about the past, then we become a component of history ourselves. History is personal, not absolute, and there is no such thing as absolute historical truth.

That is why I find the 'Dark Ages' so fascinating. For a start, there are huge problems in reconciling the historical account with the actual evidence provided by archaeological fieldwork. One has to favour one or the other, and I have chosen archaeology, not just because it is my own subject, but because it is still producing a wealth of completely unexpected new discoveries – and not only in wild, remote places, but in unexpectedly familiar locations, such as the outskirts of Southend.

I see little point in 'rubbishing' the Arthurian legends. It may be impossible ever to be certain whether there actually was a fifth-century British hero named Arthur. He may have existed, or he may not. That is all we can say with any certainty. Rather than endlessly pondering that not very enlightening question, would it not be better to view the myths of Arthur, and indeed the 'Anglo-Saxons', as interesting phenomena in their own right? That is what I have attempted to do. If I cannot reveal Arthur, I can at least try to show where and how he might have existed. I also think it is useful to examine how his story has been handled over the centuries and what its actual origins might have been – be they never so far back in time.

Arthurian legends are a reflection of over a thousand years of history and prehistory. We still do not fully understand how the earlier, prehistoric, elements came to be incorporated in the later tales, but it does seem clear from work in the Witham Valley and elsewhere that ancient traditions persisted for some three millennia within the landscape, if not in literature. As the landscape is in turn a reflection of the way people lived and organised their lives, we must assume that the ideas behind it were still common currency. Their incorporation within legends and stories that were written deliberately to invoke an earlier, perhaps more glorious, time is therefore entirely explicable.

If, as we saw in Chapter 2, the creation of Arthur may have owed more than a little to the legitimising of a Welsh élite in the face of an outside threat, then it is possible to see both Arthur and the Anglo-Saxons as symbols to do with identity. My own feeling is that both have outlived their usefulness as symbols of this sort; they have acquired much 'baggage' which we could well do without, whether it be the New Age Celtic twilight that surrounds Arthur, or the continuing belief (in certain quarters) in the superiority of Anglo-Saxon racial characteristics. Neither, to my mind, is particularly useful, truthful, or edifying. So where does that leave the question of identity? Let us first think about identity at the local level.

Local identities can be as hard to pin down as smoke. A day or two ago I was talking to a retired farmworker in the village shop. We were discussing ways of trapping eels in drainage dykes, as he had lent me his set of hooped nets, which I plan to employ (illegally) soon. I mentioned that in the peat country a few miles to the east long barbed spears, known as eel gleaves, had traditionally been used. 'Hmm,' he said, completely unimpressed. 'There's no knowing what them Black Fen boys will be up to next. They're a rum ol' bunch.' So far as he was concerned, they could have come from the moon, not Whittlesey.

Beneath the veneer of local culture lie more profound differences. As men of the Fens, my friend in the village shop and the rum old boys around Whittlesey would traditionally have been strongly nonconformist, maybe belonging to a Primitive Methodist Chapel.[1] I remember being reminded by an old man near Huntingdon (Oliver Cromwell's birthplace) that 'the Fens were for Parliament', something he was plainly proud of. Yet England as a nation is supposed to be a monarchy with an established Church – both of which I suspect my

Fen characters would have pushed out into the North Sea long ago, given half a chance.

If you spoke to the sons and daughters of Fen people today, you would be astonished by the changes that have taken place in just one generation. The strong religious nonconformity has largely gone, and Primitive Methodist Chapels are everywhere falling down and overgrown. Very few people catch eels, or even know the difference between the silt Fens, where they live, and the peat or Black Fens further east. The old Fen dialects have almost vanished, and people even dress in wholly different ways: tweeds have disappeared, and jeans are worn by all but the elderly. The traditional culture, dialect and religion of the 'Fen tiger', as men of the Fens were known in the nineteenth and early twentieth centuries, has almost entirely vanished – within at most two generations.

When we consider concepts like identity, locale or sense of place we are departing a long way from the hard and fast, supposedly definable cultural realities of archaeology or history, and in the process we may be undermining them, which is no bad thing. Identity, like history and archaeology, is a personal business. It is also something that changes through time – and space. I had not grasped the significance of this until recently when, reading a poem, it struck me that if Anglo-Saxons had actually settled down in Britain, they would have regarded not just the Britons, but themselves, differently. This change of identity would have been even more radical if they had arrived as settlers rather than as an élite warrior aristocracy, for which, as we have seen, there is no good evidence in the fifth century. We do not know how a new, insular identity would have manifested itself in the archaeological record, but to look for simplistic correlations across the North Sea is almost certainly a naive mistake.

Freddie Kramer was our first local volunteer when we opened Flag Fen to the public in 1987. He and his wife Lotte had come to England from Germany just before the outbreak of war, as Jewish refugee children of the *Kindertransport*.[2] Many of the relatives they left behind were murdered by the Nazis. It was Lotte who wrote the poem that set me thinking how identities can change not just with time, but through space.

Seesaw*

At school,
On the other side of the Channel,
I was taught
Oliver Cromwell was a hero,
A man of vision.

In England,
Living with an upper-crust family,
Democracy
In peril during the Second World War,
He was a villain.

But now,
In his native countryside
Near the Great Ouse,
The smashed cathedral glass
Receives the white light

Of the fens.
There is a sense of independence
In that black earth
Sponsoring his army of footsteps
All the way to the gallows.

Identity and culture are essentially unstable, and the attachment of a label is therefore bound to be misleading. Not only that, but labels tend to take pride of place, so that one becomes, say, English or Christian, at the expense of being what one *wants* to be. It's an imposition that I find annoying in my daily life, which is why I try to avoid attaching labels in my archaeological work. I find the 'Anglo-Saxon' label particularly irritating, because it has been used too often as an excuse to avoid thinking about some of the serious issues that archaeology ought to be addressing.

Archaeologists of the 'culture-historical' school regard such things

* From Lotte Kramer, *Earthquake and Other Poems* (Rockingham Press, 1994).

as culture, religion and language as being fundamental to the identity of the groups they study. Being perceived as indicators of identity, they are traditionally viewed as unchanging. Language and religion, for example, were believed to remain fundamentally the same. If one or both of them changed, it was likely that a new group of people had taken over. But the real world is not as simple as that. In parts of Britain, such as southern Ireland or Cornwall, for example, the 'native' British languages were replaced by English in a very short time, mainly during the eighteenth and nineteenth centuries, while in northern Wales most Welsh-speakers are actually bilingual in Welsh and English. In these instances the people remained the same, but the language changed. Religion too can change with great rapidity, as Henry VIII so clearly showed.

The adoption of Anglo-Saxon, or Early English, in south-eastern Britain was a very complete process. Few pre-English place names survive, and this has been taken as clear evidence for wholesale population change. But it is just one aspect of the profound social changes that were taking place in the fifth and sixth centuries, and it should not be taken in isolation. I am also unsure as to why language change should have to involve the exchange of people, rather than ideas. Besides, if we take a proven mass migration, such as that to North America by Europeans, it is remarkable how many significant places retain versions of their original names: Manhattan and Toronto, to name just two.

We can see this even more clearly if we look at South America, where well-established civilisations were brought crashing to the ground by a small number of European incomers. As a result, the religion of South America is Roman Catholicism, and the languages are Spanish and Portuguese. In the mighty Inca Empire of Peru, the whole system depended and focused upon the personality of the Emperor, who was regarded as having absolute temporal and spiritual authority. The incoming *conquistadores* knew nothing of this. To them he was just another human being: 'While the Emperor was venerated as a divine monarch this was no weakness, but when a handful of invaders, who cared for none of these things, struck at Atahuallpa, the head and heart of the Empire, they brought it to the dust.'[3]

In England the roots of Early English lay in Anglo-Saxon, which was probably taken up as the dominant language in south and eastern Britain in the fifth and sixth centuries. The change of language was accompanied by changes in dress and religion. It was all part of the process of 'acculturation' that was taking place around the North Sea basin at the time. The British were being influenced, but they were also influencing others themselves. Everyone involved in the process used the exchange of new ideas in their own way, to form identities that would gradually evolve into the embryonic nation states of the full medieval world.

Dr Catherine Hills of Cambridge University, who spent many years excavating the large Anglo-Saxon cemetery at Spong Hill in Norfolk, has pointed out that 'people can change their names, language, currency and political allegiances without the majority of the population being replaced'. She has in mind, of course, the hypothetical mass migration of Anglo-Saxon settlers into eastern England. She then asks two core questions: 'Did the English arrive as an intrusive band of invaders and migrants, planting themselves in eastern Britain and replacing earlier populations? Or was it a change in political allegiance that changed Britons into Anglo-Saxons?'[4] She opts for the second alternative.

I noted at the conclusion of Britain BC that the British have long seemed to respect the freedom of the individual. I still stand by that. I also believe that the British are by and large an inclusive nation. They generally accept incomers, albeit after initial resistance. This does not apply to the teeming cities alone: the Fens, for example, were home to large communities of French Huguenots in the seventeenth and eighteenth centuries. Maybe the British feel sufficiently secure in their islands not to worry about being 'swamped', as the Home Secretary recently put it. Possibly, but I think there is more to it than that.

In the post-Roman period the British Isles remained well populated, and their cultures were diverse. British or Celtic languages were spoken in the west and south-west, possibly Pictish in Scotland, Anglo-Saxon in the east, while Latin was still spoken in the Church and by élite classes in the south-west. This mix of tongues, with Anglo-Saxon at its core, gave rise to Early English.[5] The intermingling of different tongues shows that whatever their cultural differences, the various communities of Britain were in communication with one another. It is a tradition of cultural give-and-take which has left its mark on the language.

The English language is one of the glories of world culture. Unlike French, which tries unsuccessfully to exclude 'Franglais' in the interest of linguistic purity, dictionaries of the English language often include an addenda which defines new and slang words, many of which may be taken from other tongues. These new words may or may not appear in the main body of the text in subsequent editions. The English language thrives because it positively encourages the creation of new words and concepts; it succinctly and colourfully expresses what people all over the world think and believe. When it comes to defining some form of national identity that most people could subscribe to, one could do a lot worse than borrow the creative plagiarism of the English language.

Where does that leave us? To begin with, I believe we should discard the simplistic idea that invasions or mass migrations were the cause of the major changes that we see in the archaeological and historical record of the so-called 'Dark Ages'. The 'Anglo-Saxons' and their invasions have become an essential part of England's origin myth. What is worse, certainly for me as an archaeologist, is that they have also affected – no, *infected* – archaeology as well. Those much-vaunted invasions provide a false explanation for a complex of changes, each of one which deserves explanation in its own right. But they are all bundled together: language, pottery, new house forms, burial rites, etc., etc., holus-bolus, under the umbrella of mass migration.

By invoking a catch-all explanation such as 'invasion' one avoids having to think about the cause and the precise nature of the changes that took place. I believe that the all-pervading presence of the Anglo-Saxon invasions has led us to misappreciate not just the Dark Ages but Late Roman Britain too. They have stopped us thinking about the extent of actual mobility in the fifth and sixth centuries, and have set historians and archaeologists the impossible task of explaining how phenomena such as Sutton Hoo could have arisen in just two or three generations from a 'Dark Age' background, which in social terms at least must still have been as liquid as soup.

The Anglo-Saxon 'invasions' have also coloured the way we have viewed the entire period. They sit happily within the murk of a 'Dark

Age', and they encourage a view of the past as a dark, sinister place which seems to owe more to Edgar Allan Poe than to rational thought. Further, by flying in the face of what we know about the way human societies have inhabited their landscapes over the past six or seven millennia, the concept of a Dark Age Migration Period – where special rules are believed to apply – has prevented us from placing the post-Roman world into its longer-term contexts. Surely we should be thinking about Saxon England as something that possesses close links not just with Roman Britain, but with the prehistoric world as well. Instead, we take the history of England back to the start of the seventh century, at which point we stop. Everything before that is irrelevant. I wonder what the nameless king beneath the Lexden Tumulus would have thought of that.

Arthur and the Dark Ages seem made for each other. They are a Hollywood dream: pump smoke into the pre-gunpowder battle scenes and watch while the fantasy unfolds. This is what happens if one makes the mistake of confusing metaphor with history, which is not something our medieval ancestors would have done. They may have lacked our sense of historicity, and they seem to have accepted some strange origin myths, such as the Brutus stories, but I wonder to what extent they believed that these stories were the truth, the whole truth and nothing but the truth. They lived in a world where myth and legend were woven into history and where history, religion and politics were inextricably combined. Their understanding of the Arthurian legends was probably far more sophisticated in its use and appreciation of metaphor than anything we would be capable of, given our post-Renaissance, post-Enlightenment, analytical patterns of thought. I think this is apparent in the proliferation of modern Arthurian literature, where meaningless detail is relentlessly and mindlessly pursued. Meanwhile the point of the entire exercise is missed.

The Arthurian myths are a repository of clues, rather than sign-posts towards significant historical events – and they should be read as such. Over the years they have acquired their shape mainly through individual acts of literary creation by men like Geoffrey of Monmouth, Chrétien de Troyes and the elusive Thomas Malory; but these authors were themselves influenced by the stories and legends that were current in their time. They were also seeking themes that would add an air of mystical antiquity to their writing. This may help to explain why the Arthur cycle includes such a diverse mix of ancient concepts: there may be echoes of the Bronze and Iron Ages in the deposition of Excalibur in the Lake and the presence of Avalon on its Isle, not to mention the mysterious business of the sword in the stone. There are possible memories too of the 'Golden Age' of Roman Britain in the Holy Grail, and of course there is what was then current medieval mythology in the Round Table and the chivalry of its knights. There are also lessons to be learned from the way in which the Arthurian tales slipped from fashion as political documents at the start of the post-medieval period.

But there is a danger in all of this. Whether or not one accepts Arthur – or Alfred, his Anglo-Saxon surrogate – as a real figure, one is looking at someone whose deeds are largely products of more recent times. If we really want to understand what happened in Britain after the Roman period – and it is a fascinating time – we must set these largely mythological figures to one side, because they have little, of themselves, to teach us today. Further, by concentrating our attention on the battles fought between Briton and Saxon we are in danger of missing the central point: that these were more probably battles between two sets of Britons, one of which had adapted Continental customs and political systems for its own ends. If we think about the Dark Ages in these less black-and-white terms, we might arrive at a better understanding of what it was that motivated the conflict – and to what extent the battles themselves have been exaggerated in the interests of subsequent political necessity.

I am in no doubt that archaeology is the only means by which the Dark Ages can become fully illuminated. There is a huge amount of exciting new work taking place, and the more we discover, the more it becomes apparent that the fifth and sixth centuries were never truly Dark. There was no population collapse, the countryside never reverted to woodland, field systems continued in use, towns quite rapidly appeared and then stayed for good. Yes, there were major social and political changes, and yes, we can see the effects of real raiding in the Viking depredations of the mid-ninth century, that were followed by the collapse of long-distance trade. But where is the evidence for such happenings in the 'Dark Ages', when communication with mainland

Europe and the Mediterranean was a regular occurrence, by both land and sea? If we are looking for English origins, we should forget the 'Anglo-Saxons' and turn instead to the resident population, who had been there, in their millions and in their various cultures and communities, all the time. I refer, of course, to the real heroes of this book: that diverse group of people – the British.

NOTES

INTRODUCTION

1 Mark Brennand and Maisie Taylor, 'The Survey and Excavation of a Bronze Age Timber Circle at Holme-next-the-Sea, Norfolk, 1998–9', *Proceedings of the Prehistoric Society*, Vol. 69, 2003, pp.1–84.

2 Bede (ed. Bertram Colgrave and R.A.B. Mynors), *Ecclesiastical History of the English People* (Oxford Medieval Texts, Oxford University Press, 1969), pp.xviii–xix.

3 For a blow-by-blow account of the controversy see Matthew Champion, *Seahenge: A Contemporary Chronicle* (Barnwell's Timescape Publishing, Aylsham, Norfolk, 2000).

4 For a first-rate general introduction to Dark Age Britain see Michael Wood, *In Search of the Dark Ages* (BBC Books, London, revised edition 2001).

5 Edward Gibbon, *The Decline and Fall of the Roman Empire* (Random House, New York), Vol. 2, Chapter 38, pp.429–30.

6 He also noted : 'For all the expert analysis of sites and remains, and fascinating technical detail, the evidence to construct what Britons were really like is simply not there.' This surely relegates archaeology to the endnotes of history. Quoted from a review of Francis Pryor, *Britain BC: Life in Britain and Ireland Before the Romans* (HarperCollins, London, 2003) by Peter Jones, 'Founder of Friends of the Classics', *Sunday Telegraph*, 5 October 2003.

7 For an excellent textbook that covers all the archaeological periods discussed in this book see John Hunter and Ian Ralston (eds), *The Archaeology of Britain: An Introduction from the Upper Palaeolithic to the Industrial Revolution* (Routledge & Kegan Paul, London, 1999).

CHAPTER ONE – *Origin Myths: Britons, Celts and Anglo-Saxons*

1 Roy Strong, *The Spirit of Britain: A Narrative History of the Arts* (Hutchinson/Pimlico, London, 1999), p.22.

2 See Pryor, *Britain BC*, op. cit., pp.107–33.

3 Nora Chadwick, *The Celts* (Penguin Books, Harmondsworth, 1970).

4 Timothy Darvill (ed.), *The Concise Oxford Dictionary of Archaeology* (Oxford University Press, 2002).

5 T.G.E. Powell, *The Celts* (Thames & Hudson, London, 1958), p.15.

6 For a map of Celtic expansion as it was believed to have happened see ibid., p.99.

7 For post-Roman Celts see Nora Chadwick, *Celtic Britain* (Thames & Hudson, London, 1963).

8 For a well-illustrated account see Judith Herrin, 'The Fall of Constantinople', *History Today*, Vol. 53, June 2003, pp.12–17.

9 For more on Iron Age Celtic art see Paul Jacobsthal, *Early Celtic Art* (2 vols, Oxford University Press, 1944); Sir Cyril Fox, *Pattern and Purpose: A Survey of Early Celtic Art in Britain* (National Museum of Wales, Cardiff, 1958); J.V.S. Megaw, *Art of the European Iron Age: A Study of the Elusive Image* (Adams & Dart, Bath, 1970); Morna MacGregor,

Early Celtic Art in North Britain (2 vols, Leicester University Press, 1976).

10 See Pryor, *Britain BC*, op. cit., pp.406–10.

11 One of the best books of this sort is Anne Ross, *Everyday Life of the Pagan Celts* (Batsford Books, London, 1970), which still holds its own as a depiction of Iron Age life.

12 Simon James, *The Atlantic Celts: Ancient People or Modern Invention?* (British Museum Press, London, 1999), p.136.

13 Much of my discussion of 'Celticness' is based on James, ibid.

14 Quoted in Stuart Piggott, *The Druids* (Thames & Hudson, London, 1968), p.164.

15 From an excellent reference book on most matters to do with Arthur and Celticness: Bernhard Maier, *Dictionary of Celtic Religion and Culture* (Boydell Press, Woodbridge, 1997), p.104.

16 Piggott, op. cit., p.167.

17 James, op. cit., p.133.

18 My account of Anglo-Saxon historiography relies heavily on Sam Lucy, *The Anglo-Saxon Way of Death: Burial Rites in Ancient England* (Sutton Publishing, Stroud, 2000).

19 The two academic translations of the *Anglo-Saxon Chronicles* are by G.N. Garmonsway (Dent, London, 1953), and Dorothy Whitelock (Eyre & Spottiswoode, London, 1961). My personal favourite is a selection, beautifully illustrated, by Anne Savage (Heinemann, London, 1982).

20 This legend was 'excavated' by Geoffrey from the *Historia Brittonum*: N.J. Higham, *King Arthur: Myth-Making and History* (Routledge & Kegan Paul, London, 2002), p.223.

21 H.A. MacDougall, *Racial Myth in English History: Trojans, Teutons and Anglo-Saxons* (Harvest House, Montreal, 1982).

22 Lucy, op. cit., p.159.

23 Higham (2002), op. cit., p.22.

CHAPTER TWO – *The Origins and Legacy of Arthur*

1 Geoffrey of Monmouth (trans. Lewis Thorpe), *The History of the Kings of Britain* (Penguin Books, Harmondsworth, 1966), p.217.

2 Higham (2002), op. cit., p.17.

3 Leslie Alcock, *Arthur's Britain: History and Archaeology AD 367–634* (Penguin Books, Harmondsworth, 1971), p.49.

4 Higham (2002), op. cit., pp.270–1.

5 Leslie Alcock, 'Cadbury-Camelot: A Fifteen Year Perspective', *Proceedings of the British Academy*, Vol. 68, 1982, pp.355–88.

6 Leslie Alcock, *'By South Cadbury is that Camelot . . .': Excavations at Cadbury Castle, Somerset 1966–1970* (Thames & Hudson, London, 1972).

7 Geoffrey Ashe, *King Arthur's Avalon: The Story of Glastonbury* (William Collins, London, 1957).

8 Two of the best are Alcock (1971), op.cit., and Geoffrey Ashe (ed.), *The Quest for Arthur's Britain* (Pall Mall Press, London, 1968).

9 Higham (2002), op.cit., p.12.

10 The Arthurian myth-world has a huge cast of characters, usefully disentangled but rarely sourced, in Mike Dixon-Kennedy, *Arthurian Myth and Legend: An A–Z of People and Places* (Brockhampton Press, London, 1998).

11 For those wishing to journey into the world of Arthurian literature, I highly recommend Derek Pearsall, *Arthurian Romance: A Short Introduction* (Blackwell, Oxford, 2003). For medieval and earlier sources I rely mainly in this chapter on Higham (2002), op. cit. Dr Higham is unusual among scholars of medieval and earlier written sources for being an archaeologist too.

12 Higham (2002), op. cit., p.272, offers a considered response to that question.

13 Pearsall, op. cit., p.6.

14 Gildas (ed. and trans. Michael Winterbottom), *The Ruin of Britain and Other Documents* (Phillimore, Chichester, 2002).

15 Alcock (1971), op. cit., p.21.

16 Higham (2002), op. cit, p.6.

17 Ibid., p.9; for more on the *Historia Brittonum* see also pp.119–24.

18 I am grateful to Nick Higham for pointing this out to me.

19 Leslie Alcock dismissed their attribution to Nennius outright; he also chose to refer to the collection of papers that included the Welsh Annals and the *Historia* by a name of his own, the *British Historical Miscellany*. Alcock (1971), op. cit., p.44.

20 The standard text, with Latin alongside English translation, is edited by Colgrave and Mynors, op. cit.

21 Alcock (1971), op. cit., pp.45–72 . The collection of papers, copied in an Anglo-Norman hand c.1100, that includes both the *Annales Cambriae* and the *Historia Brittonum* is British Museum Harley MS 3859.

22 Monmouth (trans. Thorpe), op. cit.

23 For example, Steve Blake and Scott Lloyd, *The Keys to Avalon: The True Location of Arthur's Kingdom Revealed* (Element Books, Shaftesbury, 2000).

24 Higham (2002), op.cit., p.223.

25 Ibid., p.271.

26 Pearsall, op. cit., p.13.

27 Ibid., p.16.

28 Ibid., p.17.

29 Ibid., p.25.

30 Sir Thomas Malory (ed. Janet Cowen), *Le Morte d'Arthur* (Penguin Books, Harmondsworth, 1969).

31 From the Introduction to my favourite edition of Malory: John Matthews (ed.), *Le Morte d'Arthur* (Cassell, London, 2000), p.xiv.

32 This account of Malory's life is based on ibid., pp.xxiii–xxvii.

33 Pearsall, op. cit., p.43.

34 Richard Barber, 'Looking for the Holy Grail', *History Today*, Vol. 54, March 2004, pp.13–19. The article was based on Barber's book *The Holy Grail: Imagination and Belief* (Allen Lane, London, 2004).

35 Pearsall, op. cit., p.84.

36 The Winchester manuscript is not Malory's original, although it is much closer to it than Caxton's published version. See Pearsall, op. cit., p.88. For the Winchester manuscript see Eugene Vinaver (ed.), *The Works of Sir Thomas Malory* (Oxford University Press, 1990).

37 For an excellent account of the use of the cult of Arthur in public life see Higham (2002), op. cit., pp.226–66.

38 Ibid., pp.229–30.

39 Ibid., p 234.

40 For Arthur and the Tudors see J.J. Scarisbrick, *Henry VIII* (Pelican Books, Harmondsworth, 1971), p.355.

41 Martin Biddle (ed.), *King Arthur's Round Table: An Archaeological Investigation* (Boydell Press, Woodbridge, 2000).

42 A.C. Barefoot, 'Tree-Ring Dating the Round Table', in ibid., pp.149–94.

43 For the carpentry of the Round Table see Martin Biddle and Cecil Hewett, 'Carpentry, Condition and Sequence', in ibid., pp.105–48. The standard work on English medieval carpentry is Cecil Hewett, *English Historic Carpentry* (Phillimore, Chichester, 1980). For two excellent reviews of timber buildings see Margaret Wood, *The English Medieval House* (Random House, London, 1994), and R.W. Brunskill, *Timber Buildings in Britain* (Victor Glance, London, 1985).

44 Simon Jervis, 'The Round Table as Furniture', in Biddle, op. cit., p.31.

45 Pamela Tudor-Craig, 'Iconography of the Painting', in ibid., pp.285–333.

46 Ibid., p.333.

47 Higham (2002), op. cit., p.239.

48 For more on the Arthurising of Alfred see Barbara Yorke, 'The Most Perfect Man in History?', *History Today*, Vol. 49, October 1999, pp.8–14.

CHAPTER THREE – *Ancient Britons*

1 Barry Cunliffe, *Iron Age Communities in Britain* (Routledge & Kegan Paul, 3rd edn London, 1991), p.547.

2 Mike Parker Pearson, 'Food, Sex and Death: Cosmologies in the British Iron

Age with Particular Reference to East Yorkshire', *Cambridge Archaeological Journal*, Vol. 9, 1999, pp.43–69.

3 The fullest account of the Druids is still Piggott, op. cit. For a briefer version without the modern trappings see Cunliffe, *Iron Age Communities in Britain*, op. cit., pp.518–20. See also Graham Webster, *Boudica: The British Revolt Against Rome AD 60* (Batsford Books, London, 1978), pp.63–83.

4 Webster, op. cit., pp.131–2.

5 The earliest monuments where a variety of rituals took place were the so-called causewayed enclosures. For a good summary account of them see A. Oswald, C. Dyer and M. Barber, *The Creation of Monuments: Neolithic Causewayed Enclosures in the British Isles* (Royal Commission on the Historical Monuments of England, English Heritage, Swindon, 2001).

6 Cunliffe, *Iron Age Communities in Britain*, op. cit., p.519.

7 Richard Bradley, *The Passage of Arms: An Archaeological Analysis of Prehistoric Hoards and Votive Deposits* (Cambridge University Press, 1990).

8 See Francis Pryor, *Seahenge: A Quest for Life and Death in Bronze Age Britain* (HarperCollins, London, 2001), and *Britain BC*, op. cit.

9 In *Britain BC*, op. cit., p.414, I opt, perhaps rather conservatively, for 1.5 million.

10 Cunliffe, *Iron Age Communities in Britain*, op. cit., pp.543–6.

11 R.D. Van Arsdell, *Celtic Coinage of Britain* (Spink, London, 1989).

12 Kay Ainsworth and Jeffrey May, 'An Iron Age Coin Die from Near Alton, Hampshire', *Current Archaeology*, No. 188, 2003, p.326.

13 J.D. Hill, 'The End of One Kind of Body and the Beginning of Another Kind of Body? Toilet Instruments and "Romanisation" in Southern England During the First Century AD', in Adam Gwilt and Colin Haselgrove (eds), *Reconstructing Iron Age Societies: New Approaches to the British Iron Age*

(Oxbow Monograph 71, Oxford, 1997), pp.96–107.

14 James, op. cit., p.40.

15 For a useful summary account of the Druids see Cunliffe, *Iron Age Communities in Britain*, op. cit., pp.518–20.

16 For more on *garum* or *liquamen* see Jane Grigson, *Fish Cookery* (Penguin Books, Harmondsworth, 1975), p.369.

17 For British overseas contacts in general see Barry Cunliffe, *Facing the Ocean: The Atlantic and its Peoples* (Oxford University Press, 2001).

18 Barry Cunliffe, *Mount Batten Plymouth: A Prehistoric and Roman Port* (Oxford University Committee for Archaeology, Monograph 26, 1988); Barry Cunliffe, *Hengistbury Head, Dorset*. Vol. 1: *The Prehistoric and Roman Settlement 3500BC–AD 500* (Oxford University Committee for Archaeology, Monograph 13, 1987).

19 Ibid., p.341.

20 Barry Cunliffe, 'Britain, the Veneti and Beyond', *Oxford Journal of Archaeology*, Vol. 1, 1982, pp.39–68.

21 For a summary of the British wine trade see Peter Salway, *A History of Roman Britain* (Oxford University Press, 1993), pp.475–7.

22 R.E.M. Wheeler, *Maiden Castle, Dorset* (Report of the Research Committee of the Society of Antiquaries of London, No. 12, London, 1943). For recent work see N.M. Sharples, *Maiden Castle: Excavations and Field Survey, 1985–6* (English Heritage Archaeological Report No. 19, London, 1991).

23 An excellent popular account of Danebury is Barry Cunliffe, *Danebury: The Anatomy of an Iron Age Hillfort* (Batsford, London, 1983). Three of the key academic publications are: Barry Cunliffe, *Danebury: An Iron Age Hillfort in Hampshire*, Vol. 6: *A Hillfort Community in Perspective* (Council for British Archaeology Research Report No. 102, York, 1995); Barry Cunliffe, *The Danebury Environs Programme, the Prehistory of a Wessex Landscape*, Vol. 1:

Introduction (English Heritage and Oxford University Committee for Archaeology Monograph No. 48, Institute of Archaeology, Oxford, 2000); Rog Palmer, *Danebury, an Iron Age Hillfort in Hampshire: An Aerial Photographic Interpretation of its Environs* (Royal Commission on Historical Monuments (England), Supplementary Series No. 6, London, 1984).

24 For Maiden Castle see note 22, above. We will see that South Cadbury is famous/infamous for being a possible post-Roman 'Camelot'. Archaeologically it is more important as a Late Bronze Age and Iron Age centre, and is the subject of a major recent publication: John C. Barrett, P.W.M. Freeman and Ann Woodward, *Cadbury Castle Somerset: The Later Prehistoric and Early Historic Archaeology* (English Heritage Archaeological Report No. 20, London, 2000).

25 For a particularly well-excavated example see P.J. Fasham, *The Prehistoric Settlement at Winnall Down, Winchester* (Hampshire Field Club Monograph No. 2, 1985).

26 S.R. Bryant and R. Niblett, 'The Late Iron Age in Hertfordshire and the North Chilterns', in Gwilt and Haselgrove, op. cit., pp.270–81.

27 The work of Philip Crummy and the Colchester Archaeological Trust is, however, a notable exception to this.

28 Iron Age Silchester is the only British town which shows evidence for a grid-iron arrangement. M.G. Fulford, 'Silchester: The Early Development of a Civitas Capital', in S.J. Greep (ed.), *Roman Towns: The Wheeler Inheritance* (Council for British Archaeology Research Report No. 93, York, 1993), pp.16–33.

29 There is a huge literature on Roman and Iron Age St Albans. For a modern account with an excellent overview, see I.M. Stead and V. Rigby, *Verulamium: The King Harry Lane Site* (English

Heritage Archaeological Report No. 12, London, 1989).

30 I.M. Stead and Valery Rigby, *Baldock: The Excavation of a Roman and Pre-Roman Settlement, 1968–72* (Britannia Monograph No. 7, London, 1986); David S. Neal, Angela Wardle and Jonathan Hunn, *Excavation of the Iron Age, Roman and Medieval Settlement at Gorhambury, St Albans* (English Heritage Archaeological Report No. 14, London, 1990); Clive Partridge, *Skeleton Green: A Late Iron Age and Romano-British Site* (Britannia Monograph No. 2, London, 1981).

31 Baldock, Durobrivae and the Castor *praetorium* are featured in A.E. Brown (ed.), *Roman Small Towns in Eastern England and Beyond* (Oxbow Monograph No. 52, Oxford, 1995).

32 For a general overview see John Collis, *Oppida: Earliest Towns North of the Alps* (Department of Prehistory and Archaeology, University of Sheffield, 1984).

33 Ibid., pp.137–67.

34 Colin Haselgrove and Martin Millett, 'Verlamion Reconsidered', in Gwilt and Haselgrove, op. cit., pp.282–96.

CHAPTER FOUR – *My Roman Britain*

1 I have borrowed the title of this chapter from an old friend, colleague and highly distinguished scholar, Dr Richard Reece of University College London. His book of the same name has been a wonderful and witty inspiration to me. It also taught me the advantages of taking a personal approach to the complexities of Romano-British archaeology: Richard Reece, *My Roman Britain* (Cotswold Studies, Cirencester, 1988). It would be ludicrous to attempt a description of life and politics in Roman Britain in a single chapter. Fortunately there are some excellent general books for those who would like to learn more about the period. I can recommend two very readable

textbooks. The first, Sheppard Frere, *Britannia: A History of Roman Britain* (Routledge & Kegan Paul, London, 3rd edn 1987), guided me through my student days and is still in print; the second, Peter Salway, *A History of Roman Britain*, op. cit., is more modern and more accessible, but it is also comprehensive and authoritative. For a less concentrated, and very fully illustrated, introduction you could not do better than T.W. Potter and Catherine Johns, *Roman Britain* (British Museum Press, London, 1992). Finally, the fourth century is crucially important to our story, and Guy de la Bédoyère has just devoted a fine book to it: *The Golden Age of Roman Britain* (Tempus Books, Stroud, 1999).

2 P.V. Addyman and K.R. Fennell, 'A Dark-Age Settlement at Maxey, Northants', *Medieval Archaeology*, Vol. 7, 1964, pp.20–73; Francis Pryor, Charles French, David Crowther, David Gurney, Gavin Simpson and Maisie Taylor, *The Fenland Project*, No. 1: *Archaeology and Environment in the Lower Welland Valley* (2 vols, East Anglian Archaeology Report No. 27, Cambridge, 1985); Francis Pryor, *Etton: Excavations at a Neolithic Causewayed Enclosure Near Maxey, Cambridgeshire, 1982–7* (English Heritage Archaeological Report No. 18, London, 1998).

3 I discuss the reasons for this south–east orientation in *Britain BC*, op. cit., pp.328–31.

4 Richard Reece, 'Comment on the Coins', in Pryor et al., *The Fenland Project*, No. 1, op. cit., Vol. 1, p.164.

5 *A Matter of Time: An Archaeological Survey of the River Gravels of England* (Royal Commission on Historical Monuments [England], London, 1960).

6 Francis Pryor, *Farmers in Prehistoric Britain* (Tempus Books, Stroud, 1998), pp.109–23.

7 W.G. Simpson, 'Romano-British Settlement on the Welland Gravels', in C. Thomas (ed.), *Rural Settlement in Roman Britain* (Council for British Archaeology Research Report No. 7, London, 1966), pp.15–25.

8 E. Pollard, M.D. Hooper and N.W. Moore, *Hedges* (William Collins, Glasgow, 1974).

9 W.G. Simpson, D.A. Gurney, J. Neve and F.M.M. Pryor, *The Fenland Project*, No. 7: *Excavations in Peterborough and the Lower Welland Valley 1960–1969* (East Anglian Archaeology Report No. 61, Peterborough, 1993).

10 Addyman and Fennell, op. cit.

11 See *A Matter of Time*, op. cit., p.58.

12 Addyman and Fennell, op. cit., p.37.

13 His suggestion is the site shown in *A Matter of Time*, op. cit., Fig. 6, No. 17.

14 W.G. Simpson, 'Aspects of Land-use and Landscape Development in the Lower Welland Valley and the Surrounding Region', in Simpson et al., *The Fenland Project*, No. 7, pp.142–3.

15 C.C. Taylor and P.J. Fowler, 'Roman Fields into Medieval Furlongs?', in H.C. Bowen and P.J. Fowler (eds), *Early Land Allotment* (British Archaeological Report No. 48, Oxford, 1978), pp.159–62.

16 C.C. Taylor, *Fields in the English Landscape* (Dent, London, 1975), p.66.

17 His fold-out phase plans in the published report are superb: D.F. Mackreth, *Orton Hall Farm: A Roman and Early Anglo-Saxon Farmstead* (East Anglian Archaeology Report No. 76, Peterborough, 1996).

18 Ibid., p.xiv.

19 J.P. Wild, 'Roman Settlement in the Lower Nene Valley', *Archaeological Journal*, Vol. 131, 1974, pp.140–70.

20 Mackreth (1996), op. cit., p.88.

21 Donald Mackreth, 'Orton Hall Farm: The Saxon Connection', *Durobrivae*, Vol. 5, 1977, pp.20–1.

22 J.R. Perrin, 'Phasing and Dating Method', in Mackreth (1996), op. cit., p.xv.

23 Mackreth (1996), op. cit., p.27.

24 Gary Taylor, 'An Early to Middle Saxon Settlement at Quarrington, Lincolnshire', *Antiquaries Journal*, Vol. 83, 2003, p.276.

25 Both quotations are from Martin

Millett, *The Romanization of Britain* (Cambridge University Press, 1990), p.6.

26 J.N.L. Myres, *A Corpus of Anglo-Saxon Pottery of the Pagan Period* (2 vols, Cambridge University Press, 1977), Vol. 1, pp.125–6; see also his 'Index of Potters and Workshops', ibid., pp.68–83.

27 A broadly similar picture can be seen, for example, at West Heslerton, Yorkshire (Chapter 8), and West Stow, in Suffolk: Stanley West, *West Stow, The Anglo-Saxon Village* (2 vols, East Anglian Archaeology Report No. 24, Ipswich, 1985).

CHAPTER FIVE – *Late- and Post-Roman Britain: The Situation in the South and East*

1 F.M. Stenton, *Anglo-Saxon England* (Oxford University Press, 3rd edn 1971), p.1.

2 Salway, op. cit., p.294.

3 Based on ibid., pp.573–4.

4 For an excellent review of the Roman army of occupation see Guy de la Bédoyère, *Eagles Over Britannia: The Roman Army in Britain* (Tempus Publications, Stroud, 2001).

5 I am indebted to Guy de la Bédoyère for this suggestion.

6 As well as Guy de la Bédoyère's fine book on fourth-century Britain, I also recommend two earlier, and rather different, treatments of the subject: A.S. Esmonde Cleary, *The Ending of Roman Britain* (Routledge & Kegan Paul, London, 1989); Stephen Johnson, *Later Roman Britain* (Routledge & Kegan Paul, London, 1980).

7 De la Bédoyère (2001), op. cit., p.50.

8 M.D. Howe, J.R. Perrin and D.F. Mackreth, *Roman Pottery from the Nene Valley: A Guide* (Peterborough City Museum Occasional Paper No. 2, Peterborough, 1980).

9 Salway, op. cit., p.256.

10 The outline of later Roman history both here and later in this chapter draws heavily on ibid., pp.256–331.

11 Frere, op. cit., p.217.

12 For a good overview of the changes made to the late Roman army see Pat Southern and Karen R. Dixon, *The Late Roman Army* (Routledge & Kegan Paul, London, 1996).

13 Salway, op. cit., p.264.

14 Ordnance Survey Map of Roman Britain (Ordnance Survey, Southampton, 5th edn March 2001).

15 Andrew Sargent, 'The North–South Divide Revisited: Thoughts on the Character of Roman Britain', *Britannia*, Vol. 33, 2002, p.226.

16 The Gospel According to St John, 1.1–5.

17 Dominic Perring, '"Gnosticism" in Fourth-Century Britain: The Frampton Mosaics Reconsidered', *Britannia*, Vol. 34, 2003, pp.97–128.

18 Ibid., p.112.

19 Ibid., p.121.

20 C. Guy, 'The Lead Tank from Ashton', *Durobrivae*, Vol. 5, 1977, pp.10–11.

21 S.E. West and J. Plouviez, 'The Romano-British Site at Icklingham', *East Anglian Archaeology*, No. 3 (Ipswich, 1976), pp.63–126.

22 M. Fulford, 'Links With the Past: Pervasive "Ritual" Behaviour in Roman Britain', *Britannia*, Vol. 32, 2001, pp.199–218.

23 See Pryor, *Britain BC*, op. cit., pp.429–39.

24 Martin Henig, *The Heirs of King Verica: Culture and Politics in Roman Britain* (Tempus Books, Stroud, 2002), p.36.

25 Ibid., p.38.

26 Barry Cunliffe, 'Roman Danebury', *Current Archaeology*, No. 188, 2003, pp.345–51.

27 Ibid., p.351.

28 W.H.C. Frend, 'Pagans, Christians, and the "Barbarian Conspiracy" of AD 367 in Roman Britain', *Britannia*, Vol. 23, 1992, pp.121–32 .

29 Perring, op. cit. p.124.

30 Millett, op. cit., pp.227–30.

31 The Roman ruins in Trier are extraordinarily well preserved. See Edith Mary Wightman, *Roman Trier and the*

Treveri (Rupert Hart-Davis, London, 1970).

32 Salway, op. cit., p.320.

CHAPTER SIX – *The 'Anglo-Saxon' Origins of England*

1 D.M. Wilson, *The Anglo-Saxons* (Thames & Hudson, London, 1960), p.29.

2 Two recent reviews of the Anglo-Saxons, one early, the other late: Samantha Glasswell, *The Earliest English: Living and Dying in Early Anglo-Saxon England* (Tempus Books, Stroud, 2002); and Andrew Reynolds, *Later Anglo-Saxon England: Life and Landscape* (Tempus Books, Stroud, 1999).

3 Gildas (ed. Winterbottom), op. cit., p.26.

4 For a useful summary of recent approaches to traditional views see David Brown, 'Problems of Continuity', in Trevor Rowley (ed.), *Anglo-Saxon Settlement and Landscape* (British Archaeological Report No. 6, Oxford, 1974), pp.16–19.

5 For a balanced account of the origins of the English language see Catherine Hills, *Origins of the English* (Duckworth, London, 2003), pp.41–55.

6 Heinrich Härke, 'Kings and Warriors: Population and Landscape from Post-Roman to Norman Britain', in Paul Slack and Ryk Ward (eds), *The Peopling of Britain: The Shaping of a Human Landscape. The Linacre Lectures* (Oxford University Press, 2002), p.147.

7 Ibid., p.150.

8 N.J. Higham, *Rome, Britain and the Anglo-Saxons* (Seaby, London, 1992).

9 E.G. Bowen, *Britain and the Western Seaways* (Thames & Hudson, London, 1972).

10 Cunliffe, *Facing the Ocean*, op. cit.

11 There is a vast literature on connections across the Channel and the North Sea in prehistory. A few of the more important references are: J.J. Butler, 'Bronze Age Connections Across the North Sea', *Palaeohistoria*, Vol. 9 (entire issue), 1963; Brendan O'Connor, *Cross-Channel Relations in the Later Bronze Age* (2 vols, British Archaeological Reports International Series, No. S91, Oxford, 1980); L.P. Louwe-Kooijmans, 'A View of the Fens from the Low Countries', *Antiquity*, Vol. 62, 1988, pp.377–82.

12 Cyril Fox, *The Personality of Britain: Its Influence on Inhabitant and Invader in Prehistoric and Early Historic Times* (National Museum of Wales, Cardiff, 1932).

13 See Esmonde Cleary, op. cit., pp.188–205.

14 Salway, op. cit., p.332.

15 J.N.L. Myres, *Anglo-Saxon Pottery and the Settlement of England* (Oxford University Press, 1969).

16 Ibid., p.100.

17 Ibid., pp.63–4.

18 Myres (1977), op. cit., p.114.

19 He wrote a vast amount on the subject, but the classic summary is to be found in: C.F.C. Hawkes, 'The ABC of the British Iron Age', *Antiquity*, Vol. 33, 1959, pp.170–82.

20 Salway, op. cit., p.288.

21 Stephen Johnson, *Later Roman Britain* (Routledge & Kegan Paul, London, 1980), pp.76–7.

22 Ibid., p.82.

23 Modern opinion on Saxon shore forts has been greatly influenced by Stephen Johnson's *The Roman Forts of the Saxon Shore* (London, 1976).

24 See also Esmonde Cleary, op. cit., pp.52–3.

25 Johnson (1980), op. cit., p.76.

26 Salway, op. cit., pp.189–92.

27 A.F. Pearson, *The Roman Shore Forts: Coastal Defences of Southern Britain* (Tempus Books, Stroud, 2002). For a more detailed academic study see A.F. Pearson, *The Construction of the 'Saxon Shore' Forts* (British Archaeological Report No. 349, Oxford, 2003).

28 In addition to the two books by Andrew Pearson cited above, I also make use of an as yet unpublished

paper by him: 'Barbarian Piracy and the Saxon Shore: A Reappraisal'.

29 B.W. Cunliffe, *Excavations at Portchester Castle. I: Roman* (Society of Antiquaries Research Report No. 32, London, 1975).

30 See also J.R.L. Allen and M.G. Fulford, 'Fort Building and Military Supply Along Britain's Eastern Channel and North Sea Coasts: The Later Second and Third Centuries', *Britannia*, Vol. 30, 1999, pp.63–84.

31 See also J.R.L. Allen, E.J. Rose and M.G. Fulford, 'Re-Use of Roman Stone in the Reedham Area of East Norfolk: Intimations of a Possible "Lost" Roman Fort', *Britannia*, Vol. 34, 2003, pp.129–42.

32 Pearson, 'Barbarian Piracy and the Saxon Shore', op. cit., p.11.

33 For a useful summary of Pelagianism see Frere, op. cit., p.359.

34 Perring, op. cit., p.124fn.

35 Ibid.

36 For an archaeological essay on tradition and conservatism within ritual and religion see Richard Bradley, 'Monuments and Places', in P. Garwood, D. Jennings, R. Skeates and J. Toms (eds), *Sacred and Profane* (Oxford University Committee for Archaeology, Oxford, 1991), pp.135–40.

37 Myres (1969), op. cit., p.86.

38 For Beakers see D.L. Clarke, *Beaker Pottery of Great Britain and Ireland* (2 vols, Cambridge University Press, 1970); for Anglo-Saxon pottery see Myres (1977), op. cit.; for traditional knitting patterns see Rae Compton, *The Complete Book of Traditional Knitting* (Batsford Books, London, 1983).

39 Pryor, *Britain BC*, op. cit., p.xx.

40 Darvill, op. cit.

41 Peter Harbison and Lloyd R. Laing, *Some Iron Age Mediterranean Imports in England* (British Archaeological Report No. 5, Oxford, 1974).

42 M.U. Jones, V.I. Evison and J.N.L. Myres, 'Crop-Mark Sites at Mucking, Essex', *Antiquaries Journal*, Vol. 48, 1968, p.227.

43 M.U. and W.T. Jones, 'An Early Saxon Landscape at Mucking, Essex', in Trevor Rowley (ed.), *Anglo-Saxon Settlement and Landscape* (British Archaeological Report No. 6, Oxford, 1974), p.22.

44 Ann Clark, *Excavations at Mucking*, Vol. 1: *The Site Atlas* (English Heritage, London 1993), p.21.

45 Quoted from the dust jacket of Lucy, op. cit.

46 Ibid., p.161.

47 Ibid., p.175. The break from the 'culture-historical' approach in Britain was made by David L. Clarke, *Analytical Archaeology* (Methuen, London, 2nd edn 1978). Clarke died in 1976. The 2nd edition was revised by Bob Chapman, and is better than the 1st edition of 1968, which was very heavy going.

48 There are exceptions, however: John Pearce, 'Death and Time: The Structure of Late Iron Age Mortuary Ritual', in Gwilt and Haselgrove, op. cit., pp.174–80.

49 For a good general discussion see Rowan Whimster, *Burial Practices in Iron Age Britain: A Discussion and Gazetteer of the Evidence c.700 BC–AD 43* (2 vols., British Archaeological Report No. 90, Oxford, 1981).

50 For a useful collection of essays on mass migration and archaeology see J. Chapman and H. Hamerow (eds), *Migrations and Invasions in Archaeological Explanation* (British Archaeological Reports, International Series No. 664, Oxford, 1997).

51 Lucy, op. cit., pp.186–7.

52 M.A. Smith, 'Some Somerset Hoards and Their Place in the Bronze Age of Southern Britain', *Proceedings of the Prehistoric Society*, Vol. 25, 1959, pp.144–87.

53 The Sutton Hoo finds in the British Museum are worth a long journey to see. They are comprehensively written up by R.L.S. Bruce-Mitford in three large volumes (British Museum Publications, London, 1975, 1978 and 1983). The museum sells shorter, more accessible accounts of the finds and the

1938 excavations. For later work at Sutton Hoo and its landscape see Martin Carver (ed.), *The Age of Sutton Hoo* (Boydell Press, Woodbridge, 1992).

CHAPTER SEVEN – *Arthurian Britain: The Situation in the West and South-West*

1 In fact Durobrivae was the largest and perhaps most successful of the Romano-British 'small towns'. See D.F. Mackreth, 'Durobrivae, Chesterton, Cambridgeshire', in A.E. Brown (ed.), *Roman Small Towns in Eastern England and Beyond* (Oxbow Monograph No. 52, Oxford, 1995), pp.147–56.

2 Esmonde Cleary, op. cit.

3 De la Bédoyère (2001), op.cit. p.64.

4 Richard Reece, 'Town and Country: The End of Roman Britain', *World Archaeology*, Vol. 12, 1980, pp.77–92. The quotation is from the Note on pp.90–1.

5 My thoughts on Romano-British towns rely heavily on those of Richard Reece in ibid. and in *My Roman Britain*, op. cit.

6 Reece, *My Roman Britain*, op. cit., p.140.

7 Helena Hamerow, 'Hamwic', *British Archaeology*, No. 66, August 2002, pp.20–4.

8 The best popular book on Wroxeter is by Roger White and Philip Barker, *Wroxeter: Life and Death of a Roman City* (Tempus Books, Stroud, revised edn 2002). Three major academic reports have been published by English Heritage, in 1997, 2000 and 2002.

9 For more on the Swiss Lakes see Bryony and John Coles, *People of the Wetlands: Bogs, Bodies and Lake-Dwellers* (Thames & Hudson, 1989).

10 White and Barker, op. cit., p.19.

11 For a description of his excavation methods see Philip Barker, *Techniques of Archaeological Excavation* (Batsford Books, London, 1977).

12 There is a danger that the extent and scale of the post-Roman occupation at Wroxeter may have been overestimated; some supposedly later work could actually have taken place in Roman times. For a detailed critique of the various Wroxeter reports see a review by Professor Mike Fulford in the *Journal of Roman Archaeology*, Vol. 15, 2002, pp.639–45.

13 White and Barker, op. cit., p.121.

14 Ibid., pp.125–6.

15 See Peter Rowsome's beautifully illustrated and well-written book, *Heart of the City: Roman, Medieval and Modern London Revealed by Archaeology at 1 Poultry* (Museum of London Archaeology Service, London, 2000), pp.46–7.

16 Philip Crummy, *Aspects of Anglo-Saxon and Norman Colchester* (Colchester Archaeological Trust Report No. 1, Colchester, 1981), pp.1–4.

17 I am particularly grateful to Richard Morris for his comments and advice regarding the early Church. For an archaeological perspective on these issues see R.K. Morris, *The Church in British Archaeology* (Council for British Archaeology Research Report No. 47, London, 1983).

18 This oral tradition is based on Bede, who was using an earlier source for the story. See Bede (ed. Colgrave and Mynors), op. cit., pp.133–5.

19 Ken Dark, *Britain and the End of the Roman Empire* (Tempus Books, Stroud, 2000).

20 I discuss the restrictive nature of movement and migration throughout *Britain BC*, op. cit.

21 Ken Dark, op. cit., p.15.

22 Anthea Harris, *Byzantium, Britain and the West: The Archaeology of Cultural Identity AD 400–650* (Tempus Books, Stroud, 2003), pp.64–72.

23 Ken Dark, op. cit., p.124.

24 Charles Thomas, *Tintagel: Arthur and Archaeology* (Batsford Books, London, 1993).

25 A.D. Mills, *A Dictionary of English Place-Names* (Oxford University Press, 1991).

26 *Devon Archaeological Society Newsletter* (Exeter), No. 79, May 2001.

27 Richard Tabor (ed.), *South Cadbury Environs Project Interim Fieldwork Report, 1998–2001* (Bristol University Centre for the Historic Environment, Bristol, 2002).

28 J.M. Coles, P. Leach, S.C. Minnitt, R. Tabor and A.S. Wilson, 'A Later Bronze Age Shield from South Cadbury, Somerset, England', *Antiquity*, Vol. 73, 1999, pp.33–48.

29 John C. Barrett, P.W.M. Freeman and Ann Woodward, *Cadbury Castle Somerset: The Later Prehistoric and Early Historic Archaeology* (English Heritage Archaeological Report No. 20, London, 2000), p.323.

30 For a discussion of such places see Richard Bradley, *An Archaeology of Natural Places* (Routledge & Kegan Paul, London, 2000). The discovery of a greenstone axe in Philip Rhatz's excavations suggests the Tor was important in Neolithic times; complete polished axes are often found at special sites, such as barrows and causewayed enclosures.

31 Bradley (1990), op. cit. For an excellent and accessible review of Glastonbury archaeology see Philip Rhatz and Lorna Watts, *Glastonbury: Myth and Archaeology* (Tempus Books, Stroud, 2003).

32 Woad is best grown in or near fens and marshes. For the name see Mills, op. cit.

33 David Howlett, 'Literate Culture of "Dark Age" Britain', *British Archaeology*, No. 33, 1998, pp.10–11.

34 Charles Thomas, *Christian Celts: Messages and Images* (Tempus Books, Stroud, 1998).

35 By no means all of the word-games and encoded messages apparently concealed within these inscriptions have been accepted by scholars. See the review of the book by Charles Thomas quoted in the previous note, in *Britannia*, Vol. 31, 2000, pp.463–4.

36 Alcock (1971), op. cit., pp.246–7.

CHAPTER EIGHT – *The Making of the English Landscape*

1 W.G. Hoskins, *The Making of the English Landscape* (Hodder & Stoughton, London, 1955).

2 Ibid., p.55.

3 I am grateful to Richard Morris for this idea.

4 There is a vast amount of literature on this topic. See, for example, P.J. Fowler, *The Farming of Prehistoric Britain* (Cambridge University Press, 1983); Ian Simmons and Michael Tooley (eds), *The Environment in British Prehistory* (Duckworth, London, 1981).

5 For the extent of woodland in Anglo-Saxon times see Brian K. Roberts and Stuart Wrathmell, *An Atlas of Rural Settlement in England* (English Heritage, London, 2000), p.32.

6 Oliver Rackham is the leading authority on historical forest management. I highly recommend his fascinating and most readable book *The Last Forest: The Story of Hatfield Forest* (Dent, London, 1989).

7 Frederic Seebohm, *The English Village Community* (Longmans, Green & Co., London, 1883).

8 Mills, op. cit., p.xviii.

9 Mills tells us (ibid., p.382) that *ingas* is the Old English for 'people of, family or followers of, or dwellers at'. Birmingham means 'the homestead of the family or followers of a man called Beorma'.

10 David Hall, 'Medieval Fields in Their Many Forms', *British Archaeology*, No. 33, April 1998, pp.6–7.

11 Higham (2002), op. cit., p.23.

12 Wilson, op. cit., p.110.

13 Peter Murphy, 'The Anglo-Saxon Landscape and Rural Economy: Some Results From Sites in East Anglia and Essex', in J. Rackham (ed.), *Environment and Economy in Anglo-Saxon England* (Council for British Archaeology Research Report No. 89, York, 1994), pp.23–39.

14 Ibid., p.24.

15 O. Rackham, *The History of the Countryside* (Dent, London, 1986), pp.75–85.

16 Murphy, op. cit., p.38.

17 Rabbits were spread through Europe by the Romans, but they did not reach Britain until Norman times. See Juliet Clutton-Brock, *A Natural History of Domesticated Animals* (Cambridge University/British Museum Press, London, 1987), p.146.

18 Petra Dark, *The Environment of Britain in the First Millennium AD* (Duckworth, London, 2000).

19 As a guide to the Wall I highly recommend Guy de la Bédoyère, *Hadrian's Wall: History and Guide* (Tempus Books, Stroud, 1998). It is well-illustrated, concise, and tells you about those little points of interest that the glossy guidebooks to the large forts tend to ignore, such as the strange tumble of unfinished Roman stonework at Limestone Corner.

20 Tim Gates, 'Hadrian's Wall Amid Fields of Corn', *British Archaeology*, No. 49, November 1999, p.6.

21 Tony Wilmott published his excavations with remarkable promptness. The fully detailed report is Tony Wilmott, *Birdoswald: Excavations of a Roman Fort on Hadrian's Wall and its Successor Settlements, 1987–92* (English Heritage Archaeology Report No. 14, London, 1996). He has also produced a fine popular summary: Tony Wilmott, *Birdoswald Roman Fort: 1800 Years on Hadrian's Wall* (Tempus Books, Stroud, 2001).

22 Tony Wilmott, 'Roman Commanders, Dark Age Kings', *British Archaeology*, No. 63, February 2002, p.11.

23 D.J. Powlesland, 'West Heslerton', *Current Archaeology*, Vol. 76, 1981, pp.142–4; D.J. Powlesland, C.A. Haughton and J.H. Hanson, 'Excavations at Heslerton, North Yorkshire 1978–82', *Archaeological Journal*, Vol. 143, 1986, pp.53–173.

24 Discussed in Pryor, *Britain BC*, op. cit., pp.79–90.

25 Christine Haughton and Dominic Powlesland, *West Heslerton: The Anglian Cemetery* (The Landscape Research Centre, Yedingham, Yorkshire, 1999), Vol. 1, p.9.

26 Ibid., p.94.

27 Brian Hope-Taylor, *Yeavering: An Anglo-British Centre of Early Northumbria* (Department of the Environment Archaeological Report No. 7, HMSO, London, 1977).

28 For cursus monuments see Pryor, *Britain BC*, op. cit., pp.183–9. For Rudston see D.N. Riley, 'Air Survey of Neolithic Sites in the Yorkshire Wolds', in T.G. Manby (ed.), *Archaeology in Eastern Yorkshire* (Department of Archaeology and Prehistory, University of Sheffield, 1988), pp.89–93.

29 For the technique: P. Budd, J. Montgomery, J. Evans and P. Chenery, 'Combined Pb-, Sr- and O-Isotope Analysis of Human Dental Tissue for the Reconstruction of Archaeological Residential Mobility', in J.G. Holland and S.D. Tanner (eds), *Plasma Source Mass Spectrometry: The New Millennium* (Royal Society of Chemistry, Cambridge, 2003), pp.195–208. For its archaeological implications: Paul Budd, Andrew Millard, Carolyn Chenery, Sam Lucy and Charlotte Roberts, 'Isotopic Evidence for Archaeological Immigration and Residential Mobility in the UK', manuscript submitted to *Antiquity*, 2003; I am most grateful to Paul Budd for allowing me to see a draft of this paper prior to publication.

30 A.P. Fitzpatrick, ' "The Amesbury Archer": A Well-Furnished Early Bronze Age Burial in Southern England', *Antiquity*, Vol. 76, 2002, pp.629–30.

31 The stone is in Reading Museum. See Silchester Roman Town Project 2000, *The Silchester Ogham Stone* (Reading, 2000).

32 See, for example, E.T. Leeds, 'Anglo-Saxon Remains', in *Victoria County History: Oxfordshire*, Vol. 1 (1939), pp.346–72.

33 Information kindly provided by Paul Budd.

34 For an excellent recent collection of essays on the archaeology of the Witham Valley see Steve Catney and David Start (eds), *Time and Tide: The Archaeology of the Witham Valley* (Witham Valley Archaeological Research Committee, Lincoln, 2003).

35 See Pryor, *Britain BC*, op. cit., pp.283–7.

36 Ibid., p.285.

37 Paul Everson and David Stocker, '"Coming from Bardney . . .": The Landscape Context of the Causeways and Finds Groups of the Witham Valley', in Catney and Start, op. cit., p.10.

38 For the Thames and the Thames Valley see David Thomas Yates, 'Bronze Age Field Systems in the Thames Valley', *Oxford Journal of Archaeology*, Vol. 18, 1999, pp.157–70; D.T. Yates, 'Bronze Age Agricultural Intensification in the Thames Valley and Estuary', in Joanna Brück, *Bronze Age Landscapes: Tradition and Transformation* (Oxbow Books, Oxford, 2001), pp.65–82.

CHAPTER NINE – *Continuity and Change*

1 For an excellent discussion of what is rapidly becoming a sub-discipline in its own right see Hills, op. cit., Chapter 4, 'Bones, Genes and People', pp.57–71.

2 By M.E. Weale, D.A. Weiss, R.F. Jager, N. Bradman and M.G. Thomas, in *Molecular Biological Evolution*, Vol. 19, No. 7, 2002, pp.1008–21.

3 *Britain BC*, op. cit., p.xxvi.

4 C. Capelli et al., 'A Y Chromosome Census of the British Isles', *Current Biology*, Vol. 13, 2003, pp.979–84.

5 Quoted in Hannah Hoag, 'Y Chromosomes Rewrite British History: Anglo-Saxons' Genetic Stamp Weaker than Historians Suspected', *Science Update*, 19 June 2003, www.nature.com.

6 C.J. Arnold, 'Stress as a Stimulus for Socio-Economic Change: Anglo-Saxon England in the Seventh Century', in Colin Renfrew and Stephen Shennan (eds), *Ranking, Resource and Exchange* (Cambridge University Press, 1982), pp.124–31.

7 I am referring here to the rich 'Wessex Culture' barrows that surround and just post-date Stonehenge. See *Britain BC*, op. cit., pp.229–69.

8 Colin Renfrew was the first person to explain how barrows could have operated within the landscape. Ideas have moved on since he wrote, but his paper remains a classic: 'Monuments, Mobilisation and Social Organisation in Neolithic Wessex', in Colin Renfrew (ed.), *The Explanation of Culture Change: Models in Prehistory* (Duckworth, London, 1973), pp.539–58.

9 Arnold, op. cit., p.127.

10 J. Foster, *The Lexden Tumulus: A Reappraisal of an Iron Age Burial from Colchester, Essex* (British Archaeological Report No. 156, Oxford, 1986).

11 Philip Crummy, *City of Victory* (Colchester Archaeological Trust, Colchester, 1997).

12 Foster, op. cit. p.79; for dating see Period 5 in S.P. Needham, 'Chronology and Periodisation in the British Bronze Age', *Acta Archaeologica*, Vol. 67, 1996, pp.121–40.

13 Neil Faulkner, 'Prittlewell: Treasures of a King of Essex', *Current Archaeology*, No. 190, February 2004, pp.430–6.

14 See I.D. Margary, *Roman Roads in Britain* (John Baker, London, 3rd edn 1973), p.201.

15 *Britain BC*, op. cit., pp.344–53.

16 J.R. Mortimer, *Forty Years Researches in British and Saxon Burial Mounds of East Yorkshire* (Brown & Sons, London, 1905).

17 I.M. Stead, 'A Distinctive Form of La Tène Barrow in Eastern Yorkshire and on the Continent', *Antiquaries Journal*, Vol. 61, 1961, pp.44–62.

18 F. and H.W. Elgee, *The Archaeology of Yorkshire* (Methuen, London, 1933), p.112.

19 I.M. Stead, *The Arras Culture* (Yorkshire

258 · NOTES TO PAGES 236–240

Philosophical Society, York, 1979). See also I.M. Stead, *Iron Age Cemeteries in East Yorkshire* (English Heritage Archaeological Report No. 22, London, 1991).

CONCLUSION – *So Where Does that Leave Us?*

1 The nonconformist churches of eastern England have left us with a wonderful collection of buildings. See Christopher Stell, *An Inventory of Nonconformist Chapels and Meeting-Houses in Eastern England* (English Heritage, Swindon, 2002).

2 Caroline Sharples, 'Kindertransport: Terror, Trauma and Triumph', *History Today*, Vol. 54, March 2004, pp.23–9.

3 G.H.S. Bushnell, *The First Americans: The Pre-Columbian Civilizations* (Thames & Hudson, London, 1968), p.135.

4 Hills, op. cit., pp.10–11.

5 I am indebted to David Howlett for this.

INDEX

Page references in *italics* denote figures

P.S.

Ideas,
interviews
& features ...

About the author

About the book

Read on

The Importance of the Present

Louise Tucker talks to Francis Pryor

Personal identity, like historical identity, is closely related to place. Where is your home, and why?
I live deep in the Fens, just north of the Cambridgeshire border, about five miles inside Lincolnshire, in the area known today as South Holland (Holland = Hollow Land). We live in an isolated farmhouse, about eight miles from the Wash, that we built ourselves about fourteen years ago. It's not countryside that everyone enjoys. There are no hills and the north-easterly gales can be lethal. It's certainly not very picture postcard or Olde Worlde, but we like it because it's real, and most of the people who live here are real. So far the landscape hasn't been gentrified and tidied up to excess: woods still have dead trees and undergrowth in them and the vast arable fields that one finds in the Fens to the south have not appeared here yet. I hope those mad days of ecological destruction, in the name of chemical-based arable productivity that nobody actually wants, are over and done with.

Your book addresses, among many other subjects, what it means to be British. As somebody who has spent their working life determining what 'Britain' means from an archaeological perspective, what does being British mean to you personally?
Personally I think it's all about freedom and tolerance. I'm aware that we British are

by no means perfect – my mother's family is Irish, where views of the larger island to the east can be less than charitable, but generally speaking we are still a tolerant nation and are developing one of the most tolerant and diverse cultures on earth. I think I am still in favour of Britain remaining closely within the European Community, but I find the nationalist attitudes prevailing – indeed growing – within 'old Europe' (France, Germany and Italy) very worrying indeed. Surely the whole point of economic union is to break down, and not erect, barriers? I also think that the British tradition of liberalism is fundamental to our culture.

You 'borrowed' your grandfather's copy of Frederic Seebohm's *The English Village Community* (1883) and spent much time as a child visiting places he described. Was this the start of your interest in archaeology?
Actually my interest was first aroused a few years earlier when I was introduced to the story of the discovery of Tutankhamen's tomb by my teacher at school. The afternoon in question still lives vividly in my imagination – if not in my memory. Over the years imagination can subtly enhance memory. I'm not ashamed to admit that I've always had trouble differentiating between the two, which may be one reason why I tend to see the past through slightly rose-tinted spectacles. ▶

❝ I tend to see the past through slightly rose-tinted spectacles. ❞

3

LIFE
at a Glance

BORN

London, 1945.

EDUCATED

Read archaeology and anthropology at Cambridge, eventually taking a doctorate in 1984.

CAREER

Excavated a series of large pre-Roman sites and landscapes in the East Anglian Fens, culminating with the discovery in 1982 of timbers of a Late Bronze Age (1300–900 BC) timber causeway and religious complex at Flag Fen, Peterborough. Opened to the public in 1987, it has become one of the principal visitor attractions in the region.

FAMILY

Lives with his wife, the archaeologist Maisie Taylor, in the Lincolnshire Fens where they keep a flock of Lleyn sheep. He has a daughter by his first marriage.

The Importance ... *(continued)*

◄ 'A good field archaeologist develops a special attitude to wet or cold weather.' Nasty weather is one of the worst parts of your job, but what are the best?

The best moments for me are actually not in the trenches. I prefer to direct a dig 'hands on', from my own trench, so that I can actually experience at first hand the texture of the different deposits of the site. The modern Director/Manager tends to be more concerned with the correct filling in of the hugely over-elaborate recording system that has become standard throughout Britain – and most of Europe. So I find the actual process of excavation completely absorbing and I'm never aware that I'm having a particularly good or bad time. I only unwind and relax afterwards with the rest of the team. That's the best part of the digging day, for me. Otherwise I really enjoy the creative process of writing reports and books about my work. That's when I get the greatest intellectual satisfaction, because that's when I, and other key members of the team, transform random facts into a coherent story – into knowledge. It may sound rather pompous, but I firmly believe that the creation of new knowledge is one of the noblest things a person can aspire to.

Britain AD, like your other books, reads as story as well as history, but in contrast, as you point out, most archaeological writing is 'dull ... jargon-ridden prose'. Apart from W.G. Hoskins, which other writers, whether

archaeologists or not, have influenced you and your writing?

In my twenties and thirties I was a voracious reader of fiction, and only slowed down because now I have to read so much archaeology. I was very much influenced by Jane Austen and Ernest Hemingway – two very different writers, but both of whom were sparing in their use of words. I write as I speak and have an unfortunate tendency to be prolix at times, which is why I am so grateful to my editor at HarperCollins, Robert Lacey, who tightens up my language. I developed a personal approach to the telling of history through reading the novels of people like the American writer Thomas Wolfe (*Look Homeward, Angel* was his best-known book) and Malcolm Lowry, whose *Under the Volcano* was a masterpiece. Both authors were highly autobiographical and benefited from even more vigorous editing than Robert subjects me to (he wouldn't have liked that sentence much, either).

'Art is, after all, about ideas which can be communicated both by example and by word of mouth.' Is writing an art to you – an object in itself – or is it a means to an end?

Storytelling is an art, and writing for me is a means of telling a story. It's quite different from talking or making films, which are other ways of achieving the same ends. The important thing is the narrative and the places you visit along the route. It's the story, and the atmosphere it is able to establish, that takes the creative effort. Like any craft, ▶

> ❝ I developed a personal approach to the telling of history through reading the novels of people like the American writer Thomas Wolfe and Malcolm Lowry, whose *Under the Volcano* was a masterpiece. ❞

The Importance ... *(continued)*

◄ good writing can enhance the original creation, but not replace it. The changing pace of the narrative is important too and can be the hardest thing to judge, which is why I try never to write when I've had a glass or two of wine. I find the influence of alcohol makes it very hard to judge pace. It also makes one rather self-centred. Very occasionally I've had a drink in an effort to beat 'writer's block', but subsequently I always edit out most of what I wrote. So, to answer the question, I see writing as a means to an end. It's a craft or a trade – and none the worse for that. I'm also a sheep farmer, another craft or trade. Neither words nor sheep are simple or straightforward. Both demand respect and both require more than a lifetime to understand.

Archaeology is not a simple or accessible subject for many and yet the success of *Time Team*, your own television programmes and the arrival of hordes of visitors to the Seahenge site suggest that it is becoming increasingly fascinating and popular. Why do you think that is?
I've been asked that many times and am convinced that an interest in the past says something about people's attitude to the present. Generally speaking I have found that those who are interested in archaeology are very often people who are interested in the lives of other people. They, like me, enjoy observing human behaviour. Sometimes I fantasize about wearing a suit made from flock wallpaper and standing invisible in an Indian restaurant, listening to the people

❝ I'm also a sheep farmer, another craft or trade. Neither words nor sheep are simple or straightforward. Both demand respect and both require more than a lifetime to understand. ❞

talking at the various tables. Of course that would only work if one was indeed truly invisible and didn't know any of the diners; otherwise it would be eavesdropping or snooping – and not very pleasant. In archaeology the investigator wears a flock wallpaper suit when entering the world of the past. He or she is both invisible and anonymous. I think that's why the subject is so very appealing.

As somebody who writes very precisely and densely, how did it feel to work in television where layers and viewpoints are necessarily simplified?
The old cliché that one picture says a thousand words applies here. With film you don't need to explain every picture and can tell two or more stories simultaneously. I did the final piece-to-camera of *Britain AD* at the top of a building that overlooked the massive King's Cross redevelopment project. That setting spared me having to explain the whys and wherefores of change. As I said earlier, film-making is another route to the telling of good tales, which is why I always write my books in advance, and completely independently. The book establishes the principal narratives, which television then can develop in its own unique way. I don't have much time for those instant books-of-the-TV-series. It seems to me that sometimes they verge on intellectual prostitution.

The Arthurian myths seem to be repositories of clues that are deciphered according to personal and political ▶

> ❝ I don't have much time for those instant books-of-the-TV-series. It seems to me that sometimes they verge on intellectual prostitution. ❞

The Importance ... *(continued)*

◀ interests. In the present day puzzles presented in novels such as *The Da Vinci Code* can capture the populace's imagination in an unprecedented fashion. Why do you think we are entranced by such puzzles?

I've just watched a very good mystery film on television and it had me completely hooked for ninety minutes. In an hour I'll probably struggle to recall the details of the plot and in a year I'll re-watch the video almost as if I had never seen it before. So I don't think the explanation for the film's fascination is actually to do with what it was about. Most routine mystery stories are pretty predictable. For me the fascination has to do with security and a feeling of safety, which is why I hate books and films in which the actual detective comes under suspicion. Somehow that's not playing the game. It undermines one's nice, warm, comfortable feelings of security. And besides, apart from doing a thousand-piece jigsaw every Christmas, puzzles bore me rigid. I've never finished a crossword, and bridge leaves me cold. So I don't think that it's the solving of a mystery that matters; rather it's the process of revelation that appeals to most people. Add to that the security that we all feel in a mutually shared past, and the combination is pretty irresistible.

If you could time-travel back to any period in history, which would you choose and why?

I'm aware that I once wrote that I would swap ten years of my life for ten minutes in the

> ❝ I don't think that it's the solving of a mystery that matters; rather it's the process of revelation that appeals to most people. ❞

Bronze Age, and it made an excellent sound bite. In actual fact I would like to relive my time at university in the 1960s, but armed with what I know today. I missed so much. I also wonder how I'd react to the experience. Would I be bored after a few weeks? How would my friends of the time react to my early twenty-first-century attitudes? Were the sixties really that earth-shattering or have they been re-created in a way that suits middle-aged people today?

What do you do when you're not writing?
When not at my computer I like to do something active. So I work in the garden or on the farm. I'm not a great one for travelling any more, having spent ten years commuting across the Atlantic. I'm aware that travel enriches the mind, but when I walk into my small wood and spot a woodpecker hammering the bark of an oak tree, I might just as well be deep in the forests of Brazil. Similarly, to enjoy a pint of Bateman's best bitter in south Lincolnshire is every bit as rewarding as sipping a fine Burgundy in France. In each instance it's the quality of the experience that matters. I also believe we should think about our mental attitudes to the experience, as it happens – and not when it's over.

In the West we tend to take life for granted. We divide our days up into hours and categories, which makes for better time management, doing one thing and then moving on to something else. Life thus becomes a series of disparate events that lack a unifying narrative thread. Perhaps ▶

❝ I'm aware that travel enriches the mind, but when I walk into my small wood and spot a woodpecker hammering the bark of an oak tree, I might just as well be deep in the forests of Brazil. ❞

The Importance ... (*continued*)

◀ that's why I'm a great believer in the Buddhist view that the most important moment to experience is the present. Although I'm not a religious person myself, as I grow older I try to be aware of every moment of my life, as fully as I can. People spend too much of their time planning and looking in their diaries. Are they aware that while they are thinking about what they *intend* to do, their lives are rapidly passing them by unheeded? I think that the sheer pace of modern life is destroying the quality of the present and that it's time we slowed down, did less 'virtual' and more hands-on things and tried consciously to contemplate the here and now. Otherwise, what's the point in living at all? None of us should live entirely in the future, and archaeologists should not inhabit the past. It's the present that matters. ■

❝ As I grow older I try to be aware of every moment of my life, as fully as I can. People spend too much of their time planning and looking in their diaries. ❞

Top Ten History/
Archaeology Books

1. **Archaeology from the Earth**
   Sir Mortimer Wheeler

2. **The Making of the English Landscape**
   W.G. Hoskins

3. **Excavations at Navan Fort, 1961–71**
   D.M. Waterman

4. **Life and Death in the Bronze Age**
   Sir Cyril Fox

5. **Iron Age Communities in Britain, 3rd Edition**
   Barry Cunliffe

6. **The Passage of Arms**
   Richard Bradley

7. **The Lower Palaeolithic Occupation of Britain, 2 vols**
   John Wymer

8. **Stonehenge in Its Landscape**
   R.M.J. Cleal, K.E. Walker and R. Montague

9. **Late Stone Age Hunters of the British Isles**
   Christopher Smith

10. **Rethinking the Neolithic**
    Julian Thomas

A Writing Life

When do you write?
Early in the morning, usually between 5.30 and 9.30.

Where do you write?
In my office at home.

Why do you write?
It's what I do. I also enjoy the process of communication – I suppose you could say it's what makes us human.

Pen or computer?
Computer (since about 1979).

Silence or music?
Silence. If music's on I listen to it and the words dry up.

What started you writing?
At first it was necessity because you can't be an archaeologist and not write. Then I found I was beginning to enjoy it. Now I find I can't stop.

How do you start a book?
With an outline which I agree with my agent and publisher at great length; I then abandon it when I start to write.

And finish?
I try to do so with a flourish. A good ending is essential to a book. Leave them laughing, weeping or thinking.

Do you have any writing rituals or superstitions?
Yes: I have to write something every day in

case I lose the plot (even non-fiction should have a plot or narrative).

Which living writer do you most admire?
Seamus Heaney – for hundreds of reasons.

What or who inspires you?
I try to stay well clear of inspiration, which in my experience usually conceals self-indulgence. Almost everything I've ever written when feeling 'inspired' I have edited out the following day. There has been one exception, when I was in Ely Cathedral a few years ago. It was an inspiring moment which I wrote about later. I always find the rural landscape inspiring – even on a grey, rainy day.

If you weren't a writer what job would you do?
It would have to be something that took me outdoors. But I'd always keep a diary (possibly with one eye on eventual publication).

What's your guilty reading pleasure or favourite trashy read?
I love cartoons – everything from *Asterix* and *Tintin* to Giles and *Private Eye* – the more scurrilous the better. I like to see self-important, pompous politicians deflated. ∎

Why Archaeology Matters

By Francis Pryor

BOOKS LIKE *Britain AD* and *BC* before it have benefited enormously from changes made to town and country planning rules since 1989. I won't discuss these regulations in any detail here, as I don't want to lose every reader at the outset, but their effect on archaeology has been transforming. Quite simply, they invoke a principle that was popular in the Thatcher years, that the polluter pays. In this case it's not so much polluters as developers, which is not quite the same thing (although sometimes the two can be very close). So if I decide that I want to build a housing estate, say, on a site where it's known there was once a Romano-British farm, then I have to pay to have it excavated properly – and that might cost me upwards of £100,000. We don't know precisely what the ever-growing industry of commercial archaeology is worth, but prior to 1989 the annual spend on excavation and survey in England alone was in the order of £3–4 million. In 2004 it was around £40–50 million. I should add here that similar legislation now exists throughout the United Kingdom and Ireland – and across most of the EU.

A few years ago it became clear to me that developers and many members of the public were starting to wonder why so much money was being spent on archaeology. These were not just people, such as builders, contractors or estate agents, whose livelihoods depended on real estate development, but they included many who were self-employed and depended on their wits to earn a living. They felt that archaeology didn't really matter *that* much and that a growing industry was being spoon-fed at other people's expense. While this was happening television programmes, such as *Time Team*, were taking archaeology to ever-increasing audiences. These viewers had a very different and far more favourable opinion about the past. But could something as large as the new business of commercial archaeology really be justified on the basis of television programmes alone? Surely there has to be more to it than that?

The more I thought about it the more I became convinced that all aspects of the past were closely interlinked. Commercial archaeology was producing the huge surprises, such as that extraordinary Anglo-Saxon burial at Prittlewell (which I discuss in Chapter 9), but these would simply remain 'one-off' discoveries with no wider relevance unless they could be fitted into some sort of historical framework. That framework could best be provided by academics and others whose job was to sift through the new information, compare it with what we already knew, and then come to new insights and conclusions. Meanwhile other people were needed to reconnoitre the landscape so that businessmen could be given some idea of what their potential archaeological costs might be if they chose to develop a particular site or area. More people were needed to manage what was now being labelled as ▶

6 Prior to 1989 the annual spend on excavation and survey in England alone was in the order of £3–4 million. In 2004 it was around £40–50 million. 9

Why Archaeology Matters *(continued)*

◄ 'the archaeological resource'. These people included inspectors and administrators from organizations such as English Heritage who were given the right to decide whether certain buildings or sites should be protected for posterity by Listing or Scheduling. All of that is currently being rationalized and made simpler – which is no bad thing.

Archaeologists and historians have rather different approaches to the past, but those differences are now seen as less important than they once were. Today we both stress that we are working to understand the past and we borrow freely from each other. From this 'joined-up' approach (to use a jargon term introduced, and signally ignored, by government) has arisen a new concept, that of the 'historic environment'. The historic environment includes everything from old buildings to bumps in fields. It also includes document archives, museum collections, objects and even structures from the very recent past, such as the cruise missile hangars at Greenham Common – or indeed the protesters' encampments outside the barbed wire. So I'm hugely in favour of the historic environment, as a concept. So are all my colleagues. The trouble is, nobody else has heard of it. As a buzz-phrase it has been a complete and utter flop, with about as much sexiness and public appeal as a muddy puddle. So what are we to do?

As time passes the idea of a unified past will, I am sure, gradually gain wider acceptance. After all, we all live in the past, because the present has vanished as soon as you start to think about it. And the future

❝ The people who make the worst decisions in the here and now are those, in my experience, who ignore the lessons of history or who twist them to their own ends. ❞

will always remain both uncertain and fundamentally rooted in what has gone before. So nobody, not even the Great and the Good, can escape posterity – because the past will exist in the future. That's all we can be certain of. Now this isn't just clever word-play. It is actually very important because the people who make the worst decisions in the here and now are those, in my experience, who ignore the lessons of history or who twist them to their own ends, claiming faith or dogma of some sort as justification. I won't give examples other than to mention the complex politics of the Middle East.

I started this short discussion with commercial archaeology in Britain and have just raised Middle Eastern politics and the failure of the historic environment to catch on as a unifying concept. So how does it all hang together? I believe that the past, the present and the future are inextricably combined, and when pushy people tell one to 'get a life' and live in the twenty-first century they are missing the point. You can only appreciate just how unsustainable and overpopulated the globe is at present if you have an appreciation of what went before. That knowledge will also suggest humane and practical ways of coping with the situation, which I still believe can be turned around without the unwanted intervention of an intercontinental nuclear war, a massive pandemic of influenza or any other horrific 'solution'. Such a solution would anyhow only be short term, and in a few centuries we would find ourselves in the same situation. No, what matters is that we learn ▶

> ❝ You can only appreciate just how unsustainable and overpopulated the globe is at present if you have an appreciation of what went before. ❞

Why Archaeology Matters (*continued*)

◄ to acquire a degree of humility. We are not supermen. Human beings have never been masters of the world, and if history is anything to go by they never will. But they can only gain the humility needed to appreciate this important fact if they understand what has gone before. If you begin to understand history, you realize the limitations that humanity – in the sense of 'being human' – imposes on people.

So that's why I started to write my current books and my next on the Middle Ages. I know they are only a first and very tentative step and I will not claim more than they could deliver. Put simply, my aim is to paint a picture of the past that will allow readers to identify with it more closely. I try to make the narratives accurate and challenging, but I am aware that the past is a personal business and is also the product of one's own perspective and imagination. There are no absolute truths in history. Add to this the fact that my words will be re-interpreted when they are read, and it becomes clear that the past itself is conditioned by history. The result is a wonderfully complex, rewarding and mysterious world. ■

Have You Read?

Francis Pryor's other books

Read on

Britain BC
An authoritative and radical rethinking of the whole of British history before the coming of the Romans, based on remarkable new archaeological finds.

Seahenge
An investigation into the lives of our prehistoric ancestors, sparked by the discovery, in 1998, of the so-called Seahenge. Discovered at low tide off the north coast of Norfolk, this circle of wooden planks set vertically in the sand was likened to a ghostly 'hand reaching up from the underworld'. Now dated back to around 2020 BC, the removal and preservation of the timbers sparked controversy and raised archaeology's profile in an unexpected, and sometimes unwelcome, fashion. This book both addresses the debate but also positions it in the wider context of what we can find out about our own history through the lives of our predecessors.

Farmers in Prehistoric Britain
Unearthing the lives and work of farmers, the author uses his practical and academic knowledge to demonstrate that, despite our assumptions, farming was well established before the arrival of the Romans.

If You Loved This,
You Might Like . . .

1. **The Discovery of King Arthur**
   Geoffrey Ashe

2. **The Holy Kingdom: Quest for the Real King Arthur**
   Adrian Gilbert, Alan Wilson and Baram Blackett

3. **The Ancient Celts**
   Barry Cunliffe

4. **The Age of Arthur: A History of the British Isles**
   John Morris

5. **Avebury: Biography of a Landscape**
   Joshua Pollard and Andrew Reynolds

6. **The Significance of Monuments**
   Richard Bradley

Find Out More

Flag Fen

Francis Pryor's discovery of a Bronze Age religious site in 1982 led to the establishment of Flag Fen, a centre dedicated to that period of history. But this is no static museum: excavations continue at the site and visitors can see the results of the work in the Preservation Hall as well as visiting the permanent displays in the museum (including the oldest wheel in England), the only Roman road constructed across the Fens as well as Iron and Bronze Age roundhouses. The website at www.flagfen.com is also worth a visit, providing clear and helpful information about the exhibits and their history as well as forthcoming events.

Address: The Droveway, Northey Road, Peterborough, PE6 7QJ

Tel: + 44 (0) 1733 313414